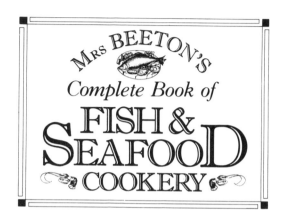

Mrs BEETON'S

Complete Book of

FISH & SEAFOOD COOKERY

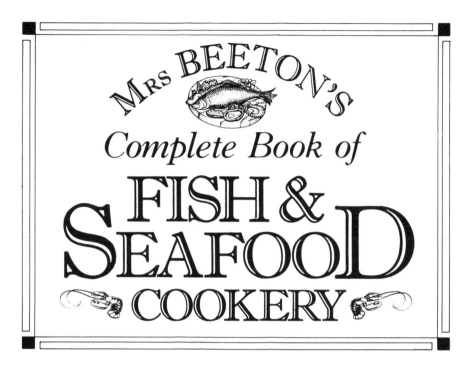

Mrs BEETON'S
Complete Book of
FISH & SEAFOOD
COOKERY

Consultant Editor **Bridget Jones**

WARD LOCK

First published 1991 by Ward Lock
Villiers House, 41/47 Strand, London WC2N 5JE

A Cassell imprint

© Text and illustrations Ward Lock Limited 1991

Designed by Cherry Randell
Edited by Jenni Fleetwood
Photography by Sue Atkinson
Home Economist: Sarah Maxwell
Illustrations by Tony Randell

Printed and bound in Great Britain by The Bath Press

British Library Cataloguing in Publication Data
Beeton, Mrs. *1836-1865*
  Mrs. Beeton's fish and seafood cookery.
  1. Food: Seafood dishes – Recipes
  I. Title   II. Jones, Bridget
  641.692

ISBN 0-7063-7005-8

*The publishers would like to thank the Sea Fish Industry Authority for their assistance in the
preparation of this book.*

CONTENTS

Useful Weights and Measures   6

Introduction   8

A Guide to Fish and Seafood   9

Preparation Techniques   18

Basic Recipes   27

Soups and Stews   46

Steamed and Sauced Fish   60

Grilled and Fried Fish   92

Baked Fish Dishes   122

Seafood Suppers and Snacks   149

Rice and Pasta Specialities   164

Pastes, Pâtés and Cold Platters   172

Glossary   188

Index   190

USEFUL WEIGHTS AND MEASURES

USING METRIC OR IMPERIAL MEASURES

Throughout the book, all weights and measures are given first in metric, then in Imperial. For example 100 g/4 oz, 150 ml/¼ pint or 15 ml/1 tbsp.

When following any of the recipes use either metric or Imperial – do not combine the two sets of measures as they are not interchangeable.

EQUIVALENT METRIC/IMPERIAL MEASURES

Weights   The following chart lists some of the metric/Imperial weights that are used in the recipes.

METRIC	IMPERIAL
15 g	½ oz
25 g	1 oz
50 g	2 oz
75 g	3 oz
100 g	4 oz
150 g	5 oz
175 g	6 oz
200 g	7 oz
225 g	8 oz
250 g	9 oz
275 g	10 oz
300 g	11 oz
350 g	12 oz
375 g	13 oz
400 g	14 oz
425 g	15 oz
450 g	16 oz
575 g	1¼ lb
675 g	1½ lb
800 g	1¾ lb
900 g	2 lb
1 kg	2¼ lb
1.4 kg	3 lb
1.6 kg	3½ lb
1.8 kg	4 lb
2.25 kg	5 lb

Liquid Measures   The following chart lists some metric/Imperial equivalents for liquids. Millilitres (ml), litres and fluid ounces (fl oz) or pints are used throughout.

METRIC	IMPERIAL
50 ml	2 fl oz
125 ml	4 fl oz
150 ml	¼ pint
300 ml	½ pint
450 ml	¾ pint
600 ml	1 pint

Spoon Measures   Both metric and Imperial equivalents are given for all spoon measures, expressed as millilitres and teaspoons (tsp) or tablespoons (tbsp).

All spoon measures refer to British standard measuring spoons and the quantities given are always for level spoons.

Do not use ordinary kitchen cutlery instead of proper measuring spoons as they will hold quite different quantities.

METRIC	IMPERIAL
1.25 ml	¼ tsp
2.5 ml	½ tsp
5 ml	1 tsp
15 ml	1 tbsp

Length   All linear measures are expressed in millimetres (mm), centimetres (cm) or metres (m) and inches or feet. The following list gives examples of typical conversions.

METRIC	IMPERIAL
5 mm	¼ inch
1 cm	½ inch
2.5 cm	1 inch
5 cm	2 inches
15 cm	6 inches
30 cm	12 inches (1 foot)

OVEN TEMPERATURES

Whenever the oven is used, the required setting is given as three alternatives: degrees Celsius (°C), degrees Fahrenheit (°F) and gas.

The temperature settings given are for conventional ovens. If you have a fan oven, adjust the temperature according to the manufacturer's instructions.

°C	°F	GAS
110	225	¼
120	250	½
140	275	1
150	300	2
160	325	3
180	350	4
190	375	5
200	400	6
220	425	7
230	450	8
240	475	9

MICROWAVE INFORMATION

Occasional microwave hints and instructions are included for certain recipes, as appropriate. The information given is for microwave ovens rated at 650-700 watts.

The following terms have been used for the microwave settings: High, Medium, Defrost and Low. For each setting, the power input is as follows: High = 100% power, Medium = 50% power, Defrost = 30% power and Low = 20% power.

All microwave notes and timings are for guidance only: always read and follow the manufacturer's instructions for your particular appliance. Remember to avoid putting any metal in the microwave and never operate the microwave empty. See also page 63.

NOTES FOR AMERICAN READERS

In America dry goods and liquids are conventionally measured by the standard 8-oz cup. When translating pints, and fractions of pints, Americans should bear in mind that the U.S. pint is equal to 16 fl oz or 2 cups, whereas the Imperial pint is equal to 20 fl oz.

EQUIVALENT METRIC/AMERICAN MEASURES

Liquid Measures

METRIC/IMPERIAL	AMERICAN
150 ml/¼ pint	⅔ cup
300 ml/½ pint	1¼ cups
450 ml/¾ pint	2·cups
600 ml/1 pint	2½ cups
900 ml/1½ pints	3¾ cups
1 litre/1¾ pints	4 cups (2 U.S. pints)

Weights

450 g/1 lb butter or margarine	2 cups (4 sticks)
100 g/4 oz grated cheese	1 cup
450 g/1 lb flour	4 cups
450 g/1 lb granulated sugar	2 cups
450 g/1 lb icing sugar	3½ cups confectioners' sugar
200 g/7 oz raw long-grain rice	1 cup
100 g/4 oz cooked long-grain rice	1 cup
100 g/4 oz fresh white breadcrumbs	2 cups

Terminology Some useful American equivalents or substitutes for British ingredients are listed below:

BRITISH	AMERICAN
aubergine	eggplant
bicarbonate of soda	baking soda
biscuits	cookies, crackers
broad beans	fava or lima beans
chicory	endive
cling film	plastic wrap
cornflour	cornstarch
courgettes	zucchini
cream, single	cream, light
cream, double	cream, heavy
flour, plain	flour, all-purpose
frying pan	skillet
grill	broil
minced meat	ground meat
shortcrust pastry	basic pie dough
shrimp	prawn
spring onion	scallion
sultana	golden raisin
swede	rutabaga

INTRODUCTION

From humble herring to luxurious lobster, on wet fish counter, in freezer or can, there is literally a fish for all occasions. All along the line, fish provides value for money, with little waste, short cooking times and excellent nutritional value.

All fish, including convenience products, can play a useful role in any well-balanced diet to provide protein, vitamins A and D, and, in some cases, valuable levels of calcium. White fish has a low fat content; the fat found in oily species such as herring and mackerel is mainly polyunsaturated. Indeed, some of the fatty acids present in oily fish may well play a positive part in promoting good health. Where the bones are eaten with the fish, in the case of whitebait, canned sardines, brisling or pilchards, a good source of calcium is provided.

Apart from cold salmon and seafood, and the use of some types of canned fish, hot dishes appear to dominate popular seafood cookery. This book attempts to redress the balance, with plenty of recipes for mousses, pâtés, spreads and cold platters suitable for starters and summer meals. Pasties and pies, perfect for picnics, feature alongside ideas for using smoked and canned fish.

Mashed and new potatoes are traditional accompaniments to white fish, but rice and pasta feature too. Simple accompaniments are usually best. Sautéed courgettes, steamed or lightly boiled French beans, grilled tomatoes and peas with plenty of chopped parsley are particularly suitable. Garnishing ideas are given in individual recipes.

Fish is simple, tasty and versatile; a traditional British food that has long been valued for making practical and nutritious meals. *Mrs Beeton's Complete Book of Fish and Seafood Cookery* explores all the basic cooking methods. Many traditional recipes are included and there are several inventive ideas to fit in with the contemporary taste for international ingredients and short-cuts to good eating.

A GUIDE TO FISH AND SEAFOOD

ABALONE

A single-shelled relation of the limpet, this large shellfish has a reputation for being tough. It is beaten to tenderise the flesh, then cooked quickly to prevent it from toughening again. Soups and Oriental dishes incorporating abalone are available in cans; the frozen shellfish is sometimes sold at Oriental supermarkets.

ANCHOVY

A relation of the herring, the fresh anchovy is a small round fish, 7.5-15 cm/3-6 inches in length. Canned anchovy fillets are salted for at least a month before being packed in either olive or vegetable oil.

BRILL

A large flat fish, similar to turbot but slightly more oval and smaller, weighing up to 4.5 kg/10 lb. Small brill may be cooked whole but the fish is usually sold as fillets. Brill is available from June to February and is at its best during June and July.

CARP

There are many species of this round freshwater fish. Carp is popular in China and eastern Europe. Wild carp can have a muddy taste; the live fish should be kept in clean water for 24 hours before being killed. The carp available in specialist fish-mongers comes from fish farms. The two farmed varieties are mirror carp, which is covered in scales, and leather carp which has a tough skin and fewer, large scales. They are available from June to March but not in April and May, the breeding season.

You will have to order carp well in advance to be sure of obtaining a fish for a specific occasion. Fish weighing less than 900 g/2 lb are not worth preparing and those above 3.5-4 kg/8-9 lb are very coarse. Farmed fish usually weigh between 1-2.5 kg/2¼-5½ lb, the best weight for eating. The firm white flesh has large flakes and a distinctive taste which is not to everyone's liking. Although carp is very bony, the bones are long and large, therefore easy to avoid.

CATFISH

There are both sea and freshwater species. The sea fish is the most common and it is also known as rock fish, wolf fish or spotted catfish. This fish has a long body which tapers towards the tail to resemble a large tadpole. The skin is brown-beige with a mottled, dark pattern of inverted 'V' shapes along its length. A long dorsal fin extends from the head to the tail. The flesh is white and fine flavoured as the catfish feeds on mussels and whelks. It is usually sold as fillets between February and July.

Freshwater catfish has dark skin and whiskers on either side of the head. Its white flesh resembles that of pike.

CAVIAR

The soft roe, or eggs of sturgeon which are processed with speed and care. They are lightly salted to flavour and preserve them, then vacuum packed. Cans of Russian caviar are marked 'malassol', indicating that the contents are lightly salted.

Beluga caviar – the most expensive – is grey in colour; the eggs are large. It comes from the largest variety of sturgeon, the beluga, which can live for up to a century and may grow to be a huge fish.

Pressed caviar is made of very small, immature eggs or those that may have been slightly crushed or damaged in production.

CLAMS

There are many types of clam, ranging from the giant species to the small, striped Venus clam of the Mediterranean which is likely to be 2.5-4 cm/1-1½ inches long.

Fresh clams are available all year but you will have to order them in advance. Prepare as for mussels. Canned and frozen clams are also available.

COCKLES

Small molluscs with ridged shells which look heart-shaped when viewed from the side. Cockles are usually cooked and shelled before being sold in local markets. Fresh cockles must be purged overnight and prepared as for mussels (page 25). They are most readily available in jars, preserved in vinegar.

COD

Probably the most popular white fish, cod has firm, white flesh and a good flavour. This is a large fish which is sold prepared, either in fillets, cutlets or steaks. The fillets are thick and therefore versatile. Although the battered cod on sale at fish and chip shops is not often skinned, it is best to skin cod fillets before cooking. Codling are young cod.

Smoked cod fillet and smoked cod's roe (page 14) are both readily available. See also Salt Cod (page 14).

COLEY

A relative of the cod, coley has thicker skin, darker flesh, a coarse texture and stronger taste. Although it is not much favoured as a fish for grilling or frying, it makes good pies, fish cakes or sauced dishes. Coley is usually sold in fillets. Frozen, pre-formed

coley steaks are also popular and quick to prepare.

Pollock is an American term for coley. In this country, the fish is also known as saithe or coalfish.

CONGER EEL

A sea eel which grows to great length (up to 3 metres/9 feet). Sold skinned and cut in steaks, conger is firm and meaty with large bones. Unlike most fish, conger requires comparatively long cooking in sauce until tender, otherwise it can be tough. Conger steaks are used in Mediterranean fish stews, such as bouillabaisse or bourride.

CRAB

World-wide, there is an enormous variety of edible crabs. The brown crab is the species most often sold in Britain, both live and cooked. As with all live crustaceans, crabs should be lively when bought. Avoid limp-clawed specimens that look thoroughly dead. Live crabs should feel heavy for their size. Give the crabs a shake and avoid any that make swishing noises; a sign that they contain water.

When buying a cooked crab, make sure that it looks clean and fresh and that the legs and claws are tight against the body. Cooked crab is also sold ready dressed, with all meat removed and presented in the cleaned shell. Buy from a reputable source.

Soft shell crabs are small shore crabs that have shed their hard covering in spring or autumn and have not had time to acquire new ones. These are cooked and eaten whole.

CRAWFISH

Also known as langouste or spiny lobster, this is a marine crustacean which looks rather like a large lobster without claws. It differs from the lobster in that the shell of the live animal is red, although some species are darker than others. A prized seafood, crawfish is not often found on the supermarket fish counter, although it may be available at a large wholesale fish market. The American use of the term crawfish to describe crayfish is confusing. Crayfish, a freshwater species, is not readily available.

DAB
A small flat fish of the plaice family, in season all year. Dabs are cleaned (gutted), trimmed and cooked whole by grilling or frying.

DOVER SOLE
Dover sole has a fine flavour and firm delicate flesh. The fish yields small fillets, so it is usually grilled or fried whole. The fishmonger will clean and skin the fish for you – the tough skin is slit at the tail end and easily pulled away from the flesh.

EEL
Freshwater eel are considered superior to conger eel as they have rich, oily flesh. Although they are available all year, they are best during the winter months when fully mature, dark-skinned specimens are on sale. Young, yellow-coloured eels are inferior.

Since eels have to be cooked absolutely fresh, they are usually sold live. Fishmongers selling eels keep them in tanks or buckets of water and kill, then skin them as required. They should be cooked on the day of purchase.

Elvers, tiny eels resembling short spaghetti and measuring about 5 cm/2 inches in length, are a traditional West Country speciality, fried with bacon. Cold elver cake is cooked, pressed elvers, served in slices.

Smoked eel fillets are a speciality from the Netherlands and Scandinavian countries. It is also an East Anglian delicacy. Available from delicatessens and larger supermarkets, smoked eel is skinned and ready to serve. It has a delicate flavour and it is good served very simply with soured cream and chives, and thin, buttered bread.

FLOUNDER
A flat fish which is similar in size to plaice. It has brown and yellow blotchy markings and a rough patch on its head. Flounder is available from March to November and it may be cooked whole or as fillets. The flesh is delicate but not outstanding.

GRAYLING
A freshwater fish of the salmon and trout family. Grayling is seldom sold commercially but the firm white flesh and good flavour make for excellent eating.

GREY MULLET
A round fish with large scales, grey mullet is available from September to February. This fish is not related to red mullet and it is quite different in size, appearance and taste.

Grey mullet vary in size, the largest farmed mullet being over 60 cm/24 inches long, although the majority are about 45 cm/18 inches long. The white flesh is of good quality but it bruises and becomes soft easily, so the fish should be handled and scaled with care. Mullet is usually cooked whole, by baking or poaching; it is also a good candidate for the barbecue.

GURNARD
These are an group of ugly – looking fish with bony, angular heads. Both red and grey gurnard are available, the latter being slightly more brown-beige in colour than grey. Red gurnard, available from July to February, is better quality than the grey fish. Red gurnard must not be confused with red mullet which is usually smaller and not as ugly.

The flesh is firm and the flakes are large with a fairly strong flavour. Gurnard may be cooked whole or filleted. Also known as gurnet.

HADDOCK

A firm white fish which is not as large as cod, yielding thinner fillets with smaller, slightly less firm flakes. Haddock is distinguished by a black line which runs along its length and a thumbprint mark behind the gills. Readily available as fillets, haddock may be grilled, fried, braised or used instead of cod.

Smoked haddock varies enormously in quality and colour. Some fillets are dyed a bright golden hue, others are naturally pale. Good fishmongers clearly distinguish between the different types.

Finnan haddock are small fish that are split and smoked on the bone over peat or oak. They are pale gold, with the tail still intact. They look slightly dry compared to smoked haddock fillets that are processed by other methods, but are actually superior in flavour. The name derives from the Scottish village, Findon, where the haddock were originally smoked by this method.

HAKE

From the same family as cod and haddock, hake is longer and slimmer in shape. It has a finer flavour than its relatives and firm, white flesh. Available from June to March, hake is most often sold as steaks or cutlets.

HALIBUT

Available from June to March, halibut is the largest of the flat fish. It is sold fresh and frozen, as fillets or steaks. Its firm, white flesh has a fine flavour. Halibut may be cooked by almost any method but it should be kept moist during cooking, either by the addition of a sauce or by frequent basting.

HERRING

An oily fish of silvery appearance which is known for its tasty flesh and multitude of bones, herring is similar in size to small or medium mackerel. It is best to bone the fish before cooking. Herrings may be grilled, fried, baked or soused and are also available preserved as rollmops in brine or in vinegar. Salted herring fillets packed in oil have an excellent flavour. Herring fillets are also canned in oil, mustard sauce or a variety of other sauces.

Kippers are smoked herrings, either split and opened out or filleted. Bloaters are whole, lightly smoked herrings.

HUSS

Also known as dogfish, flake or tope, huss is a member of the shark family. It does not have bones but is a tough, cartilaginous fish with a characteristic, slightly chewy texture which is not to everyone's taste. Huss often appears on fish and chip shop menus; in some areas the battered and deep fried form is greatly favoured.

At the wet fish shop it is usually sold skinned and prepared for cooking. The flesh has a very slight pink tinge. Huss may be barbecued or grilled on kebabs, but is also suitable for braising.

JOHN DORY

A deep-bodied fish which looks alarming, mainly because of its large mouth and long, prickle-like fins. When headless and cleaned the fish is reduced to two-thirds of its original weight. The flesh has a good flavour and texture. Available all year, the fish is good grilled, poached or baked and served cold.

LAVER BREAD

Cooked and puréed laver seaweed, a Welsh speciality. Resembles spinach in flavour but has a dark, almost black, colour. Oatmeal is added to thicken the purée which is coated in more oatmeal and fried in the shape of soft cakes. Served with bacon.

LEMON SOLE

This is not related to true sole (referred to as Dover sole in this book). Lemon sole is a flat fish, larger than Dover sole and not as expensive. Lemon sole has good flavour which, as the name suggests, has a hint of lemon. It may be cooked whole but it is also large enough to yield good fillets. Available from April to February.

LOBSTER

Live lobsters are dark in colour – almost black – and turn red on cooking. Although cooked lobsters are available both fresh and frozen in ice, live ones are only stocked by the busiest and most cosmopolitan fish-mongers. However, most good fishmongers or fish counters at large supermarkets will order a live lobster on request.

Lobster meat, extracted from the tail and claws, is firm, white and sweet. If you are buying a live lobster, look for one which is quite perky and heavy for its size.

Cooked lobster should be clean and bright in appearance with a tightly curled tail. Always follow the instructions on the packaging for thawing and using frozen lobster.

MACKEREL

An oily fish with distinctive green-blue markings, mackerel are available all year.

Tasty dark flesh and large bones are typical of this fish which may be grilled, fried, poached, soused, baked or barbe-cued. The fish may be cooked whole, split or filleted.

Smoked mackerel fillets or whole smoked mackerel are widely available, sometimes with additional seasonings.

MEGRIM

A small flat fish which is a pale brown-gold in colour. Available from May to March. The fillets are not exceptionally flavour-some; they tend to be slightly dry as well as bland.

MONKFISH

This weird-looking fish has a huge ugly head, so the tail flesh is usually sold skinned and prepared for cooking. The flesh is firm and has an excellent flavour; it is also ex-pensive. It may be cooked by all methods and served either hot or cold. Available all year, also known as angler fish or angel fish.

MUSSELS

Dark, oval bivalves, these shellfish are in season from September to March. Apart from the familiar dark-shelled mussels, there are also brown-shelled species and very large New Zealand mussels with green shells.

Smoked mussels vary in quality from small, shrunken offerings, sometimes canned in oil, to lightly smoked, large mussels that retain a delicate texture.

Pickled mussels in vinegar or brine are a poor substitute for fresh mussels; however frozen mussels are a good alternative. These are available frozen on the half shell.

OCTOPUS

These molluscs are popular in Mediterra-nean countries where they may be served stewed or fried whole when small. They are not so readily available as squid (page 16) which is more versatile.

OYSTERS

There are many varieties of oyster and they vary in size. In Britain, Colchester and Whitstable are known for their oyster beds and for the excellent quality of their shell-fish. British oysters are known as 'native' to distinguish them from imported types.

Oysters are, of course, known for the fact that they are eaten raw, with a squeeze of lemon or perhaps a dash of Tabasco. To be served this way, they must be absolutely fresh and newly opened, displayed on ice.

Smoked oysters vary enormously in qual-ity. The best are succulent and lightly smoked; the worst are strong, synthetic in flavour and oily.

PERCH

A freshwater fish, olive-green in colour with vertical black stripes. Good to eat but bony, perch is usually filleted, then poached or fried.

PIKE

A large, fierce freshwater fish of medium size. Those weighing up to 3 kg/6½ lb are best for cooking. Pike flesh is soft, with many fine bones. The flavour is valued for making traditional dishes such as quenelles, when the flesh is puréed and sieved. Not readily available.

PILCHARDS

These are usually large sardines (page 15).

PLAICE

A familiar flat fish which is available either whole or as fillets. Fine, slightly soft flesh and a delicate flavour are characteristic of plaice. The fish may be fried, grilled, baked, stuffed or poached.

POLLACK

Not to be confused with pollock (the American name for coley) pollack is a white-fleshed member of the cod family. Its flesh is slightly watery and not such good quality as cod.

PRAWNS

See also Shrimps (page 15). Good fish-mongers usually sell two varieties of this crustacean: cold water prawns and Medi-terranean prawns, also known as king prawns or jumbo prawns. The smaller more familiar cold water prawns are available cooked, either peeled or in their shells. They are also readily available frozen. Mediterranean prawns are usually sold cooked and in their shells. Uncooked Medi-terranean prawns are sometimes available. They are a grey colour and turn pink on cooking. The usual way of buying uncooked Mediterranean prawns is peeled and frozen.

Confusion arises over the terms prawn and shrimp because Americans use only the latter. American cooks refer to shrimp and jumbo shrimp; both are larger than those available in Britain.

REDFISH

Available all year, the redfish can grow up to 1 metre/3¼ feet long. Another ugly-looking specimen, the redfish is often dis-played whole or filleted. The flesh is not noted for exceptional flavour.

ROE

Roes are the testes of a male fish or the ovaries of the female.

Soft roes come from the herring. They are often cooked in butter and served on toast. Pressed roes are sold canned, for slicing and frying or grilling.

Smoked cod's roe is used for making Taramasalata (page 175).

Lumpfish roe is served in the same way as caviar. It is salted and usually dyed. Norwegian types are less salty than some others.

SALMON

Both farmed and wild salmon are available. Wild salmon, caught in rivers and lochs, is in season from February to the end of August. Excellent farmed salmon is avail-able all year, as steaks, fillet portions or whole fish.

From June to the beginning of August small, one-year-old farmed salmon are available.

Sea trout or salmon trout are in season from March to July. Smaller than salmon, these are caught in the sea. The flesh is similar in colour to salmon but has the flaky texture of trout. The bone structure is the same as for trout.

SALT COD

Also known as *bacalao*, this is cod fillet which is preserved by salting. Available from continental delicatessens, it is widely used in Mediterranean countries. The salted fillets must be soaked in cold water for 24 hours before use. Not to be confused with Italian dried cod (stockfish) which is unsalted.

SARDINES

These small, flavoursome fish are available from February to July. They are also frozen and are of good quality. Usually cooked whole by grilling, sardines are delicious when barbecued. They may also be stuffed, either whole or boned and rolled.

SCALLOPS

These shellfish are usually sold separated from their shells. They have a nugget of firm white flesh and a bright moon-shaped coral which should be a good red colour. Unopened scallops should be placed in a warm oven for a few moments until their shells begin to open. Place rounded shell down to catch precious juices. Carefully prize the white flesh and coral away from the shell, discarding the grey-brown frill and dark intestine.

Queen scallops are a small species, sold without roe as small rounds of very pale pink muscle. Canned queen scallops are also available but they are very disappointing.

Frozen scallops are often available from delicatessens or Oriental stores and they can be excellent. Scallops should be cooked gently and briefly; otherwise they become leathery.

SCAMPI

Also known as langoustine, Dublin Bay prawns or Norway lobsters, these are orange-red crustaceans which look like miniature lobsters. They have long claws and curled tails. They must not be confused with Mediterranean prawns or crawfish, neither of which has claws. Remember, too, that uncooked Mediterranean prawns are grey rather than pink. Scampi are bright red-pink when alive; they retain this colour when cooked. The tail contains the meat. They are not readily available but an advance order at a good fishmongers may secure them.

Breaded scampi tails are available frozen.

Check the wording on the packet to ensure that they are exactly that and not 'scampi-style' portions which are not the real thing.

SEA BASS

A fine-flavoured, large scaly fish which is grey in colour, sea bass is in season from August to March. The fish may be baked, poached or barbecued whole. Although the fishmonger will fillet the fish, the fillets are surprisingly small.

SEA BREAM

Several types of bream (including a fresh-water fish) are available from June to February. Known as porgy in America, bream has a good flavour. Look out for red bream, black bream and gilt head bream which is dark grey-blue with silvery lower sides. The edge of the gill is scarlet and the fish has a bright golden stripe running across its forehead between the eyes. Also known as gilthead.

SEA TROUT

See Salmon.

SHARK

Although many of the fish described here belong to the shark family, you can also buy shark steaks as such. Larger fishmongers may even display whole shark.

The tough, leather-like skin has to be removed before cooking as it shrinks and spoils the flesh. The flesh is firm, meaty and rather cartilaginous, a texture which not everyone likes. The flavour is not particularly noteworthy.

SHRIMPS

Both brown and pink shrimps are available, although the brown ones are usually a regional speciality. They resemble very small prawns and are sold cooked in their shells. Peeling shrimps is a time-consuming task but the excellent flavour is ample reward. Shrimps are available canned but not frozen.

SKATE

A member of the shark family, also known as ray. Wings of skate are available from May to February. The flesh is cartilaginous and characteristically has a faint odour of ammonia which disappears when the fish is rinsed or blanched in acidulated water. Any strong smell of ammonia indicates that the fish is not as fresh as it should be.

SNAILS

While snails are not, strictly speaking, seafood, they are members of the same family as periwinkles, limpets and whelks (right) and are habitually classified alongside these related molluscs. There are many types of snail. They are now commercially farmed. The wild snail (or 'garden snail') was traditionally collected but today the favoured variety is the Burgundy or Roman snail.

Processing live snails is a complicated business. They must be kept in a basket or ventilated box for a week to purge their systems. The next stage is salting, to remove all the slime. They are then washed, boiled, removed from their shells and boiled again until tender.

Prepared snails are sold in cans, often with clean shells as part of the packaging. The snails are placed in the shells, then topped with garlic butter. They are heated through in the oven and served in dimpled snail dishes with tongs to hold the shells and special forks for extracting the snails. The shells can be thoroughly washed, dried and used again and again. See page 24.

SPRATS

Available from October to March, these small fish may be grilled or deep fried. They are usually gutted and their backbones are removed.

SQUID

Squid is sold prepared or whole from May to September. Many supermarkets sell battered squid rings, or *calamari*, ready for baking or frying.

SWORDFISH

Available all year, swordfish steaks are firm and meaty. They have a good flavour and are ideal for grilling or barbecuing. Since it can become rather dry during cooking, swordfish benefits from frequent basting or cooking in butter or oil.

TROUT

A freshwater fish that is now inexpensive due to extensive farming. Available fresh and frozen, also as prepared fillets. Rainbow trout has pale pink, delicately flavoured flesh. For sea trout or salmon trout, see Salmon.

TUNA

There are several different species of tuna, all large. It is available throughout the year, either fresh or frozen. The dark sculptured flesh is dry; it benefits from marinating and frequent basting during cooking. Tuna is sold as portions or steaks and is ideal for barbecuing and for cooking in a sauce.

Canned tuna in oil or brine is a familiar – and useful – storecupboard item.

TURBOT

A large flat fish, turbot has firm white meat with a good flavour. It is available from April to February and is usually sold as steaks or fillets. Special turbot kettles are available for cooking whole fish.

WHELKS AND WINKLES

These are both sea snails. Whelks are carnivores and winkles are herbivores. Winkles, the smaller of the two, are traditionally picked from their shells by using a pin. Both are usually sold cooked and shelled. Whelks are available from February to August; winkles from September to April.

WHITEBAIT
Small young herring and sprat fry, whitebait is available fresh from February to June. Frozen whitebait is on sale throughout the year. They are cooked whole by deep frying. The fish are eaten whole.

WHITING
A member of the cod family, whiting has slightly soft white flesh which tends to be rather bland and uninteresting. It is usually sold filleted but is sometimes available whole. Available from June to February.

EXOTIC FISH
The following are just a few examples of the exotic fish which are sometimes available. Many are from tropical regions including the west coast of Africa, the Seychelles, the Pacific Ocean and the Indian Ocean. They make good eating and many look attractive when cooked and served whole.

Croakers or Drums Light brown fish with a red-tinged belly. Available all year.

Emperors or Emperor Bream A striking fish, available all year, this has golden fins, tail and nose on an otherwise grey-silver body.

Groupers A golden dorsal line, hints of orange-gold speckles and a bright orange-gold eye make this a decorative species. Available all year.

Jacks Colourful fish, tinged blue, yellow and red. Available all year.

Parrot Fish A striking fish, either blue or brightly coloured, available all year.

Pomfret Available all year, a deep bodied fish with a small face. Tinged pale gold to grey.

Snappers Available all year. The red snapper is the most common.

PREPARATION TECHNIQUES

The basic techniques outlined below are, on the whole, interesting rather than essential because the majority of good fishmongers will prepare the fish for you. However, the advice on handling live crustaceans and shellfish should be followed carefully. If you are lucky enough to have a fisherman in the family, you may find the information on cleaning fish (page 26) useful.

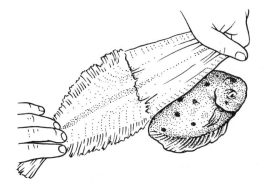

SKINNING FLAT FISH (Dover sole, plaice etc)

1 Lay the fish on a clean surface, light skin down. Cut through the skin at the tail end. Slip the point of a knife under the skin to separate a flap from the flesh. Dip your fingers in salt to prevent slipping and hold the fish down firmly by its tail, then pull the skin off, working towards the head. Cut the skin neatly around the head. Turn the fish over and repeat on the second side.

FILLETING FLAT FISH

1 Lay the fish on a clean surface with the tail towards you. Use a sharp pointed knife to cut the flesh down to the bone around the head. Cut straight down the middle of the back, from head to tail.

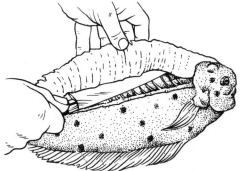

2 Starting at the head end of the fillet, cut the flesh off the bones working from the middle towards the side of the fish. Slide the point of the knife down the bones, keeping it close to them all the time, and lift the fillet of fish away as it is cut free.

BONING A POUCH IN FLAT FISH

1 Cut a slit down the backbone, from head to tail. Carefully ease the point of the knife under the flesh, cutting it off the bones on one side. Work right against the bone down to the side but do not cut through to the skin of the fish. Repeat on the second side to reveal the bones.

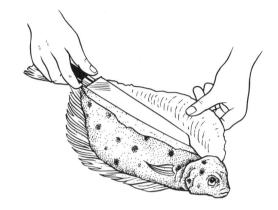

2 Use a pair of kitchen scissors to snip the backbone at the head and tail ends. Make two more snips along its length. Use the point of a knife and scissors to remove all the bones from the cavity, leaving a pouch ready for stuffing.

FILLETING ROUND FISH (mackerel, herring etc)

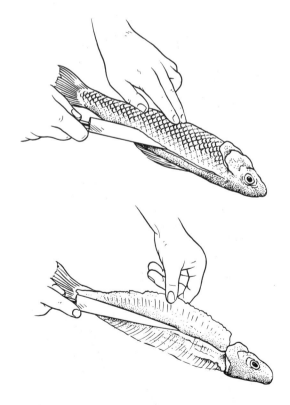

1 Cut the flesh down to the bone around the head. Hold the fish firmly with one hand and cut along its length down to the backbone.

2 Starting at the head again, cut the flesh away from the bones, easing the fillet back as you cut. Work close to the bones. Turn the fish over and repeat on the second side.

Note: If you ask the fishmonger to fillet a round fish, for example mackerel, you will often be given a flat, boned whole fish. Therefore, if you want two fillets from each fish, make this clear when you ask to have them filleted.

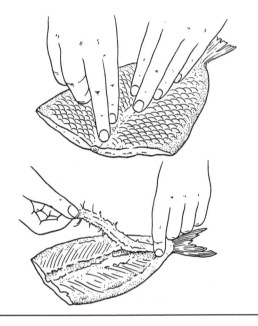

BONING ROUND FISH

1 Ensure that the cleaned fish has been slit right down to the tail. The head must be removed. Lay the fish, skin up, flat on a board. Press the flesh firmly along the backbone.

2 Turn the fish over and lift the backbone off from the tail end. It should come away easily, lifting most of the bones with it. Remove any stray bones.

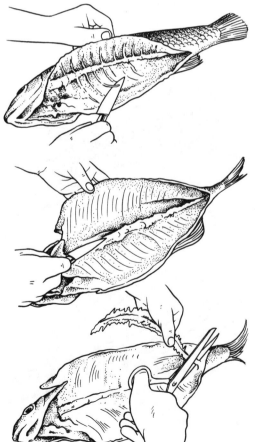

BONING WHOLE ROUND FISH

This is a technique for removing the bones while keeping the head and tail intact, for instance when stuffing the body cavity of a whole fish.

1 Make sure the body cavity of the fish is slit all along its length. Slide the point of a knife under each bone to free it from the flesh. Work from the backbone outwards.

2 Use a pair of kitchen scissors to snip through the backbone at the head and tail ends. Use the point of a knife to free the backbone, and lift it away. Remove any stray bones.

SKINNING FISH FILLETS

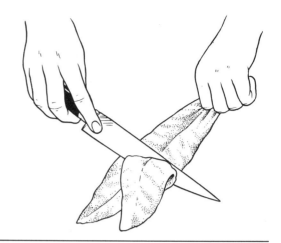

1 Lay the fillet on a board, skin down. Rub your fingers in salt. Hold the tail end firmly, then cut the flesh away from the skin. Hold the knife at an acute angle and use a sawing motion to remove the flesh in one piece, folding it back as you cut from the tail end towards the head.

SCALING FISH

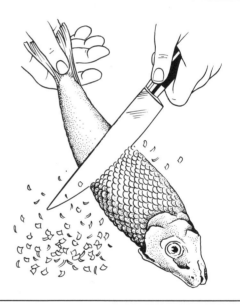

1 Hold the fish in a clean sink and have cold water running slowly to wash away the scales as you work. Scrape off the scales from the tail towards the head, occasionally rinsing the knife and fish. A messy task, also known as descaling.

BONING FISH STEAKS OR CUTLETS

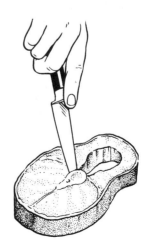

1 Use a thin, pointed knife and cut down around the bone to free the flesh from it. In the case of cutlets it is sometimes easier to snip the end of the bone free with kitchen scissors.

CLEANING COOKED CRAB

1 Twist off the claws and legs. Tap the edge of the shell firmly on a board to loosen the body slightly. Turn the crab upside down on a board with the mouth and eyes away from you. Pull off the tail. Use both thumbs to ease the body up and out of the shell.

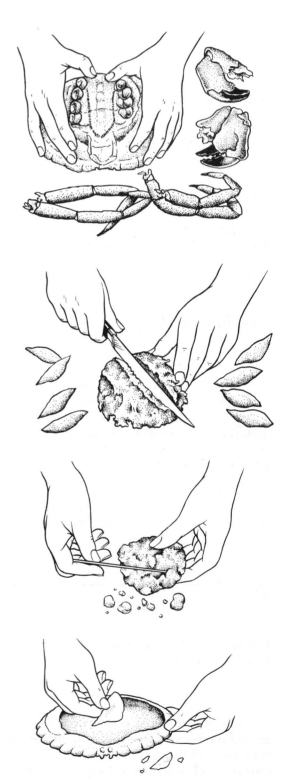

2 Discard the stomach sac, located just behind the mouth, and remove the soft gills around the body. The gills are known as dead men's fingers because of their appearance. Cut the body in half.

3 Pick out the white meat from the body and the brown meat from inside the shell. Crack the claws and legs, then pick out the white meat.

4 Trim the shell: tap away the shell edge around the groove and remove it. This gives a neat shell which should be thoroughly scrubbed in hot soapy water and rinsed with boiling water, then dried.

5 To dress crab, mix the brown meat with a small quantity of fresh breadcrumbs, a dash of lemon juice and salt and pepper to taste. Arrange it in the sides of the clean shell. Arrange the white meat in the middle. Chopped parsley, hard-boiled egg and lemon may be added as a garnish.

CLEANING LOBSTER

1 Twist off the claws and legs. Lay the lobster on a board with the shell down. Use a heavy, sharp knife and rolling pin or meat mallet to split the lobster down the middle.

2 Discard the dark intestinal tract which runs down the length of the body. Discard the spongy gills from the head end. Scoop out and save any red coral. The soft, brown liver may be saved and used to flavour a sauce. Remove the firm white tail meat.

3 Clean out the head end of the shell, wash and dry it. The shell may be used to serve the cold dressed lobster, sauced lobster or lobster gratin. Crack the claws and pick out the meat.

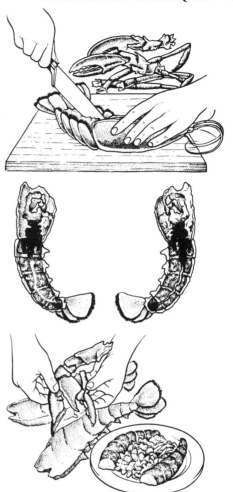

PEELING PRAWNS

1 Break off and discard the head.

2 Pull the shell apart from underneath and slip it all off, leaving just the tail in place. Break off the tail.

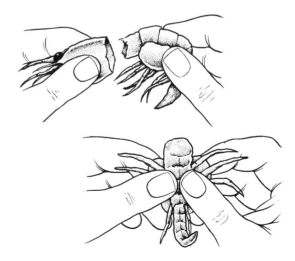

CLEANING SQUID

1 If the tentacles are to be used, cut them off first and set them aside. Cut off and discard the beak from the centre of the tentacles. Pull the head and the attached parts out of the sac: discard the head parts.

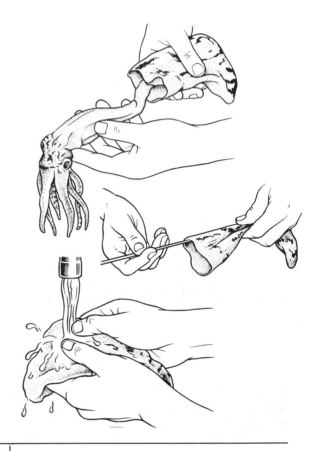

2 Remove the transparent 'pen' from inside the body.

3 Rub off the mottled skin under running water, at the same time rubbing off the small flaps on either side of the body, leaving the body clean and white.

KILLING AND COOKING LIVE CRAB AND LOBSTER

There are two options: freezing or cooking in cold water.

Freezing Place the live crab or lobster in a clean polythene carrier bag in the freezer and leave it there for 5-7 hours or overnight.

Cover with cold water in a large saucepan, add a little salt and bring slowly to the boil. Lower the heat and simmer for 15 minutes per 450 g/1 lb, plus 10 minutes. Lobster is cooked when the shell has turned a bright pink. Drain well and cool. Allow an extra 5 minutes for shellfish that are frozen hard night through.

Cooking from Live Place the crab or lobster in a large pan of cold salted water and put a tight-fitting lid on the pan. Heat gently to boiling point, then cook as above.

Killing by Stabbing The method of stabbing lobsters behind the head or crabs between the eyes is not to be recommended. Freezing is much more humane.

PREPARATION OF SHELLS FOR SERVING

If empty shells are to be used for serving, they must first be thoroughly scrubbed and boiled in clean water for 5 minutes, then drained and dried. This applies particularly to shells from scallops or oysters which are not cooked with the shellfish.

STUNNING AND SKINNING EELS

Conger eel is sold skinned and cut into steaks. Freshwater eels are kept alive until they are prepared. The fishmonger will usually do this for you as it is not a pleasant task. If, however, you have to prepare an eel, the following may prove valuable:

First stun the eel by banging its head firmly against a hard surface. Then stab it through the back of the head to kill it.

Slit the skin around the head using a strong sharp knife. Using pliers, loosen the skin, then, holding the head firmly in a piece of cloth, pull back the skin from head to tail in one piece. Cut off and discard head.

The eel may be hung by the head from a meat hook and the skin pulled off.

PREPARING MUSSELS

Thoroughly scrub the shells and scrape off any barnacles. Discard any open shells which do not close when tapped. Pull away the dark hairy 'beard' which protrudes slightly from the shell.

Cook mussels in a small amount of boiling liquid over high heat. Put a tight-fitting lid on the saucepan. Shake the pan occasionally and cook for about 5 minutes, until all the shells have opened. The mussels cook in the steam of the liquid. They should not be overcooked or they will toughen. Discard any shells that have not opened after cooking.

Note: The above method is also used for cockles and clams. Bought farmed shellfish should not be sandy; however leaving the shellfish in a cold place in a bucket of salted water overnight allows time for them to expel any sand they may contain.

OPENING OYSTERS

Ideally a special, short-bladed, tough oyster knife should be used. Do not use your favourite light kitchen knife as the blade may break. Select a fairly blunt, short, strong knife or similar implement. Hold the oyster with the curved shell down. Insert the point of the knife into the hinged end of

the shell and prize it open. Take care as the tough shell is difficult to open and a knife which slips can cause a nasty injury.

OPENING SCALLOPS

Scallops are usually sold prepared. To open them at home place them in a warm oven for a few moments, until the shells part slightly. Then prize the shells apart and cut the nugget of white muscle and coral free.

ASK THE FISHMONGER

Knowing the basics of fish preparation makes it easier when shopping. Always ask the fishmonger to clean (gut) whole fish (trout, mackerel, bass, mullet and so on), stating clearly whether you want the head and tail on or off. Filleting is a task for the fishmonger. Most will also bone, scale and skin fish. Some fishmongers may even cut large fillets into serving portions.

These are not attributes of the model fishmonger; they are services you can reasonably expect, for no extra charge, but you must be reasonable in making a request. At busy times, select your purchase, explain the preparation required and call back later. A polite request achieves a lot more than a haughty demand. Most fishmongers are highly skilled and only too ready to help.

SEAFISH QUALITY AWARD

Look out for the symbol above. It is displayed by fishmongers who have satisfied the judges that they not only sell quality fish, but also score in terms of quality and operation of the premises, storage, equipment, staff, handling and presentation.

CLEANING FISH

If possible, ask the fishmonger or fisherman to clean (gut) fish for you. If you have to do this at home, lay several thicknesses of clean newspaper on the work surface and place the fish on greaseproof paper on top. Slit the fish down its belly, then scrape out the innards. Transfer the fish to a plate; repeat with other fish. Wrap the newspaper tightly around the innards at once, and place in an outdoor waste bin. Wash down all surfaces, utensils and your hands. Thoroughly rinse the fish, then pat it dry with absorbent kitchen paper.

Other methods Round fish may also be cleaned through the gills to avoid splitting the body open. Similarly, whole flat fish (plaice and Dover or lemon sole) have only small pockets of innards that are removed through a small slit below the head. The fishmonger will clean fish in this way for you but always remember to ask for a specific cleaning method such as through the gills.

RULES TO REMEMBER

Buying Fish and Seafood
■ Buy from a reputable source – the premises should look clean and smell fresh.

■ Wet fish should look moist and bright. All eyes should be bright and moist, markings on skin should be bright. Fish fillets should be moist, clean and unbroken.

■ Ready-to-eat fish and seafood (for example, smoked mackerel) should never be handled immediately after raw fish. The fishmonger should pick up the ready-to-eat fish with an implement or in a bag. This rule is particularly important if the fishmonger has been cleaning raw fish. He should either wear gloves for this operation or wash his hands thoroughly when the fish has been cleaned.

■ Make fish the last item you buy on a shopping trip, take it home quickly (in a chiller bag on hot days) and unpack it at once.

■ Rinse and dry the fish, then put it in a dish and cover it with cling film. Place in the refrigerator and cook it within 24 hours.

Handling Fish
■ Use a clean board, preferably made of plastic material. Wooden boards should always be scrubbed and rinsed in boiling water, then allowed to dry after use.

■ Use a sharp, narrow-bladed, pointed knife for preparing fish.

■ Kitchen scissors are useful for snipping off fins and for cutting bones. Wash them well after use.

■ Never prepare raw fish and cooked food using the same utensils, unless the utensils have been thoroughly washed and dried.

■ Always keep fish covered and chilled before cooking.

Freezing Fish
■ Bought frozen fish is frozen soon after it is taken from the sea. It is frozen speedily at low temperatures for best results.

■ Fish for home freezing should be freshly caught or bought fresh from a reputable fishmonger. Do not freeze bought fish which has been frozen and thawed before sale. Freeze fish immediately after purchase. This applies particularly to oily fish such as mackerel.

■ Always clean and prepare fish for cooking before freezing it.

■ Pack fish in heavy polythene bags, excluding as much air as possible.

■ White fish may be stored for 3-4 months; oily fish keeps for 2-3 months in a domestic freezer at −18°C/0°F.

BASIC RECIPES

This chapter provides a selection of essential stocks, sauces, stuffings and flavoured butters. In addition, there are a few useful ideas for garnishing fish and seafood dishes.

BASIC FISH STOCK

This simple fish stock can be used for poaching fish, making soups or sauces, or in batters for frying fish. It should always be freshly made and will not keep unless frozen.

fish bones and trimmings without gills
   which cause bitterness
5 ml/1 tsp salt
1 small onion, sliced
2 celery sticks, sliced
4 white peppercorns
1 bouquet garni

Break up any bones and wash the fish trimmings, if used. Put the bones, trimmings or heads in a saucepan and cover with 1 litre/1¾ pints cold water. Add the salt.

Bring the liquid to the boil and add the vegetables, peppercorns and bouquet garni. Lower the heat, cover and simmer gently for 30-40 minutes. Do not cook the stock for longer than 40 minutes or it may develop a bitter taste.

Strain the stock through a fine sieve into a clean saucepan or measuring jug and use as required.

MAKES 1 LITRE/1¾ PINTS

WHITE WINE FISH STOCK

Adding wine or cider gives this fish stock extra piquancy. Use it for cooking fish or shellfish, for poaching fish quenelles, for marinating herrings or as a basis for sauces or fish soups.

100 ml/3½ fl oz dry white wine or
   dry cider
800 g/1¾ lb white fish heads, trimmings
   and bones
1 large onion, thinly sliced
1 large carrot, thinly sliced
4-5 mushroom stalks
1 blade of mace
6 peppercorns
1 bouquet garni

Put the wine or cider into a large saucepan with 1 litre/1¾ pints water. Wash the fish heads and trimmings and break up the bones. Add them to the pan with the remaining ingredients.

Heat the liquid to simmering point, cover the pan and simmer for 30 minutes. Leave to cool, then strain the stock through a fine sieve into a clean saucepan or measuring jug. Use as required.

MAKES 1 LITRE/1¾ PINTS

ASPIC JELLY

In Mrs Beeton's day, making aspic jelly was a lengthy and uneconomical process, involving the slow boiling in stock of two calf's feet (or 450 g/1 lb cracked veal knuckles with 100 g/4 oz pork rind). Today's method, using gelatine, is faster but equally effective.

1 litre/1¾ pints fish, chicken or vegetable
    stock, cooled
125 ml/4 fl oz white wine (see Variation)
30 ml/2 tbsp white wine vinegar
40-50 g/1½-2 oz gelatine
1 bouquet garni
whites and crushed shells of 2 eggs

Before you begin, scald a large enamel or stainless steel (not aluminium) saucepan, a piece of clean muslin or thin white cotton, a metal sieve and a whisk in boiling water, as the merest trace of grease may cause cloudiness in the finished jelly. For the same reason, skim off any fat on top of the stock.

Put the stock into the saucepan with the remaining ingredients and heat gently. Stir with the whisk until the gelatine softens, then bring the liquid to just below boiling point, whisking constantly. A thick white crust of foam will develop on the top. Remove the whisk. As soon as the liquid rises to the top of the pan, remove it from the heat. Leave to stand briefly until the foam falls back into the pan, then heat the stock in the same way once or twice more, until the liquid is crystal clear. If the stock was fairly clear before clarifying, then one boiling may be sufficient; a very cloudy stock needs at least two boilings.

Line the sieve with the muslin and place it over a perfectly clean bowl. Strain the crust and liquid very gently through the muslin into the bowl. Try not to break the crust as it acts as an extra filter. The aspic should be sparkling clear; if necessary repeat the process a second time, remembering to scald the equipment again. Use as directed in recipes.

MAKES 1 LITRE/1¾ PINTS

VARIATION

SHERRY ASPIC If using the aspic with red meats or game, substitute half the white wine with dry sherry.

COURT BOUILLON

This is the traditional stock used for poaching salmon, salmon trout or any other whole fish. It is discarded after use.

500 ml/17 fl oz dry white wine or dry cider
30 ml/2 tbsp white wine vinegar
2 large carrots, sliced
2 large onions, sliced
2-3 celery sticks, chopped
6 parsley stalks, crushed
1 bouquet garni
10 peppercorns, lightly crushed
salt and pepper

Put the wine in a large stainless steel or enamel saucepan. Add 1 litre/1¾ pints water, with the remaining ingredients.

Bring the liquids to the boil, lower the temperature and simmer for 30 minutes. Cool, then strain and use as required.

MAKES 1.5 LITRES/2¾ PINTS

MRS BEETON'S TIP Parsley stalks impart valuable flavour to stocks and other simmering liquids. The leaves and sprigs may be cut off and saved.

LEMON AND HERB STUFFING

50 g/2 oz margarine
100 g/4 oz fresh white breadcrumbs
30 ml/2 tbsp chopped parsley
2.5 ml/½ tsp chopped fresh thyme
grated rind of ½ lemon
salt and pepper

Melt the margarine in a small saucepan. Add the breadcrumbs, herbs and lemon rind. Add salt and pepper to taste, then use as required.

SUFFICIENT FOR 8 × 75 G/3 OZ THIN FISH FILLETS

RICE AND OLIVE STUFFING

50 g/2 oz butter
1 onion, finely chopped
2 celery sticks, finely chopped
50 g/2 oz stuffed green olives, chopped
100 g/4 oz cooked long-grain rice
1.25 ml/¼ tsp dried sage
1.25 ml/¼ tsp dried thyme
salt and pepper

Melt the butter in a small saucepan. Add the onion and celery and fry gently for 3-4 minutes until soft.

Stir in the olives, rice and herbs. Cook gently for 3 minutes, then add salt and pepper to taste. Use as required.

SUFFICIENT FOR 1 × 1.4 KG/3 LB WHOLE FISH

 MRS BEETON'S TIP As a guide, 50 g/2 oz uncooked rice will yield 100-150 g/4-5 oz cooked rice.

TOMATO STUFFING

2 large ripe tomatoes, peeled, seeded and chopped
1 red pepper, seeded and chopped or 2 canned pimientos, chopped
1 garlic clove, crushed
50-75 g/2-3 oz fresh wholemeal breadcrumbs
salt and pepper

Mix the tomatoes, pepper or pimientos and garlic in a bowl. Add enough breadcrumbs to absorb the juice from the tomatoes. Add salt and pepper to taste, then use as required.

SUFFICIENT FOR 1.5 KG/3¼ LB WHITE FISH

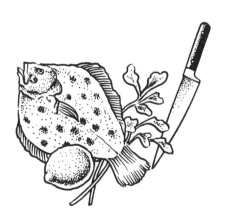

MUSHROOM STUFFING

1 rindless streaky bacon rasher, chopped
100 g/4 oz button mushrooms with stalks,
  chopped
100 g/4 oz fresh white breadcrumbs
knob of butter or margarine
pinch of grated nutmeg
salt and pepper
1 egg

Put the bacon in a heavy-bottomed sauce-pan over moderate heat for about 2 minutes or until the fat runs.

Add the mushrooms and fry very gently for 3-5 minutes, stirring frequently. When the mushrooms soften, remove the pan from the heat and stir in the breadcrumbs, butter or margarine and nutmeg. Add salt and pepper to taste.

Beat the egg in a cup until it is just liquid, then stir enough of the beaten egg into the stuffing to bind it. Use as required.

SUFFICIENT FOR 8 × 75 G/3 OZ THIN FISH FILLETS

> **MRS BEETON'S TIP**   It is a good idea to keep a stock of breadcrumbs in a sealed polythene bag in the freezer. They thaw very swiftly and can be used in a wide variety of sweet and savoury dishes.

OYSTER STUFFING

Once a common food, oysters are central to many traditional English dishes. Rich in protein and full of flavour, they make an excellent stuffing for a whole fish such as grey mullet.

6 fresh or canned oysters
100 g/4 oz fresh white breadcrumbs
50 g/2 oz shredded suet or melted butter
5 ml/1 tsp chopped mixed fresh herbs
pinch of grated nutmeg
salt and pepper
1 egg

If using fresh oysters, open them over a saucepan (see Mrs Beeton's Tip), then simmer them very gently in their own liquor for 10 minutes. Canned oysters need no cooking.

Drain the oysters, reserving the liquor, and cut into small pieces.

In a bowl, mix the breadcrumbs with the suet or melted butter. Add the oysters, herbs and nutmeg, with salt and pepper to taste.

Beat the egg in a cup until it is just liquid, then stir it into the oyster mixture, adding a little of the reserved oyster liquor, if necessary, to bind.

SUFFICIENT FOR 1 × 1.1 KG/2½ LB WHOLE FISH

> **MRS BEETON'S TIP**   Use a strong knife or special oyster knife to open the oysters (see page 25), working it between the shells to cut the ligament hinge which keeps the shells together.

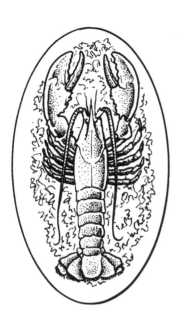

*E*GG STUFFING

15 g/½ oz butter, softened
1 hard-boiled egg, finely chopped
75 ml/5 tbsp fresh white breadcrumbs
2.5 ml/½ tsp chopped parsley
salt and pepper
milk

Cream the butter in a small bowl. Add the egg, breadcrumbs and parsley, with salt and pepper to taste. Mix well, adding just enough milk to bind the mixture. Use as required.

SUFFICIENT FOR 2 × 75 G/3 OZ THIN WHITE FISH FILLETS

MRS BEETON'S TIP To prevent a dark ring from forming around the yolk of a hard-boiled egg, plunge the egg into cold water immediately after cooking and for at least 5 minutes thereafter.

---

*F*ISH FORCEMEAT

25 g/1 oz plain flour
125 ml/4 fl oz Basic Fish Stock (page 27)
25 g/1 oz butter
salt and pepper
1 egg
225 g/8 oz white fish fillet, skinned and finely flaked
grated rind and juice of ½ lemon

Sift the flour on to a sheet of greaseproof paper. Bring the stock and the butter to the boil in a small saucepan. Heat gently until the butter melts.

When the butter has melted, bring the liquid rapidly to the boil and add all the flour at once. Immediately remove the pan from the heat and stir the flour into the liquid to make a smooth paste which leaves the sides of the pan clean. Add salt and pepper to taste. Set aside to cool slightly.

Beat the egg in a cup until it is just liquid, then add it gradually to the cooled mixture, beating well after each addition.

Beat the raw flaked fish into the mixture with the grated lemon rind. Add lemon juice to taste. Use as required.

SUFFICIENT FOR 12 × 75 G/3 OZ THIN FISH FILLETS, 8 FISH CUTLETS OR 4 × 350 TO 450 G/12 OZ TO 1 LB WHOLE FISH

MRS BEETON'S TIP When grating citrus fruit, work over a sheet of foil, using a clean pastry brush to extricate all the rind from the grater. Tip the rind into the bowl or saucepan, then use the brush to sweep in any lingering shreds.

MAYONNAISE

Buy eggs from a reputable supplier and make sure they are perfectly fresh. Immediately before cracking the eggs wash them in cold water and dry them on absorbent kitchen paper.

2 egg yolks
salt and pepper
5 ml/1 tsp caster sugar
5 ml/1 tsp Dijon mustard
about 30 ml/2 tbsp lemon juice
250 ml/8 fl oz oil (olive oil or a mixture of
olive and grapeseed or sunflower oil)

Place the egg yolks in a medium or large bowl. Add salt and pepper, the sugar, mustard and 15 ml/1 tbsp of the lemon juice. Whisk thoroughly until the sugar has dissolved. An electric whisk is best; or use a wire whisk and work vigorously.

Whisking all the time, add the oil drop by drop so that it forms an emulsion with the egg yolks. As the oil is incorporated, and the mixture begins to turn pale, it may be added in a slow trickle. If the oil is added too quickly before it begins to combine with the eggs, the sauce will curdle.

The mayonnaise may be made in a blender or food processor. The egg mixture should be processed first, with 10 ml/2 tsp of the oil added right at the beginning. With the machine running, add the oil drop by drop at first, then in a trickle as above.

When all the oil has been incorporated the mayonnaise should be thick and pale. Taste the mixture, then stir in more lemon juice, salt and pepper, if necessary. Keep mayonnaise in a covered container in the refrigerator for up to 5 days.

MAKES ABOUT 300 ML/½ PINT

VARIATIONS

AÏOLI Add 2 fresh large crushed garlic cloves to the yolks with the seasonings.

ROUILLE Add 2 fresh large crushed garlic cloves to the yolks. Omit the mustard. Add 15 ml/1 tbsp paprika and 1.25 ml/¼ tsp cayenne pepper to the yolk mixture before incorporating the oil.

> **MRS BEETON'S TIP** All is not lost if the mixture curdles. Stop adding oil immediately the sauce shows any sign of curdling. Take a clean bowl and place a fresh egg yolk in it. Whisk the yolk well with 5 ml/1 tsp of the curdled mixture. Whisking vigorously, add the remaining curdled mixture drop by drop. Make sure each drop of curdled mixture is incorporated before adding more.

TARTARE SAUCE

2 hard-boiled egg yolks
2 egg yolks
salt and pepper
15 ml/1 tbsp white wine vinegar
300 ml/½ pint oil (olive oil or a mixture of
olive with grapeseed or sunflower oil)
15 ml/1 tbsp chopped capers
15 ml/1 tbsp chopped gherkin
30 ml/2 tbsp chopped parsley
15 ml/1 tbsp snipped chives

Sieve the hard-boiled egg yolks into a bowl. Add one of the raw yolks and mix thoroughly, then work in the second raw yolk. Stir in salt and pepper to taste and mix to a paste with the vinegar.

Beating vigorously, gradually add the oil, drop by drop, as for making mayonnaise (left). When all the oil has been incorporated and the mixture is thick, stir in the capers, gherkin and herbs.

MAKES ABOUT 300 ML/½ PINT

Channel Chowder (page 47), and Spanish Fish Soup (page 48)

Mediterranean Crab Soup (page 51) and Norwegian Fish Soup (page 55)

Moules Marinière (page 57)

Eel Casserole (page 59) and Cod Portugaise (page 65)

Sweet and Sour Hake (page 68)

Plaice Mornay (page 67) and Sole Veronique (page 70)

Poached Trout with Prawn Sauce (page 84) and Pike Quenelles (page 85)

Carp with Mushrooms (page 86) and Golden Grilled Cod (page 95)

WHITE SAUCE

The recipe that follows is for a thick coating sauce.

50 g/2 oz butter
50 g/2 oz plain flour
600 ml/1 pint milk, Basic Fish Stock
    (page 27) or a mixture
salt and pepper

Melt the butter in a saucepan. Stir in the flour and cook over low heat for 2-3 minutes, without browning.

With the heat on the lowest setting, gradually add the liquid, stirring constantly. If lumps begin to form, stop pouring in liquid and stir the sauce vigorously, then continue pouring in the liquid when smooth. Increase the heat to moderate and cook the sauce, stirring, until it boils.

Lower the heat and simmer for 1-2 minutes, beating briskly to give the sauce a gloss. Add salt and pepper to taste.

MAKES 600 ML/1 PINT

VARIATION

POURING SAUCE Follow the recipe above, but use only 40 g/1½ oz each of butter and flour. The sauce should flow freely, barely masking the spoon.

MRS BEETON'S TIP White Sauce can be made by the all-in-one method. Simply combine the butter, flour and liquid in a saucepan and whisk over moderate heat until the mixture comes to the boil. Lower the heat and simmer for 3-4 minutes, whisking constantly until the sauce is thick, smooth and glossy. Add salt and pepper to taste.

BÉCHAMEL SAUCE

Marquis Louis de Béchameil is credited with inventing this French foundation sauce. For a slightly less rich version, use half white stock and half milk.

1 small onion, thickly sliced
1 small carrot, sliced
1 small celery stick, sliced
600 ml/1 pint milk
1 bay leaf
few parsley stalks
1 thyme sprig
1 clove
6 white peppercorns
1 blade of mace
salt
50 g/2 oz butter
50 g/2 oz plain flour
60 ml/4 tbsp single cream (optional)

Combine the onion, carrot, celery and milk in a saucepan. Add the herbs and spices, with salt to taste. Heat to simmering point, cover, turn off the heat and allow to stand for 30 minutes to infuse, then strain.

Melt the butter in a saucepan. Stir in the flour and cook over low heat for 2-3 minutes, without browning. With the heat on the lowest setting, gradually add the milk, stirring constantly.

Return the pan to moderate heat, stirring until the mixture boils and thickens to a coating consistency. Lower the heat when the mixture boils and simmer the sauce for 1-2 minutes, beating briskly to give the sauce a gloss. Stir in the cream, if used, and remove the sauce from the heat at once. Do not allow the sauce to come to the boil again. Check the seasoning and add salt if required.

MAKES ABOUT 600 ML/1 PINT

HOLLANDAISE SAUCE

This is the classic sauce to serve with poached salmon or other firm fish.

45 ml/3 tbsp white wine vinegar
6 peppercorns
½ bay leaf
1 blade of mace
3 egg yolks
100 g/4 oz butter, softened
salt and pepper

Combine the vinegar, peppercorns, bay leaf and mace in a small saucepan. Boil rapidly until the liquid is reduced to 15 ml/1 tbsp. Strain into a heatproof bowl and leave to cool.

Add the egg yolks and a nut of butter to the vinegar and place over a saucepan of gently simmering water. Heat the mixture gently, beating constantly until thick. Do not allow it to approach boiling point.

Add the remaining butter, a little at a time, beating well after each addition. When all the butter has been added the sauce should be thick and glossy. If the sauce curdles, whisk in 10 ml/2 tsp cold water. If this fails to bind it, put an egg yolk in a clean bowl and beat in the sauce gradually.

Season the sauce lightly with salt and pepper and serve lukewarm.

MAKES ABOUT 125 ML/4 FL OZ

☀ **MICROWAVE TIP** A quick and easy Hollandaise Sauce can be made in the microwave. Simply combine 30 ml/2 tbsp lemon juice with 15 ml/1 tbsp water in a large bowl. Add a little salt and white pepper and cook on High for 3-6 minutes or until the mixture is reduced by about two-thirds. Meanwhile place 100 g/4 oz butter in a measuring jug. Remove the bowl of lemon juice from the microwave oven, replacing it with the jug of butter. Heat the butter on High for 2½ minutes. Meanwhile add 2 large egg yolks to the lemon juice, whisking constantly. When the butter is hot, add it in the same way. Return the sauce to the microwave oven. Cook on High for 30 seconds, whisk once more and serve.

SIMPLE VARIATIONS ON BASIC SAUCES

Add one of the ingredients shown to the basic recipe (in this chapter), when the sauce is cooked.

	Cheese, grated (Cheddar)	Eggs, hard-boiled and chopped	Anchovy essence	Parsley, chopped	Tomato Purée	Mushrooms, sliced and cooked in butter	Mustard, made mild	Capers chopped
White Sauce	100 g/4 oz	3-4		60 ml/4 tbsp		175 g/6 oz	45-60 ml/3-4 tbsp	
Béchamel Sauce		3	30 ml/2 tbsp		30 ml/2 tbsp	100 g/4 oz		45 ml/3 tbsp
Hollandaise Sauce					15 ml/1 tbsp			15 ml/1 tbsp
Mayonnaise			15 ml/1 tbsp	30 ml/2 tbsp	15 ml/1 tbsp		10-15 ml/2-3 tsp	15 ml/1 tbsp

BLACK BUTTER

Black butter is a bit of a misnomer. The beurre noir *so beloved of the French should be a rich golden brown. It is the perfect accompaniment to fried or poached skate.*

150 g/5 oz butter
30 ml/2 tbsp chopped parsley
15 ml/1 tbsp chopped capers
10-15 ml/2-3 tsp wine vinegar

Heat the butter in a heavy-bottomed frying pan until deep golden brown but not burnt. Add the parsley and capers. Pour into a heated jug.

Add the vinegar to the frying pan and bring to the boil. Immediately add it to the butter mixture. Stir and use at once.

MAKES ABOUT 200 ML/7 FL OZ

BUTTER SAUCE

30 ml/2 tbsp finely chopped onion or
    shallot
30 ml/2 tbsp white wine vinegar
225 g/8 oz unsalted butter, chilled
salt and white pepper
lemon juice to taste

Place the onion or shallot and vinegar in a saucepan. Add 45 ml/3 tbsp water and bring to the boil. Boil until the liquid is reduced by half.

Meanwhile, cut the butter into chunks. Reduce the heat to the lowest setting so that the liquid is below simmering point. Whisking constantly, add a piece of butter. Continue adding the butter, one piece at a time, whisking to melt each piece before adding the next.

The sauce should be pale, creamy in appearance and slightly thickened – rather like single cream. Take care not to let the mixture become too hot or it will curdle.

Remove the pan from the heat when all the butter has been incorporated. Taste the sauce, then add salt, white pepper and lemon juice to taste. Serve at once with poached fish.

MAKE ABOUT 250 ML/8 FL OZ

FRESH TOMATO SAUCE

30 ml/2 tbsp olive oil
1 onion, finely chopped
1 garlic clove, crushed
1 rindless streaky bacon rasher, chopped
800 g/1¾ lb tomatoes, peeled and
    chopped
salt and pepper
pinch of sugar
15 ml/1 tbsp chopped fresh basil or
    5 ml/1 tsp dried basil

Heat the oil in a saucepan and fry the onion, garlic and bacon over gentle heat for 5 minutes.

Stir in the remaining ingredients except the basil, cover the pan and simmer gently for 30 minutes.

Rub the sauce through a sieve into a clean saucepan or purée in a blender or food processor until smooth. Add the basil.

Reheat the sauce. Check the seasoning before serving and add more salt and pepper if required.

MAKES ABOUT 600 ML/1 PINT

MAITRE D'HOTEL BUTTER

**50 g/2 oz butter
2-3 large parsley sprigs, finely chopped
salt and pepper
few drops of lemon juice**

Beat the butter until creamy in a small bowl. Add the parsley, a little at a time, beating until well combined. Season the mixture with salt and a small pinch of pepper. Add a few drops of lemon juice to intensify the flavour. Use at once or press into small pots, tapping the pots while filling to knock out all the air. Cover with foil and refrigerate until required. Use within 2 days.

MAKES 50 G/2 OZ

☆ **FREEZER TIP** A convenient way to freeze this butter is to shape it into a roll on a piece of foil or freezer paper. Roll it up in the paper, overwrap in a polythene bag, seal, label and freeze. The frozen butter can then be cut into slices as required, using a warm knife.

GARLIC BUTTER

**1 garlic clove, crushed
50-75 g/2-3 oz butter, softened**

Put the crushed garlic in a bowl and add enough butter to give the desired flavour. Use at once or press into small pots, tapping the pots while filling to knock out all the air. Cover with foil and refrigerate until required. Use within 2 days.

MAKES 50-75 G/2-3 OZ

HERB BUTTER

Herb butter may be prepared using one or more herbs. When mixing herbs, balance strong and mild types. Although dried herbs may be used, fresh ones give a superior flavour. Parsley and dill work well.

**50 g/2 oz butter, softened
30 ml/2 tbsp chopped parsley
2.5 ml/½ tsp chopped fresh thyme or
    1.25 ml/¼ tsp dried thyme
salt and pepper**

Beat the butter until creamy in a small bowl. Add the herbs, beating until well combined. Season the mixture with salt and a small pinch of pepper. Use at once or press into small pots, tapping the pots while filling to knock out all the air. Cover with foil and refrigerate until required. Use within 2 days.

MAKES 50 G/2 OZ

DEVILLED BUTTER

A pat of this butter, placed on fish steaks while grilling, imparts a delicious flavour.

**100 g/4 oz butter, softened
generous pinch of cayenne pepper
generous pinch of white pepper
1.25 ml/¼ tsp curry powder
1.25 ml/¼ tsp ground ginger**

Beat all the ingredients together in a small bowl, using the back of the spoon to combine them thoroughly. Check the seasoning. Use at once or press into small pots, tapping the pots while filling to knock out all the air. Cover with foil and refrigerate until required. Use within 2 days.

MAKES 100 G/4 OZ

GARNISHES FOR FISH AND SEAFOOD

Suggestions for garnishing are included throughout the book. Lemon is a simple, classic garnish. It may be sliced, halved, quartered or cut into wedges so that the juice may be squeezed out. Dill, fennel, parsley, basil and thyme are all suitable herbs. The following are a few more elaborate ideas:

Diced Peppers Finely diced peppers (red, green, yellow or orange) make a colourful garnish. Use only small amounts – as little as 5 ml/1 teaspoon per portion – and toss them quickly in hot oil. These look effective if placed in small mounds with sprigs of parsley or halved slices of lemon.

Tiny Pasta Shells Cook some tiny pasta shells (the size to use in soup) in advance. Rinse them under cold water, drain well and set aside. Just before serving, toss them in hot olive oil or butter, then spoon them on to a small nest of shredded lettuce, or into a ring of diced tomato.

Buttered Crumbs Cook some fresh breadcrumbs in butter until crisp and golden. Mix in chopped parsley and a little grated lemon rind. Good on pale fish dishes.

Croûtons Fry 1 cm/½ inch cubes of bread in a mixture of butter and oil until golden, stirring often. Drain on absorbent kitchen paper.

Hard-boiled Egg Chop hard-boiled egg and mix with chopped parsley, dill or snipped chives. Chopped white and sieved yolk, arranged in alternate lines, is a classic garnish, particularly good on kedgeree or sauced fish. Add coarsely grated lemon rind, dill or parsley for colour, if liked.

Fleurons To make pastry fleurons, roll out 215 g/7½ oz puff pastry on a floured board. Cut into rounds, using a 5 cm/2 inch cutter. Move the cutter halfway across each round and cut in half again, making a half moon and an almond shape. Arrange the half moons on a baking sheet, brush with beaten egg and bake in a preheated 200°C/400°F/gas 6 oven for 8-10 minutes. The almond shapes may either be baked as biscuits, or rerolled and cut into more fleurons.

Lemon Twists Lemon twists are easy to make and they look most effective. If you like, use a canelle knife to score a lemon from top to bottom at regular intervals so that the slices will have an attractive scalloped appearance. Cut lengthways halfway through the fruit, using one of the pared lines as a guide, then cut the fruit in slices. Twist each slice away from the cut.

Fried Parsley Select perfectly fresh parsley sprigs, wash swiftly and lightly and dry thoroughly on absorbent kitchen paper. Heat oil for deep frying to 180-190°C/350-365°F. Prepare a double layer of absorbent kitchen paper on a plate. Drop the parsley into the hot oil and cook for a few seconds, until bright green and crisp. Drain on the paper and serve freshly cooked. This is a classic accompaniment for fried fish.

Vegetable Julienne Blanched or lightly steamed fine strips of vegetables make a colourful garnish for poached, steamed, grilled, baked or breadcrumb-coated fish. Blanch fine strips of carrot, celery and/or celeriac: prepare the vegetables and a saucepan of boiling water in advance. Immerse the vegetables in rapidly boiling water for a few seconds, simply to heat them and to accentuate their colour and flavour. Drain and arrange on the fish, either sprinkling them in neat lines on top or grouping the vegetables in tidy mounds around the fish.

Spring Onion and Cucumber Finely shredded spring onion and thin strips of cucumber combine well as an Oriental-style garnish.

SOUPS AND STEWS

A chapter of classic dishes for all occasions, including chowders, bisques and wholesome stews. Many seafood soups are virtually stews, ideal for serving as main dishes rather than starters.

*B*OUILLABAISSE

This famous French dish had its origins in Marseilles where it depends for its success on the use of fresh Mediterranean fish and shellfish, good olive oil, sun-warmed local tomatoes and other vegetables and fresh herbs. The fish content varies but always includes the rascasse or scorpion fish. Angler fish, John Dory, red mullet and crawfish are invariably present and other fish include weever, gurnard and whiting. Mussels or baby crabs are sometimes added in their shells.

Bouillabaisse is more a stew than a soup. Vegetables are an essential flavouring, particularly tomatoes and onions. Fresh herbs such as fennel leaves and saffron are added. The shellfish are put in first; the firm-fleshed fish a few minutes later.

The stew is boiled fast for 12-20 minutes. This process of boiling serves to thicken the soup as well as extract full flavour from the seafood. The fish should be cooked through but should not be allowed to disintegrate.

When ready to serve, the fish broth is strained over slices of crisp baked (not toasted) bread, and the fish is served separately with bowls of rouille – a spicy mayonnaise flavoured with cayenne pepper and paprika as well as garlic. Aïoli, a garlic mayonnaise, may also be served with the bouillabaisse.

Although the purist will insist that bouillabaisse can only be prepared in France, using a wide variety of locally caught fresh fish, it is possible to prepare a perfectly good dish along the lines of bouillabaisse, making use of whatever fresh fish and seafood are available. Since fresh live scampi are not always easy to obtain, take advantage of fresh mussels, when in season, and add some whole uncooked Mediterranean prawns, with their shells if possible.

1 small French bread stick, thickly sliced
1 red mullet, cleaned, scaled and trimmed
1 red gurnard, cleaned, scaled and trimmed
350 g/12 oz whiting fillet, skinned
350 g/12 oz monkfish fillet, skinned
60 ml/4 tbsp olive oil (or more, see method)
2 onions, chopped
2 garlic cloves, crushed
2 celery sticks, sliced
1 kg/2¼ lb tomatoes, peeled and roughly chopped
salt and pepper
600 ml/1 pint dry white wine
1 bouquet garni
1 whole uncooked lobster, killed by freezing (page 24)
6 uncooked Mediterranean prawns, in shells if possible or 12 cooked prawns in shells
2.5 ml/½ tsp saffron threads or 1.25 ml/¼ tsp saffron powder
plenty of chopped fresh parsley
Rouille and Aïoli to serve (page 32)

Set the oven at 160°C/325°F/gas 3. Lay the bread slices on a baking sheet and bake them for about 30 minutes until dry and crisp but not toasted.

Rinse the whole fish and dry on absorbent kitchen paper. Cut the fish fillets into large chunks. Set aside on a plate. Heat the olive oil in a very large saucepan – more oil may be added if liked.

Add the onions, garlic and celery and cook, stirring frequently over low heat for 15 minutes, until the onion is soft. Stir in the tomatoes with plenty of salt and pepper, then stir over high heat until the tomatoes are soft. Pour in the wine and add 1.1 litres/ 2 pints water. Add the bouquet garni and bring to the boil.

When the soup is boiling add the lobster. Put a lid on the pan and regulate the heat so that the liquid boils without spilling over. Cook for 15 minutes.

Next add the gurnard and boil for 3 minutes with the lid off. Add the mullet and boil for 2 minutes more. Lastly add the chunks of fish fillet and the uncooked prawns (if used). Boil for a final 3 minutes, or until all the fish is cooked but not breaking up. If cooked prawns in shells are used they should be added last – their contribution to flavour will be small.

Pound the saffron threads to a powder with a pestle in a mortar. Stir in a little of the hot soup to dissolve the saffron, then add the liquid to the pan. Saffron powder may be sprinkled directly into the soup. Add plenty of parsley and taste the liquid. Add more salt and pepper if required. Ladle the fish into a large warmed serving bowl. Arrange some of the slices of bread in soup plates and ladle the soup over them. Offer the remaining bread separately, with Rouille and Aïoli.

SERVES 6

CHANNEL CHOWDER

Illustrated on page 33

25 g/1 oz butter
450 g/1 lb onions, chopped
½ green pepper, seeded and chopped
75 g/3 oz rindless streaky bacon rashers, chopped
450 g/1 lb huss fillets, skinned and cut into bite-sized pieces
450 g/1 lb tomatoes, peeled, seeded and roughly chopped
1 bay leaf
salt and pepper
125 ml/4 fl oz Basic Fish Stock (page 27)
chopped parsley to garnish

Set the oven at 180°C/350°F/gas 4. Melt the butter in a flameproof casserole. Add the onions, pepper and bacon and fry gently for 4-5 minutes.

Add the fish to the casserole with the chopped tomatoes. Place the bay leaf on top and add plenty of salt and pepper.

Pour in the fish stock, cover and bake for 45 minutes. Remove the bay leaf. Serve hot, garnished with the parsley.

SERVES 4

SPANISH FISH SOUP

Illustrated on page 33

225 g/8 oz monkfish fillet
225 g/8 oz sea bass fillet, skinned
225 g/8 oz hake steak, skinned and boned
15 ml/1 tbsp olive oil
3 onions, finely chopped
2 garlic cloves, crushed
30 ml/2 tbsp plain flour
5 ml/1 tsp chopped parsley
15 ml/1 tbsp vinegar
1 bay leaf
450 g/1 lb mussels
salt and pepper
croûtons (page 45) to garnish

Cut the monkfish, sea bass and hake into small pieces and put into a large saucepan with the oil, onions, garlic, flour, parsley, vinegar and bay leaf. Cover and marinate for 30 minutes at room temperature.

Meanwhile, wash, scrape and beard the mussels, following the instructions on page 25.

Add 1 litre/1¾ pints water to the fish in the pan, with salt and pepper to taste. Bring to the boil, lower the heat and simmer for 15 minutes.

Add the mussels and simmer for 5 minutes or until open. Remove any mussels that remain shut, together with the bay leaf.

Using a slotted spoon, ladle a few pieces of fish and several mussels into each individual soup bowl, top with broth and garnish with croûtons. Serve at once.

SERVES 4

SOUTHWOLD COD SOUP

25 g/1 oz butter
20 ml/4 tsp olive oil
2 large onions, thinly sliced
1 large carrot, thinly sliced
2 celery sticks, thinly sliced
225 g/8 oz potatoes, peeled and diced
5 ml/1 tsp curry powder
1 bouquet garni
salt and pepper
575 g/1¼ lb cod fillet, skinned and cut
  into small pieces
45 ml/3 tbsp white wine (optional)
25 g/1 oz cornflour
125 ml/4 fl oz milk
75 ml/5 tbsp single cream

Melt the butter in the oil in a deep saucepan. Add all the vegetables and fry gently for 10 minutes.

Stir in the curry powder and cook for 3 minutes. Stir in 750 ml/1¼ pints boiling water. Add the bouquet garni, with salt and pepper to taste. Add the fish and bring the soup back to simmering point. Cover and simmer for 3-5 minutes until the fish is tender.

Using a slotted spoon, transfer the best pieces of fish to a bowl. Ladle in a little of the soup stock and keep hot.

Reduce the remaining soup by simmering, uncovered, for 15 minutes. Remove the bouquet garni. Rub the soup through a sieve into a clean pan, or process in a blender or food processor. Add the wine, if used, and reheat the soup.

Meanwhile, blend the cornflour with a little of the milk in a bowl. Stir in the rest of the milk. Add the mixture to the soup, stirring constantly. Bring to the boil and cook for 2-3 minutes, stirring constantly. Add the fish, remove the pan from the heat and stir in the cream. Serve at once.

SERVES 4 TO 6

VARIATIONS

Haddock or skate may be used instead of cod.

*F*ISH BALL SOUP

50 g/2 oz fresh root ginger, peeled and
    finely chopped
1 spring onion, finely chopped
15 ml/1 tbsp dry sherry
1 egg white
225 g/8 oz firm white fish fillet, skinned
    and cut into pieces
25 ml/5 tsp cornflour
salt
25 g/1 oz lard
snipped chives to garnish

CHINESE CHICKEN STOCK
  2 chicken quarters
  ½ onion, thickly sliced
  1 large carrot, thickly sliced
  ¼ celery stick, thickly sliced
  1 thin slice fresh root ginger
  5 ml/1 tsp dry sherry

Make the stock. Put the chicken quarters in a heavy-bottomed pan. Add 2 litres/3½ pints water and bring to the boil. Skim, lower the heat, cover and simmer for 1½ hours. Remove the chicken from the stock and set aside for use in another recipe.

Add the vegetables to the stock, cover and simmer for 20 minutes. Stir in the root ginger and sherry, with salt to taste. Remove the lid and simmer for 10 minutes more. Strain the stock into a clean sauce-

pan, making it up to 1.25 litres/2¼ pints with water if necessary. Skim off any fat on the surface and set aside.

To make the fish balls, sieve the root ginger and spring onion into a bowl containing 75 ml/5 tbsp water. Stir briskly. Alternatively, process the root ginger, spring onion and water in a blender or food processor. Strain the liquid into a clean bowl, discarding any solids. Add a further 75 ml/ 5 tbsp water to the liquid, with the sherry and the egg white. Whisk until smooth.

Place the fish in a basin or large mortar and pound it to a paste. Alternatively, purée the fish in a food processor. Transfer 15 ml/1 tbsp of the sherry mixture to a shallow bowl and add the fish. Stir in the cornflour, salt and lard, and mix thoroughly so that the ingredients bind together. The mixture should be soft and malleable; add more of the sherry mixture as necessary.

Form the fish mixture into balls about 4 cm/1½ inches in diameter and drop them into a large saucepan of cold water. Bring the water to the boil, lower the heat and simmer until the fish balls rise to the surface. Remove with a slotted spoon.

Bring the saucepan of Chinese chicken stock to the boil. Drop in the fish balls and heat through for 1-2 minutes. Serve immediately, garnished with the chives.

SERVES 6

☆ **FREEZER TIP** The shaped fishballs may be frozen before cooking. Open freeze them on a baking sheet lined with freezer film, then pack in polythene bags when firm. Cook from frozen in soup, deep fried or stir fried.

*E*EL SOUP

25 g/1 oz butter
450 g/1 lb eel, skinned and cut into chunks
1 large onion, sliced
1 bouquet garni
1 blade of mace
1 strip of lemon rind
5 ml/1 tsp lemon juice
salt and pepper
25 g/1 oz cornflour
30 ml/2 tbsp milk
100 ml/3½ fl oz single cream

Melt the butter in a saucepan, add the eel and onion and fry gently for 10 minutes until the onion is soft and pale gold. Add 1.25 litres/2¼ pints water and boil.

Add the bouquet garni, mace, lemon rind and juice, with salt and pepper to taste. Lower the heat, cover and simmer very gently for 30 minutes or until the eel fillets start to come away from the bones.

Strain the soup into a clean pan. Discard the bones. Cut the fillets into pieces and place in a heated dish. Keep warm.

In a cup, blend the cornflour to a paste with the milk. Stir the mixture into the soup, bring to the boil, and cook for 2-3 minutes, stirring constantly until thick and smooth. Check the seasoning.

Off the heat, add the cream and the pieces of eel. Return the pan to the heat and warm through gently. Do not boil.

SERVES 6

MRS BEETON'S TIP If conger eel is used, increase the cooking time by about 15 minutes or until tender.

*C*REAM OF SCALLOP SOUP

100 g/4 oz butter
3 large onions, finely chopped
225 g/8 oz carrots, finely chopped
12-16 large scallops
1 thyme sprig
½ bay leaf
45 ml/3 tbsp chopped parsley
salt and pepper
150 ml/¼ pint dry white wine
1.25 litres/2¼ pints Basic Fish Stock
    (page 27)
800 g/1¾ lb potatoes, diced
250 ml/8 fl oz single cream
pinch of cayenne pepper

Melt 75 g/3 oz of the butter in a large heavy-bottomed saucepan. Cut the remaining butter into small cubes and chill until required. Add the onions and carrots to the melted butter and fry gently for 15 minutes.

Add the scallops and herbs to the pan, with salt and pepper to taste. Pour in the wine and fish stock, bring to the boil, lower the heat and simmer for 10 minutes.

Using a slotted spoon, transfer the scallops to a heated dish and keep warm. Add the potatoes to the soup and cook for about 15 minutes or until soft. Rub the soup through a sieve or remove the thyme sprig and bay leaf, then process in a blender or food processor.

Transfer the soup to a clean saucepan and stir in the cream. Chop the reserved scallops into 2 or 3 pieces each and add them to the pan. Heat gently to just below boiling point, stir in the chilled butter, sprinkle with cayenne and serve.

SERVES 6

MEDITERRANEAN CRAB SOUP

Illustrated on page 34

25 g/1 oz butter
225 g/8 oz onions, sliced
1 clove garlic, peeled but left whole
575 g/1¼ lb tomatoes, chopped
1 bunch of herbs (parsley, basil, fennel or tarragon)
pinch of powdered saffron
small strip of lemon rind
10 ml/2 tsp lemon juice
pinch of grated nutmeg
salt and pepper
45 ml/3 tbsp dry white wine
1(1.5 kg/3¼ lb) cooked fresh crab or 1(213 g/7½ oz) can crab meat, drained
125 ml/4 fl oz single cream
chopped parsley to garnish

Melt the butter in a deep saucepan. Add the onions and garlic and fry gently for 10 minutes. Add the tomatoes, herbs, saffron, lemon rind and juice. Stir in the nutmeg, with salt and pepper to taste. Heat to simmering point, cover and simmer for 20 minutes.

Add the wine and boil for 2 minutes. Pick the crab meat from the shell and add it to the pan. Alternatively, add the canned crab meat. Stir in 1 litre/1¾ pints water. Bring to the boil, lower the heat, cover the pan, and simmer for 20 minutes.

Rub the soup through a wire sieve into a clean saucepan, or remove the herbs and purée in a blender or food processor. Add more salt and pepper if required, stir in the cream and reheat gently without boiling. Serve sprinkled with chopped parsley.

SERVES 4 TO 6

 MRS BEETON'S TIP If fresh tomatoes are expensive, use 2(397 g/ 14 oz) cans of chopped tomatoes instead. Drain them before use, reserving the juice in a large measuring jug. Make up the juice to 1 litre/1¾ pints with water, and add with the crab meat.

CRAB AND CORN BISQUE

600 ml/1 pint milk
225 g/8 oz brown and white crab meat, mixed
salt and pepper
50 g/2 oz butter
50 g/2 oz plain flour
1(275 g/10 oz) can sweetcorn kernels, drained
75 ml/5 tbsp double cream
chopped parsley to garnish

Combine the milk and crab meat in a heavy-bottomed saucepan, add salt and pepper to taste and simmer for 10 minutes. Purée in a blender or food processor.

Melt the butter in the pan, stir in the flour and cook for 1 minute, stirring constantly. Add the crabmeat purée gradually, stirring to make a smooth sauce. Bring to the boil, lower the heat and simmer until thickened.

Add the sweetcorn kernels and simmer for 5 minutes. Remove from the heat, stir in the cream and serve, garnished with chopped parsley.

SERVES 3 TO 4

SMOKED HADDOCK CHOWDER

450 g/1 lb smoked haddock fillet, skinned
750 ml/1¼ pints milk
50 g/2 oz butter
1 small onion, finely chopped
100 g/4 oz mushrooms, finely chopped
40 g/1½ oz plain flour
250 ml/8 fl oz single cream
freshly ground black pepper

Put the haddock fillets into a saucepan with the milk and heat to simmering point. Simmer for about 10 minutes until just tender. Drain the fish, reserving the cooking liquid, remove the skin and shred lightly.

Melt the butter in a clean pan, add the onion and mushrooms and fry gently for about 10 minutes until soft. Do not allow the onion to colour.

Stir in the flour and cook for 1 minute, stirring constantly. Gradually add the fish-flavoured milk, stirring until smooth. Bring to the boil, lower the heat and simmer until thickened.

Off the heat, add the cream and the shredded haddock. Return the pan to the heat and warm through gently. Do not allow the soup to boil after adding the cream. Top with a generous grinding of black pepper and serve at once.

SERVES 4 TO 6

MRS BEETON'S TIP Reserve a few perfect mushrooms for a garnish if liked. Slice them thinly and sprinkle a few slices on top of each portion of soup. It is not necessary to cook the mushrooms.

LOBSTER BISQUE

shell, trimmings and a little of the flesh of
   1 small or medium cooked lobster
1 onion, thinly sliced
1 carrot, thinly sliced
1 garlic clove, thinly sliced
1 bay leaf
1 blade of mace
5 ml/1 tsp lemon juice
5 ml/1 tsp anchovy essence
125 ml/4 fl oz white wine
750 ml/1¼ pints Basic Fish Stock
   (page 27)
salt and pepper
15 ml/1 tbsp cooked lobster coral
   (optional)
50 g/2 oz butter
25 g/1 oz plain flour
125 ml/4 fl oz single cream

Crush the lobster shell and put it in a heavy-bottomed saucepan with the trimmings. Flake the flesh finely, setting a few neat pieces aside for the garnish. Add the flesh to the pan with the onion, carrot and garlic. Put in the bay leaf, mace, lemon juice, anchovy essence and wine and bring to the boil. Cook briskly for 3-5 minutes (see Mrs Beeton's Tip). Add the fish stock and a little salt. Bring to the boil, lower the heat and simmer for 1 hour.

Strain the soup through a metal sieve into a large jug or bowl, rubbing through any pieces of firm lobster. Pound the lobster coral (if used) with half the butter in a small bowl, then rub through a clean sieve into a bowl. Set the coral butter aside.

Melt the remaining butter in a saucepan and stir in the flour. Cook for 1 minute, stirring, then gradually add the strained soup. Bring to the boil, stirring constantly. Add the reserved lobster coral butter or plain butter, stirring all the time.

Off the heat, add the cream and the reserved lobster pieces, with salt and pepper, if required. Return the pan to the heat and warm through gently. Do not allow the soup to boil after adding the cream. Serve at once.

SERVES 4 TO 6

> **MRS BEETON'S TIP** It is important to boil the lobster trimmings and flesh in the wine for at least 3 minutes. The alcohol in the wine extracts much of the flavour from the lobster, vegetables and herbs.

SHRIMP AND CIDER BISQUE

Cooked whole prawns, thawed if frozen, may be used instead of the shrimps in this bisque.

750 ml/1¼ pints Basic Fish Stock
   (page 27)
225 g/8 oz cooked whole shrimps
45 ml/3 tbsp soft white breadcrumbs
50 g/2 oz butter
pinch of grated nutmeg
5 ml/1 tsp lemon juice
100 ml/3½ fl oz cider
salt and pepper
1 egg yolk
125 ml/4 fl oz single cream

Pour the fish stock into a large saucepan. Shell the shrimps and add the shells to the pan. Set the shrimps aside. Bring the stock and shrimp shells to the boil, cover and cook for 10 minutes. Strain into a large measuring jug or bowl.

Put the breadcrumbs in a small bowl with 250 ml/8 fl oz of the strained stock. Set aside to soak for 10 minutes.

Meanwhile, melt 25 g/1 oz of the butter in a saucepan. Add the shrimps and toss over gentle heat for 5 minutes. Add the nutmeg, lemon juice and breadcrumb mixture and heat gently for 5 minutes. Beat in the rest of the butter.

Process the mixture in a blender or food processor or rub through a sieve into a clean saucepan. Gradually add the cider and the remaining stock. Bring to the boil, remove from the heat and add salt and pepper to taste.

In a small bowl, mix the egg yolk with the cream. Stir a little of the hot soup into the egg mixture, mix well, then add the contents of the bowl to the soup, stirring the bisque over low heat until it thickens. Serve at once.

SERVES 4 TO 6

> **MRS BEETON'S TIP** The unused egg white may be frozen. It is a good idea to freeze several egg whites together in usable quantities of 2, 3 or 4. Whisk lightly before freezing in lidded containers. Thaw for 2-3 hours before use. 1 egg white is equal to about 30 ml/2 tbsp.

MUSSEL SOUP

800 g/1¾ lb mussels
125 ml/4 fl oz white wine
20 ml/4 tsp lemon juice
750 ml/1¼ pints Basic Fish Stock
    (page 27)
25 g/1 oz butter
30 ml/2 tbsp plain flour
salt and pepper
20 ml/4 tsp chopped parsley
1 egg yolk
75 ml/5 tbsp single cream

Wash, scrape and beard the mussels following the instructions on page 25. Put them in a large saucepan with the wine and lemon juice. Add 250 ml/8 fl oz of the fish stock, cover the pan tightly and simmer for 8-10 minutes or until the mussels have opened. Discard any that remain shut.

Strain the cooking liquid through muslin or a very fine sieve into the remaining fish stock. Shell the mussels.

Melt the butter in a deep saucepan. Stir in the flour and cook gently for 1 minute. Gradually add the fish stock, stirring constantly. Bring to the boil and cook for 2 minutes, still stirring. Add salt and pepper to taste and stir in the parsley.

In a small bowl, mix the egg yolk with the cream. Stir a little of the hot soup into the egg mixture, mix well, then add the contents of the bowl to the soup, stirring the bisque over low heat until it thickens. Add the mussels and reheat gently, without boiling. Serve at once.

SERVES 4 TO 6

CLAM CHOWDER

450 g/1 lb fresh or canned clams
4 rindless unsmoked streaky bacon
    rashers, chopped
2 celery stalks, chopped
2 onions, finely chopped
30 ml/2 tbsp plain flour
600 ml/1 pint milk
450 g/1 lb potatoes, diced
15 ml/1 tbsp chopped parsley
salt and pepper

Prepare the clams, following the instructions on page 25. If using canned clams, drain them, reserving the can juices. Cut any large clams into bite-sized pieces.

Heat the bacon in a heavy-bottomed saucepan until the fat starts to run. Raise the heat and fry the bacon until crisp, then remove the pieces with a slotted spoon, drain on absorbent kitchen paper and set aside.

Add the celery and onions to the hot bacon fat and fry gently for about 10 minutes or until golden. Add the clams and fry gently for 3-4 minutes.

If canned clams have been used, measure the juices and make up to 600 ml/1 pint with milk. Add the flour to the vegetable and clam mixture and cook for 1 minute, stirring. Gradually add the milk, or milk and clam juices, stirring constantly until the soup begins to thicken.

Add the potatoes and parsley, with salt and pepper to taste. Simmer for about 20 minutes or until the potatoes are cooked. Add the bacon pieces and serve at once.

SERVES 4

NORWEGIAN FISH SOUP

Illustrated on page 34

1 small onion, roughly chopped
¼ celeriac, roughly chopped
1 leek, trimmed, sliced and washed
2 carrots, roughly chopped
1.5 litres/2¾ pints Basic Fish Stock
   (page 27)
1 rindless bacon rasher, roughly chopped
30 ml/2 tbsp tomato purée
25 g/1 oz butter
15 ml/1 tbsp plain flour
salt ● 100 ml/3½ fl oz dry sherry
dill sprigs to garnish

FISH BALLS
   225 g/8 oz firm white fish fillet, skinned
     and cut into pieces
   25 ml/5 tsp cornflour
   1 egg white
   15 ml/1 tbsp chopped dill

Combine all the vegetables in a large saucepan. Add the stock and bacon, bring to the boil and cook for about 20 minutes. Strain the stock, add the tomato purée and mix well.

To make the fish balls, pound the fish to a coarse paste or process it briefly in a food processor. Thoroughly mix in the cornflour, a good pinch of salt, the egg white and dill. Wet your hands and shape the mixture into small balls.

Melt the butter in a large saucepan, add the flour and cook until nut brown but not burnt. Gradually add the stock, stirring constantly. Bring to the boil, lower the heat and add the fish balls. Simmer for 5 minutes, stirring, until the fish balls rise. Stir in salt to taste and the sherry. Garnish with dill.

SERVES 6

CULLEN SKINK

1 large finnan haddock on the bone
1 onion, finely chopped
450 g/1 lb potatoes, halved
salt and pepper
25 g/1 oz butter
150 ml/¼ pint single cream
250 ml/8 fl oz milk
chopped parsley to garnish

Put the haddock in a large saucepan with the onion. Add 1 litre/1¾ pints water. Bring to the boil, lower the heat and simmer for 20 minutes. Lift out the fish and remove the skin and bones, returning these to the stock. Flake the fish roughly and set it aside in a clean saucepan. Simmer the stock for a further 45 minutes.

Meanwhile cook the potatoes in a saucepan of lightly salted water for about 30 minutes or until tender. Drain and mash them with the butter.

Strain the fish stock into the pan containing the flaked fish. Set aside 60 ml/4 tbsp of the cream in a small jug. Add the remaining cream to the pan with the milk. Stir in the mashed potato and heat through, stirring to make a thick soup. If a thinner soup is preferred, add more milk.

Check the seasoning. The soup is unlikely to need salt, but pepper may be added, if liked. Ladle into individual bowls, drizzling a little of the reserved cream on to the surface of each portion. Sprinkle with chopped parsley and serve at once.

SERVES 4

———————— ◈ ————————

FISHERMAN'S HOT POT

2 slices of white bread
25 g/1 oz butter
45 ml/3 tbsp oil
50 g/2 oz piece of white cabbage,
    shredded
2 leeks, trimmed, sliced and washed
1 large onion, chopped
225 g/8 oz white fish fillet, skinned and cut
    into 2.5 cm/1 inch cubes
150 ml/¼ pint Muscadet or other dry
    white wine
45 ml/3 tbsp tomato purée
1 chicken stock cube
1 bouquet garni
1 garlic clove, crushed
salt and pepper
chopped parsley to garnish

Remove the crusts from the bread, cut it into cubes and spread on a baking sheet. Dry out in a 150°C/300°F/gas 2 oven for 10-15 minutes, then set aside.

Melt the butter in the oil in a large saucepan. Add the vegetables, cover and cook gently for 7-8 minutes until soft. Do not allow the leeks and onions to colour.

Add the fish cubes and fry for 3 minutes, turning occasionally, until firm on all sides. Pour in the wine and add 1 litre/1¾ pints water. Stir in the tomato purée and crumble in the stock cube. Add the bouquet garni, crushed garlic and salt and pepper to taste.

Heat the stew to simmering point and cook for 20 minutes. Discard the bouquet garni. Pour into a serving dish and sprinkle with the chopped parsley. Serve with the toasted bread cubes.

SERVES 4

FRENCH FISH STEW

25 g/1 oz butter
30 ml/2 tbsp oil
1 small onion or shallot, chopped
8 button mushrooms, sliced
1 kg/2¼ lb haddock fillets, skinned and
    thinly sliced
350 ml/12 fl oz dry still cider
150 ml/¼ pint single cream
15 ml/1 tbsp arrowroot
100 ml/3½ fl oz milk or water
pinch of ground mace
salt and pepper
chopped parsley to garnish

Melt the butter in the oil in a deep saucepan. Add the onion or shallot and fry for 3-4 minutes until soft but not brown. Add the mushrooms and cook for 2 minutes, stirring occasionally.

Add the fish and cook for 8 minutes, turning several times. Remove from the heat and drain off the oil. Add the cider to the pan, cover, return to the heat and simmer for 8 minutes. Stir in the cream, then remove from the heat.

In a cup, mix the arrowroot to a paste with a little of the milk or water. Stir into the stew with the remaining milk or water. Add the mace, with salt and pepper to taste.

Return the saucepan to a moderate heat and stir until the sauce thickens. Sprinkle with chopped parsley and serve at once.

SERVES 4

MOULES MARINIERE

Illustrated on page 35

1.6 kg/3½ lb mussels
1 onion, sliced
2 garlic cloves, cut in slivers
1 carrot, sliced
1 celery stick, sliced
1 bouquet garni
125 ml/4 fl oz white wine
25 g/1 oz butter
25 g/1 oz plain flour
salt and pepper
chopped parsley to garnish

Wash, scrape and beard the mussels following the instructions on page 25. Put them in a large saucepan. Tuck the sliced vegetables among the mussels and add the bouquet garni.

Pour over 125 ml/4 fl oz water and the wine. Place over moderate heat and bring to the boil. As soon as the liquid begins to boil, shake the pan 2 or 3 times, cover it tightly and cook for about 5 minutes until the mussels have opened. Discard any that remain shut. With a slotted spoon transfer the mussels to a deep dish and keep hot.

Strain the cooking liquid through muslin or a very fine sieve into a smaller saucepan. In a cup, cream the butter with the flour.

Place the small saucepan over moderate heat and add the butter and flour in small pieces, whisking thoroughly. Bring to the boil, whisking, then add salt and pepper.

Pour the thickened cooking liquid over the mussels, sprinkle with chopped parsley and serve with plenty of chunky bread.

SERVES 4 TO 6

MUSSELS IN WHITE SAUCE

1.6 kg/3½ lb mussels
50 g/2 oz butter
25 g/1 oz plain flour
1 egg yolk
30 ml/2 tbsp double cream
lemon juice
chopped parsley to garnish

Wash, scrape and beard the mussels following the instructions on page 25. Put them in a large saucepan with 250 ml/8 fl oz water. Place over moderate heat and bring to the boil. As soon as the liquid boils, shake the pan 2 or 3 times, cover it tightly and cook for about 5 minutes until the mussels have opened. Discard any that remain shut. Remove the mussels with a slotted spoon, shell them and keep them hot.

Strain the cooking liquid through muslin or a very fine sieve into a measuring jug. Reserve 250 ml/8 fl oz of the liquid.

Melt half the butter in a saucepan, add the flour and cook for 1 minute over low heat, stirring constantly. Do not allow the flour to colour. Remove from the heat and gradually add the reserved cooking liquid, whisking constantly.

Over moderate heat, bring the sauce to the boil. Lower the heat and simmer for 5 minutes. Beat the egg yolk and cream together in a small bowl, then add to the sauce with lemon juice to taste. Stir in the remaining butter with the reserved shelled mussels. Heat through but do not allow to boil. Serve immediately, garnished with chopped parsley.

SERVES 2 TO 3

MATELOTE OF EELS

Eels, mushrooms and wine make a marvellous combination in this stew, made to a traditional recipe.

800 g/1¾ lb eels, skinned and cut into
    7.5 cm/3 inch pieces
seasoned flour for coating
50 g/2 oz butter
400 ml/14 fl oz Basic Fish Stock (page 27)
125 ml/4 fl oz dry red wine
25 g/1 oz plain flour
12 button mushrooms, sliced
salt and pepper

Toss the pieces of eel in seasoned flour. Melt half the butter in a saucepan, add the eel and fry gently for 10 minutes until lightly browned, turning the pieces frequently.

Pour in the stock and wine and bring to the boil. Lower the heat, cover the pan and simmer for 30 minutes or until the eel flesh starts to come away from the bones.

Meanwhile, melt the remaining butter in a saucepan, add the flour and cook gently until nut brown in colour. Do not allow the butter to burn. Set the pan aside.

Drain the eel pieces, discarding the bones, and keep them warm in a serving dish. Strain the stock into a large measuring jug. Gradually add the stock to the browned butter and flour mixture, stirring constantly. Return the pan to the heat and bring to the boil, stirring.

Lower the heat, add the sliced mushrooms and simmer for 3-4 minutes. Add salt and pepper to taste and pour the mixture over the eel pieces. Serve at once, with plenty of wholemeal bread.

SERVES 4

STEWED EELS

1 kg/2¼ lb eels, skinned and cut into
    7.5 cm/3 inch pieces
salt and pepper
1 large onion studded with 3 cloves
1 strip of lemon rind
500 ml/17 fl oz chicken or vegetable stock
75 ml/5 tbsp port
45 ml/3 tbsp double cream
50 g/2 oz plain flour
cayenne pepper
few drops of lemon juice

Lay the pieces of eel in a saucepan large enough to hold them in a single layer. Sprinkle lightly with salt and pepper. Add the onion and lemon rind and pour over the stock and port. Cover the pan and bring the liquid to the boil. Lower the heat and simmer for 30 minutes or until the eel fillets start to come away from the bones.

Drain the eel pieces, discarding the bones, and keep them warm in a serving dish. Strain the stock into a clean saucepan. Mix the cream and flour together in a small bowl and stir in enough of the hot stock to make a thin cream. Add this to the stock and place the pan over moderate heat, stirring until the sauce thickens.

Add cayenne and lemon juice to taste, pour the mixture over the eel pieces and serve at once.

SERVES 4

VARIATION

STEWED CONGER EELS Use 4 (200 g/7 oz) conger steaks and substitute Madeira for the port. Conger eel may take longer to cook, therefore allow an extra 15 minutes, checking frequently.

EEL CASSEROLE

Illustrated on page 36

2 onions, sliced in rings
1 garlic clove, crushed
1 bouquet garni
salt and pepper
800 g/1¾ lb eels, skinned and cut into
    5 cm/2 inch pieces
250 ml/8 fl oz red wine
75 g/3 oz butter
100 g/4 oz mushrooms, halved if large
50 g/2 oz plain flour

GARNISH
    croûtons (page 45)
    peeled cooked prawns
    herb sprigs (oregano) to garnish

Put the onion rings in a large saucepan with the garlic and bouquet garni. Add salt and pepper to taste, then lay the pieces of eel on top. Pour over the wine and simmer for 20 minutes or until the eel flesh starts to come away from the bones.

Meanwhile heat 25 g/1 oz of the butter in a small frying pan, add the mushrooms and fry for about 5 minutes until soft. Transfer to a heated serving dish.

With a slotted spoon, remove the pieces of eel from the stock, discard the bones and add to the mushrooms in the serving dish. Remove and discard the bouquet garni. Mix the remaining butter with the flour in a small bowl.

Boil the stock for about 5 minutes to reduce slightly, then add the butter and flour mixture, a little at a time, whisking until the sauce thickens to the desired consistency. Pour over the fish and mushrooms, garnish and serve at once.

SERVES 4 TO 5

CASSEROLE OF LING

Ling is one of the largest fish in the cod family. It is a long fish, with a bronze-green or brown skin and firm white flesh. Cod or haddock may be substituted for ling fillet.

575 g/1¼ lb ling fillet, skinned and cut
    into 5 cm/2 inch pieces
25 g/1 oz butter
1 large onion, sliced
100 g/4 oz mushrooms, halved if large
25 g/1 oz plain flour
400 ml/14 fl oz tomato juice
pinch of mixed herbs
salt and pepper

Set the oven at 200°C/400°F/gas 6. Arrange the ling pieces in a shallow ovenproof dish.

Melt the butter in a saucepan, add the onion and mushrooms and fry for 3-4 minutes until the onions start to colour. Sprinkle in the flour and cook for 1 minute, stirring.

Stir in the tomato juice and bring to the boil, stirring constantly. Add the herbs, with salt and pepper to taste, then pour the sauce over the fish. Cover the dish with foil and bake for 30 minutes. Serve at once.

SERVES 4

MRS BEETON'S TIP   Do not peel or wash the mushrooms; simply wipe them clean with a piece of absorbent kitchen paper. Trim the base of each stem and cut in half or quarters if large.

STEAMED AND SAUCED FISH

In Mrs Beeton's day steamed fish was considered suitable food for invalids, children and the aged, and recipes tended to be rather dull. Although basic methods remain the same, the wealth of international ingredients now at our disposal means that the plainest cooking techniques can be used to produce exciting, flavoursome results.

STEAMING

Steaming is a method of cooking food in water vapour, producing moist results and retaining the maximum flavour of the food.

EQUIPMENT

The traditional, and simplest, method of steaming fish and seafood is to sandwich it between two plates and to place it over a saucepan of boiling water; however, there are alternatives.

A saucepan-top steamer placed in or on a container over boiling water may be used to cook fish and seafood. Alternatively, foods such as rice may be cooked in the pan, with the seafood steamed directly on top so that its juices flavour the food below.

A bamboo steamer placed on a wok is ideal for cooking fish and seafood. Oriental-style techniques and seasonings perfectly complement the light taste and texture of these ingredients.

Free-standing electric steamers come and go; all the rage one day and not available the next. Depending on the shape of the steaming compartment, an electric steamer can be useful for cooking fish.

Improvising is not difficult and a metal cooling rack placed in a roasting tin of water makes a good platform on which to steam small whole salmon trout, whole trout or a small curved whole salmon. A foil covering with a tightly crumpled edge will usually keep in the steam.

SELECTING FISH FOR STEAMING

Fish fillets are ideal for this cooking method. Plaice, Dover or lemon sole, portions of cod or haddock fillet and smoked fish fillets are all suitable. Thin fillets may be rolled or folded, with herbs or other flavourings placed inside for flavour.

Shellfish, such as scallops, mussels and oysters, are excellent steamed.

Oily fish, on the other hand, do not benefit from being cooked by this method; mackerel, herring and sardines are better baked or grilled.

Size imposes restrictions on the choice of fish for this cooking method: whole fish do not fit well into the majority of steamers but it is worth improvising – curling a whole fish or steaming a fish in sections for later assembly – especially when it comes to fish like salmon and trout that benefit from being steamed.

FLAVOURING AND SEASONING

The choice of flavouring ingredients for any dish should be considered alongside the cooking method. Steaming produces fairly intense results, therefore strong ingredients (onion or garlic) can be rather overpowering in the finished dish.

Here are some ideas:

Fresh Herbs There is a herb to flavour every food. Where fish is concerned the more delicate herbs are ideal. Dill and parsley are, of course, the classics; try lemon thyme, fresh basil, fennel, coriander leaves, lemon balm and lemon grass too. Fresh rosemary, savory, majoram and oregano tend to be too strong for steamed fish; these herbs should be used judiciously with all seafood, however cooked.

Dried herbs can also be too intense with steamed fish and seafood; if you must use them, do so with caution.

Fresh Root Ginger Ginger's reputation as a robust flavouring is based on the dried and ground product, for fresh root ginger has a citrus-like tang and a hint of heat in its make-up. The preparation of fresh ginger plays an important role in determining its eventual impact in a dish: for just a hint of flavour a few slices of ginger may be added to a dish, then removed before serving. At the other end of the spectrum, grated ginger may be used liberally with other spices to maximise its warming properties. Peeled, thinly sliced and shredded ginger, added in carefully measured quantities are a compromise between the two, contributing plenty of zest with some heat.

Combine ginger with spring onions, soy sauce, carrots and celery to flavour strips of plaice, chunks of cod or mussels. Add a hint of ginger and lemon to scallops, lemon sole rolls or squid rings.

Lemon or Lime Lemon is another favourite flavouring for fish. The rind (grated, cut in strips or shredded), the juice or just a slice or two of fruit may be used when steaming fish.

Lime also goes well with all types of fish and seafood. Use rind, juice and slices for steaming.

Soy Sauce Combined with spring onions and fresh root ginger, soy sauce gives steamed fish a wonderful Oriental flavour that is the perfect foil to plain cooked rice. Whole fish such as plaice, grey mullet, bass or snapper may be cooked with this strong seasoning.

Vegetables Celery, fennel, carrots and spring onions are useful for flavouring and adding colour to steamed fish. Cut the vegetables finely so that they give up their flavour and cook perfectly in the same time as the seafood.

STEAMING METHODS

Little by way of special preparation is needed for fish steamed between two plates. Lay fillets flat and add the chosen flavouring; a sprinkling of lemon juice, some chopped parsley or dill, seasoning and a knob of butter produces excellent results.

If the fish is placed in a perforated, saucepan-top steamer or in a bamboo steamer, there are several options to consider. The cooking juices may be saved and served as a sauce or allowed to drip away into the water below. The flavouring ingredients may be placed on the fish or, in the plainest possible style of cooking, in the water below to scent the steam. The seafood may be put in a covered container or left uncovered so that some moisture collects to yield extra cooking liquor.

Allowing the cooking juices from white fish fillets or pieces to drip away tends to give bland results, unless the juices are absorbed by rice or couscous placed below the fish. Whole fish such as trout, salmon and bass cooked this way are protected from loss of flavour by their skin. In addition, flavouring ingredients may be tucked into the body cavity of whole fish.

Wrapping Seafood Fish may be wrapped before being placed in a perforated steamer. Foil and roasting bags are ideal for retaining all the juices and flavouring. Greaseproof paper and cooking parchment may also be used but tend to become soft and allow loss of liquor and some flavour.

Leaves may be used to wrap seafood, imparting their own flavour as well as helping to retain the fish juices. Iceberg or cos lettuce leaves and vine leaves may be blanched to soften them before use as a wrapping for whole trout or red mullet. Herbs and other flavourings may be placed inside the fish or on the leaves before wrapping.

Cooking in Dishes The seafood may be placed in a suitable dish with the chosen flavouring ingredients. The dish may be covered or left open, in which case condensed steam will collect in it. The uncovered method is ideal when very brief cooking is required and when flavourings such as soy sauce are added, resulting in just the right amount of full-flavoured, thin sauce. Thinly cut strips of fish or shellfish may be cooked this way.

Cooking Directly on Other Food Fish can be steamed directly on other moist food with which it is being served. For example, fillets of smoked haddock may be laid on two-thirds cooked rice when making kedgeree. When the pan is covered the fish will cook in the steam from the rice. The fillets should be lifted off carefully at the end of cooking.

Similarly, fish may be laid on vegetables – a bed of spinach is ideal – and steamed gently in the cooking vapour.

POACHING

This is probably one of the most popular cooking methods for cooking fish and seafood. Poaching means cooking very gently in liquid. It is ideal for tender fish, allowing additional flavouring ingredients to be cooked with the fish to produce liquor which may be thickened or reduced, then served as a sauce.

Poaching is also used for cooking fish roes. Cod's roe is usually bought freshly boiled or smoked. Herring roes (soft roes, from the male fish) are not sold cooked. Poach them in Court Bouillon (page 28) for 15 minutes, then drain and press until cold, when they may be sliced and fried or grilled.

Very fresh trout may be cooked 'au bleu'. In this method the natural slime on the skin of the fish is not rinsed off but is retained to give a soft slate blue covering to the lightly simmered fish (see Glossary, page 188).

FLAVOURING POACHED FISH

Poaching is often just one step in the overall cooking process. For example, fillets may be poached until barely cooked and the flesh flaked off them for adding to rice, pasta, pie fillings, croquettes and fish cakes. The poaching liquor is frequently saved and used to flavour the dish.

If poaching is to be the sole method of cooking used for the seafood, flavourings should be carefully closen. Herbs and vegetables may be added to the poaching liquid. If the liquid is discarded or strained after poaching, these ingredients may be roughly cut and briefly simmered in the liquid before the fish is added. If the poaching liquid is reduced or thickened, then served without being strained, ingredients such as onion should be parcooked in a little oil or butter to ensure they are completely cooked in the finished dish.

POACHING LIQUID

Fish stock (page 27) or Court Bouillon (page 28) are used for poaching whole fish such as salmon, when the liquid is discarded after cooking and cooling.

Wine is usually combined with water or stock for poaching fish and seafood, with the resultant liquor served as a sauce. Flour or cornflour may be used to thicken the sauce or the liquid may be reduced by rapid boiling after the seafood has been removed.

Milk is used for poaching fish which is to be served in a creamy sauce or for cooking white fish for fish cakes. The milk is added to the mashed potatoes.

Canned tomatoes may also be used for poaching, making a simple sauce at the same time.

OVERCOOKING – THE ULTIMATE CRIME

Overcooking steamed or poached fish really is a crime because it results in tasteless seafood with a ruined texture. The plainer the cooking, the more important it is to ensure that the fish is cooked to perfection. The flesh should be just firm, still moist and just cooked. When steaming fish, always check part-way through the time to make sure that it is neither cooking too rapidly nor for too long.

When poaching fish the liquid should barely simmer. Boiling liquid will break delicate fillets and toughen seafood such as scallops or squid. The crucial words are time and temperature. Keep the cooking time short and the temperature low and check the fish frequently.

Poached fish which is to be served cold should be removed from the heat when it is three-quarters cooked, then allowed to cool in the liquid. The residual heat completes the cooking and ensures that the fish is moist.

MICROWAVE COOKING

This is a moist method which produces results comparable with those achieved by steaming. It is also a very quick cooking method which may be used successfully for fish.

Mussels and scallops may be cooked in the microwave but take care not to overcook them or they will become rubbery.

Remember the rules – no metal containers, metal trimmings, skewers or fastenings. Use dishes that withstand the heat of cooking and avoid putting food in the corners of oblong dishes.

When cooking fish in the microwave always cover it unless it is well coated in sauce (for example raw fish added to a white sauce for cooking). The thin end of fillets should be folded or tucked under the thicker part of the same fillet. Alternatively, when more than one fillet is cooked, they may be overlapped to protect thin areas from overcooking.

Fish cutlets should be arranged with the thick parts towards the outside of the dish. The thin flaps should be folded into the body cavity space. A wooden cocktail stick through the flaps will hold them in place.

It is most important to read and follow the microwave manufacturer's instructions and suggested timings for cooking fish.

COD WITH CREAM SAUCE

6 (100 g/4 oz) cod steaks or portions
75 g/3 oz butter
250 ml/8 fl oz Basic Fish Stock (page 27)
milk (see method)
25 g/1 oz plain flour
30 ml/2 tbsp double cream
15 ml/1 tbsp lemon juice
salt and pepper

Rinse the fish and pat dry on absorbent kitchen paper. Melt half the butter in a frying pan, add the cod and fry quickly on both sides to seal without browning.

Add the stock, cover the pan and simmer gently for 20 minutes. Drain the fish, reserving the cooking liquid in a measuring jug, place on a warmed dish and keep hot. Make the cooking liquid up to 300 ml/ ½ pint with milk.

Melt the remaining butter in a saucepan, add the flour and cook for 1 minute, stirring. Gradually add the reserved cooking liquid and milk mixture, stirring constantly. Bring to the boil, lower the heat and simmer for 4 minutes, stirring occasionally.

Remove the pan from the heat and stir in the cream and lemon juice. Add salt and pepper to taste and spoon a little sauce over each fish portion. Serve at once.

SERVES 6

> **MRS BEETON'S TIP** The stock used as the basis for this recipe should be pale in colour. Avoid adding the skin of the fish when making it, as this would darken it.

CURRIED COD

800 g/1¾ lb cod fillets, skinned
50 g/2 oz butter
1 large onion, sliced
15 ml/1 tbsp plain flour
10 ml/2 tsp curry powder
500 ml/17 fl oz Basic Fish Stock (page 27)
15 ml/1 tbsp lemon juice
salt and pepper
cayenne pepper

Rinse the fish and pat dry. Cut into pieces about 2.5 cm/1 inch square. Melt the butter in a saucepan and fry the cod lightly for 2-3 minutes. Using a slotted spoon, transfer the pieces to a warmed dish and keep hot.

Add the onion to the butter remaining in the pan and fry gently for 3-4 minutes until soft. Stir in the flour and curry powder and fry for 5 minutes, stirring constantly to prevent the onion from becoming too brown.

Pour in the stock and bring to the boil, stirring constantly. Lower the heat and simmer for 15 minutes. Strain the sauce into a clean saucepan, adding lemon juice, salt and pepper and cayenne to taste. Carefully add the fish to the pan, stir gently and bring to simmering point.

Simmer for about 10 minutes, until the fish has absorbed the flavour of the sauce. Stir occasionally to prevent sticking. Serve at once, with boiled rice if liked.

SERVES 6

VARIATION

QUICK COD CURRY Use cold cooked fish, omitting the preliminary frying. Serve with a mixture of plain yogurt and chopped cucumber.

COD PORTUGAISE

Illustrated on page 36

75 ml/5 tbsp oil
1 large onion, finely diced
2 garlic cloves, crushed
45 ml/3 tbsp plain flour
225 g/8 oz tomatoes, peeled, seeded and
   chopped
1 green pepper, seeded and diced
125 ml/4 fl oz dry white wine
2.5 ml/½ tsp dried thyme
10-12 stuffed green olives
salt and pepper
575 g/1¼ lb cod fillet, skinned and cut
   into 4 pieces

GARNISH
   lemon wedges
   thyme sprigs

Heat 30 ml/2 tbsp of the oil in a saucepan. Add the onion and garlic and fry gently for 4-5 minutes until soft. Add half the flour and cook for 1 minute, stirring.

Add the tomatoes and green pepper and stir in the wine, with 125 ml/4 fl oz water. Add the thyme and bring to the boil, stirring. Lower the heat, cover and simmer for 10 minutes, stirring occasionally. Add the olives, stir gently and simmer for 5 minutes.

Meanwhile, season the remaining flour with salt and pepper in a shallow bowl, add the pieces of fish and coat on all sides. Heat the remaining oil in a frying pan, add the fish and fry for 10 minutes, turning once.

Remove the pieces of fish with a fish slice and arrange on a warmed serving dish. Pour the sauce over, garnish and serve at once.

SERVES 4

FISH PUDDING

fat for greasing
450 g/1 lb white fish fillet (cod, haddock,
   hake, ling), skinned and finely chopped
100 g/4 oz shredded suet
50 g/2 oz fresh white breadcrumbs
30 ml/2 tbsp chopped parsley
salt and pepper
few drops of anchovy essence
2 eggs, lightly beaten
125 ml/4 fl oz milk

Grease a 600 ml/1 pint pudding basin. Prepare a steamer or half fill a large saucepan with water and bring to the boil.

Combine the fish, suet, breadcrumbs and parsley in a bowl. Mix well and season with salt, pepper and anchovy essence.

Stir in the eggs and milk. Spoon the mixture into the prepared basin, cover with greased greaseproof paper or foil and secure with string.

Put the pudding in the perforated part of the steamer, or stand it on an old saucer or plate in the saucepan of boiling water. The water should come halfway up the sides of the basin. Cover the pan tightly and steam the pudding over gently simmering water for 1½ hours.

Leave for 5-10 minutes at room temperature to firm up, then turn out on to a warmed serving plate. Serve with a parsley or mushroom sauce, if liked.

SERVES 4

*H*ADDOCK FLORENTINE

50 g/2 oz butter
1 kg/2¼ lb fresh spinach
salt and pepper
100 ml/3½ fl oz Basic Fish Stock (page 27)
100 ml/3½ fl oz dry white wine
1 kg/2¼ lb haddock fillets, skinned
1.25 ml/¼ tsp grated nutmeg
50 g/2 oz Parmesan cheese, grated

MORNAY SAUCE
1 small onion
1 small carrot
1 small celery stick
600 ml/1 pint milk
1 bay leaf
few parsley stalks
1 thyme sprig
1 clove
6 white peppercorns
1 blade of mace
50 g/2 oz butter
50 g/2 oz plain flour
1 egg yolk
25 g/1 oz Gruyère cheese, grated
25 g/1 oz Parmesan cheese, grated
60 ml/4 tbsp single cream
pinch of grated nutmeg

Start by making the sauce. Combine the onion, carrot, celery and milk in a saucepan. Add the herbs and spices, with salt to taste. Heat to simmering point, cover, turn off the heat and allow to stand for 30 minutes to infuse. Strain into a measuring jug.

Melt the butter in a saucepan. Stir in the flour and cook over low heat for 2-3 minutes, without allowing the mixture to colour. Remove the pan from the heat and gradually add the flavoured milk, stirring constantly.

Return the pan to moderate heat, stirring until the mixture boils and thickens to a coating consistency. When the mixture boils, lower the heat and simmer for 1-2 minutes, beating briskly. Cool slightly.

Beat the egg yolk in a small bowl. Add a little of the sauce and mix well. Add the contents of the bowl to the sauce and heat gently, stirring. Do not allow the sauce to boil. Stir in the cheeses until melted. Add the cream and nutmeg. Cover the surface of the sauce closely with damp greaseproof paper and set aside.

Using 25 g/1 oz of the butter, grease a shallow ovenproof serving dish. Tear the spinach leaves from the stalks and place in a large saucepan with the remaining butter. Add salt and pepper to taste. Cover with a tight-fitting lid and cook gently for about 15 minutes, shaking the pan occasionally.

Meanwhile, combine the stock and white wine in a large saucepan. Bring to simmering point, add the fish and poach for 7-10 minutes.

Drain the spinach throughly in a colander, pressing out all free liquid with the back of a wooden spoon. Put the spinach on the base of the prepared dish. Remove the fish fillets with a slotted spoon and arrange them on top. Keep hot.

Boil the fish stock until reduced by half. Reheat the sauce, stirring frequently. Add the reduced fish stock, season with salt, pepper and nutmeg and pour the sauce over the fish. Sprinkle with the grated Parmesan and brown under a hot grill. Serve at once.

SERVES 4

———————— ◆ ————————

GEFILTE FISH

This mixture may also be used to stuff a whole fish such as carp, which is then poached whole.

1 large carrot, sliced
3 onions
10 ml/2 tsp salt
pinch of pepper
fish bones and fish head (if available)
1 kg/2¼ lb haddock, cod or whiting fillets
2 eggs, lightly beaten
30 ml/2 tbsp medium matzo meal or fresh
    white breadcrumbs
5 ml/1 tsp caster sugar

Put the carrot into a saucepan. Slice 1 onion and add it to the pan with 1 litre/1¾ pints water, the salt, pepper and fish bones. Bring to the boil, lower the heat and simmer for 30 minutes.

Meanwhile, mince the raw fish or process it roughly in a food processor. Put it into a large bowl. Mince or grate the remaining onions and add them to the bowl with the eggs, matzo meal or breadcrumbs and sugar. Stir in salt and pepper to taste.

With wet hands, form the mixture into 12-14 balls. Add to the fish stock and simmer gently for 1 hour.

Transfer the fish balls to a serving plate, using a slotted spoon. Set aside to cool. Strain the stock into a clean bowl, reserving the cooked carrot slices. Chill the stock.

When the fish balls are cold, decorate each one with a slice of cooked carrot. Serve with the chilled stock.

SERVES 4

PLAICE MORNAY

Illustrated on page 38

fat for greasing
350 ml/12 fl oz milk
1 onion, finely chopped
1 carrot, finely chopped
1 celery stick, finely chopped
1 bouquet garni
salt and pepper
8 plaice fillets
25 g/1 oz butter
25 g/1 oz plain flour
100 g/4 oz Gruyère cheese, grated
50 g/2 oz Parmesan cheese, grated
1.25 ml/¼ tsp mustard powder
chervil sprigs to garnish

Grease a shallow flameproof dish. Combine the milk, vegetables and bouquet garni in a saucepan. Add salt and pepper to taste. Bring to the boil, lower the heat and simmer for 10 minutes. Set aside to cool.

Fold the plaice fillets in three, skin side inwards. Strain the flavoured milk into a deep frying pan and heat to simmering point. Add the fish and poach for 6-8 minutes or until the fish is cooked. Using a slotted spoon, transfer the fish to the prepared dish. Cover with buttered greaseproof paper and keep warm. Reserve the cooking liquid in a jug.

Melt the butter in a saucepan, add the flour and cook for 1 minute, stirring. Gradually add the reserved cooking liquid, whisking constantly until the sauce thickens.

Mix the cheeses and stir half the mixture into the sauce, with the mustard. Remove the buttered paper from the fish, pour the sauce over the top and sprinkle with the remaining cheese mixture. Brown briefly under a hot grill. Garnish and serve.

SERVES 4

SWEET AND SOUR HAKE

Illustrated on page 37

450 g/1 lb hake fillet, skinned and cut into
    2.5 cm/1 inch cubes
cornflour for coating
oil for deep frying
1 green pepper, seeded and finely
    chopped

MARINADE
    2 spring onions, finely chopped
    15 ml/1 tbsp medium-dry sherry
    30 ml/2 tbsp soy sauce
    15 ml/1 tbsp finely chopped fresh
        root ginger

SAUCE
    1 (227 g/8 oz) can pineapple cubes in
        natural juice
    30 ml/2 tbsp cornflour
    30 ml/2 tbsp soy sauce
    15 ml/1 tbsp medium-dry sherry
    5 ml/1 tsp malt vinegar
    5 ml/1 tsp oil

Make the marinade by combining all the ingredients in a shallow dish large enough to hold all the fish cubes in a single layer. Add the fish cubes, cover the dish and marinate for 1-2 hours, stirring several times.

Meanwhile make the sauce. Drain the pineapple cubes, reserving the juice in a measuring jug. Make up to 90 ml/6 tbsp with orange juice or water if necessary. Reserve the pineapple cubes.

Put the cornflour in a small saucepan. Add about 30 ml/2 tbsp of the pineapple juice and mix to a smooth paste, then stir in the remaining pineapple juice, soy sauce, sherry, vinegar and oil. Bring to the boil, stirring constantly, then lower the heat and simmer for 3 minutes.

Drain the fish cubes, discarding the marinade. Spread the cornflour for coating in a shallow bowl, add the fish cubes and shake the bowl until all the cubes are well coated.

Put the oil for frying into a deep wide saucepan to a depth of at least 7.5 cm/ 3 inches. Heat the oil to 180-190°C/350-375°F or until a cube of bread added to the oil browns in 30 seconds. If using a deep-fat fryer, follow the manufacturer's instructions.

Fry the fish cubes, a few at a time, for 2-3 minutes until evenly browned. Drain on absorbent kitchen paper, transfer to a warmed serving dish and keep hot.

Add the reserved pineapple cubes to the sweet and sour sauce and heat through. Pour the sauce over the fish, sprinkle with the chopped green pepper and serve at once.

SERVES 4

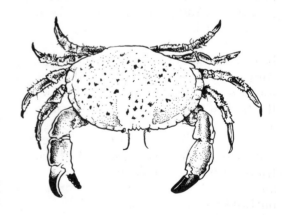

SOLE WITH SHERRY AND BEAN SAUCE

This unusual dish owes its flavour to a fermented bean sauce, which is available from Chinese supermarkets. It is dark, rich and strongly flavoured. When buying bean sauce be careful to distinguish between types that are salty and mild, and others that are very hot, with red chillies.

450 g/1 lb Chinese egg noodles
salt
3 garlic cloves, crushed
4 spring onions, finely chopped
2.5 cm/1 inch piece of fresh root ginger
    peeled and shredded
90 ml/6 tbsp fermented black bean sauce
30 ml/2 tbsp sugar
45 ml/3 tbsp corn oil
1 lemon sole, about 575 g/1¼ lb
45 ml/3 tbsp dry sherry
oil for deep frying
browned almonds (see Mrs Beeton's Tip)
    to garnish

Cook the noodles in a large saucepan of boiling salted water for about 5 minutes or follow packet instructions. Drain thoroughly and set aside to cool completely.

Mix the garlic, spring onions, ginger, bean sauce and sugar in a bowl. Heat the corn oil in a saucepan, add the bean sauce mixture and 30 ml/2 tbsp water. Bring to the boil, stirring constantly. Cover the pan and remove it from the heat.

Leave the head and tail on the fish, but trim the fins and remove the gills. Rinse and dry well. Rinse the fish again inside and out with the sherry, catching the liquor in a bowl. Place the fish in a dish and sprinkle with the reserved sherry. Cover and place in the perforated top section of a large steamer. Alternatively, cook fish between 2 plates over a saucepan of boiling water for 10-15 minutes.

Meanwhile put the oil for deep frying into a deep wide saucepan to a depth of at least 7.5 cm/3 inches. Heat the oil to 180-190°C/350-375°F or until a cube of bread added to the oil browns in 30 seconds. If using a deep-fat fryer, follow the manufacturer's instructions.

Put some of the noodles into a wire basket and lower them carefully into the hot fat. Fry for 2-3 minutes until crisp and golden brown. Drain on absorbent kitchen paper and keep hot while frying the rest of the noodles.

Transfer the fish to a serving dish. Add the cooking liquid from the fish to the sauce and reheat it to boiling point, then pour it over the fish. Garnish with the almonds and serve with the crisp noodles.

SERVES 3-4

> **MRS BEETON'S TIP** To brown or roast almonds, spread them out in a foil-lined grill pan. Place under moderate heat, shaking the pan frequently to prevent the almonds from burning or acquiring dark scorch spots.

SOLE VERONIQUE

Illustrated on page 38

4 large lemon sole fillets
2 shallots, chopped
50 g/2 oz mushrooms, finely chopped
2 parsley sprigs • 1 bay leaf
salt and pepper
125 ml/4 fl oz dry white wine
25 g/1 oz butter
30 ml/2 tbsp plain flour
125 ml/4 fl oz milk
100 g/4 oz small seedless white grapes,
　　halved
juice of ½ lemon
30 ml/2 tbsp single cream

GARNISH
　　Fleurons (see page 45)
　　chopped parsley

Set the oven at 190°C/375°F/gas 5. Arrange the fillets in a shallow ovenproof dish. Sprinkle the shallots, mushrooms, herbs and seasoning over. Pour in the wine, with 125 ml/4 fl oz water. Cover the dish and bake for 15 minutes.

Using a slotted spoon and a fish slice, carefully transfer the fish to a warmed serving dish and keep hot. Tip the cooking liquid into a saucepan and boil until reduced to about 125 ml/4 fl oz.

Meanwhile melt the butter in a clean pan and stir in the flour. Cook for 1 minute, stirring, then gradually add the reduced cooking liquid with the milk, stirring constantly until boiling. Set aside a few grapes and stir the rest into the sauce.

Remove the sauce from the heat and stir in the lemon juice and cream. Pour over the fish, garnish with the pastry fleurons, sprinkle with parsley and serve at once.

SERVES 4

JOHN DORY IN WHITE WINE

fat for greasing
8 John Dory fillets
50 g/2 oz butter
salt and pepper
350 ml/12 fl oz dry white wine
25 g/1 oz plain flour
2 egg yolks
125 ml/4 fl oz double cream
50 g/2 oz peeled cooked prawns to garnish

Grease a shallow baking dish. Set the oven at 190°C/375°F/gas 5.

Roll up the fish fillets, arrange them in the dish and dot with half the butter. Sprinkle with plenty of salt and pepper, pour over half the wine and cover with buttered greaseproof paper. Bake for 20 minutes.

Meanwhile melt the remaining butter in a small saucepan. Add the flour and cook for 1 minute, stirring constantly. Add the remaining wine with 125 ml/4 fl oz water, stirring constantly, and cook until the sauce boils.

Using a slotted spoon, carefully transfer the fish to a warmed serving dish and keep hot. Whisk the cooking liquid into the sauce.

Beat the egg yolks and cream in a small bowl. Add a little of the sauce and mix well. Add the contents of the bowl to the sauce and heat gently, stirring. Do not allow the sauce to boil.

Pour the sauce over the fish, garnish with the prawns and serve at once.

SERVES 4

MACKEREL NICOISE

4 small mackerel
25 g/1 oz butter
30 ml/2 tbsp olive oil
1 large onion, finely chopped
1 garlic clove, crushed
125 ml/4 fl oz medium-dry white wine
10 ml/2 tsp tomato purée
pinch of powdered saffron
salt and pepper
225 g/8 oz tomatoes, peeled, seeded and
    chopped

GARNISH
    parsley sprigs
    stoned black olives
    lemon slices

Rinse the fish inside and out and pat dry on absorbent kitchen paper. Melt the butter in the oil in a large frying pan. Add the onion and garlic and fry for 3-4 minutes until soft but not coloured. Place the fish on top.

Mix the wine and tomato purée together and pour over the fish. Season with the saffron, salt and pepper. Bring the liquid to simmering point and poach the fish for 10 minutes.

Using a slotted spoon and a fish slice, carefully transfer the fish to a warmed serving dish and keep hot. Add the chopped tomatoes to the cooking liquid and boil briskly for 5 minutes, stirring occasionally.

Pour the sauce over the fish, garnish with parsley, olives and lemon slices and serve at once.

SERVES 4

RED MULLET WITH TOMATOES AND OLIVES

150 ml/¼ pint olive oil
1 onion, finely chopped
1 garlic clove, crushed
25 g/1 oz parsley, chopped
225 g/8 oz tomatoes, peeled, seeded and
    chopped
5 ml/1 tsp tomato purée
salt and pepper
1 bouquet garni
4 (225 g/8 oz) red mullet, cleaned and
    scaled
8 black olives, stoned
75 ml/5 tbsp dry white wine
lemon slices to garnish

Heat 100 ml/3½ fl oz of the olive oil in a saucepan, add the onion and fry for 3-4 minutes until lightly browned. Add the garlic and parsley, with the chopped tomatoes. Stir in the tomato purée, with salt and pepper to taste, and add the bouquet garni. Simmer for 15 minutes.

Heat the remaining oil in a deep frying pan and fry the fish gently for 5 minutes, turning once.

When the sauce is cooked, remove the bouquet garni and add the olives and wine. Drain the excess oil from the frying pan. Pour the sauce over the fish, cover the pan and cook for 10 minutes more.

Carefully transfer the fish and sauce to a warmed serving dish. Serve at once, garnished with lemon slices.

SERVES 4

SALMON TROUT WITH AVOCADO SAUCE

1 (1.8-2 kg/4-4½ lb) salmon trout
Court Bouillon (page 28)

SAUCE
    2 avocados
    30 ml/2 tbsp lime or lemon juice
    45 ml/3 tbsp oil
    salt and pepper

Clean the salmon trout, if necessary, but leave the head and tail on.

Place the fish in a kettle or suitable pan and pour in the court bouillon to cover the fish by at least 3.5 cm/1¼ inches. Top up with water if necessary. Bring the liquid to a bare simmer, cover the pan tightly and cook for about 30 minutes or until the thickest part of the fish yields slightly when pressed.

Carefully transfer the fish to a board or platter. Skin as much of the fish as possible. Turn the fish on to a serving platter, or carefully turn it over, and strip off the remaining skin. Cover loosely with a cloth and set aside to cool.

Make the sauce by mashing the avocado flesh in a bowl with the remaining ingredients until it has the consistency of thick mayonnaise. A food processor or blender may be used, but take care not to over-process the mixture.

When the fish is cold, use a little of the sauce to mask it. Serve the remaining sauce separately.

SERVES 6 TO 8

SCALLOPED HADDOCK

fat for greasing
450 g/1 lb potatoes, halved and cooked
salt and pepper
75 g/3 oz butter
15-30 ml/2-3 tbsp single cream
250 ml/8 fl oz milk
30 ml/2 tbsp chopped onion
1 blade of mace
225 g/8 oz smoked haddock
25 g/1 oz plain flour
30 ml/2 tbsp chopped parsley
30 ml/2 tbsp double cream
browned breadcrumbs

Grease 4 shallow individual ovenproof dishes. Set the oven at 200°C/400°F/gas 6. Mash the potatoes until smooth. Beat in 25 g/1 oz of the butter and the single cream.

Combine the milk, onion and mace in a deep frying pan. Bring to simmering point, add the fish and poach gently for 5-8 minutes. Using a slotted spoon, transfer the fish to a large plate. Remove any skin and flake the fish, then divide it between the dishes. Reserve the cooking liquid.

Melt half the remaining butter in a saucepan, add the flour and cook for 1 minute, stirring. Gradually add the reserved cooking liquid and boil, stirring. Add seasoning, parsley and double cream. Pour the sauce over the fish. Sprinkle with the breadcrumbs.

Spoon the creamed potato into a piping bag fitted with a large star nozzle and pipe a border of mashed potato around the edge of each dish. Dot the remaining butter over the breadcrumbs. Stand the dishes on a large baking sheet and bake for 4-5 minutes until browned.

SERVES 4

Spicy Fish Slices (page 97) and Prawn Curry (page 87)

Lobster Thermidor (page 89)

Coquilles St Jacques Mornay (page 90)

Cod Cutlets with Shrimp Stuffing (page 96)

Grilled Kippers (page 99) and Goujons of Plaice (page 100)

Sole Colbert (page 102)

Fish Cakes and Whitebait (both on page 104)

80

Monkfish and Bacon Kebabs (page 105)

HAM AND HADDIE

125 ml/4 fl oz milk
575 g/1¼ lb Finnan haddock on the bone
25 g/1 oz butter
4 (100 g/4 oz) slices cooked ham
pepper
45 ml/3 tbsp double cream

Pour the milk into a large frying pan. Heat to just below boiling point, add the haddock, lower the heat and simmer for 10-15 minutes or until the fish is cooked.

Using a slotted spoon and a fish slice, transfer the fish to a large plate. Remove the skin and bones from the fish and flake the flesh. Reserve the cooking liquid in a jug.

Melt the butter in a clean frying pan and add the ham slices. Heat through, turning once, then arrange the ham slices in a warmed flameproof dish. Spoon the flaked fish over the ham and pour the reserved cooking liquid over. Add pepper to taste, then drizzle the cream over the dish. Brown quickly under a hot grill before serving.

SERVES 4

JUGGED KIPPERS

4 kippers
4 pats chilled Maître d'Hôtel Butter
  (page 44)

Put the kippers, tail end up, in a tall heatproof jug. Pour boiling water into the jug to cover all but the tails of the fish. Cover the jug with a cloth and leave to stand for 5 minutes.

Tilt the jug gently over a sink and drain off the water (see Mrs Beeton's Tip). Put each kipper on a warmed plate and serve topped with a pat of maître d'hôtel butter.

SERVES 4

> **MRS BEETON'S TIP** Do not attempt to pull the kippers out of the jug by their tails – they may well part company with the body of the fish.

SKATE IN BLACK BUTTER

1-2 skate wings, total weight about
  800 g/1¾ lb
1 litre/1¾ pints Court Bouillon (page 28)
25 g/1 oz butter
salt and pepper
30 ml/2 tbsp capers
30 ml/2 tbsp chopped parsley
75 ml/5 tbsp wine vinegar

Rinse and dry the skate and cut it into serving portions. Put the fish in a deep frying pan and cover with the court bouillon. Bring to simmering point and simmer for 15-20 minutes or until the fish is cooked.

Using a slotted spoon and a fish slice, lift out the fish and transfer to a wooden board. Scrape away the skin. Place the fish in a warmed ovenproof dish and keep hot.

Pour off the court bouillon from the frying pan, add the butter to the pan and heat until it is a rich golden-brown. Spoon over the fish, sprinkle with salt and pepper to taste and scatter the capers and parsley over the top. Pour the vinegar into the pan, swill it around while heating quickly, then pour it over the fish. Serve at once.

SERVES 3 TO 4

*H*OT POACHED SALMON

Serve hot poached salmon with Hollandaise Sauce (page 42). Cold poached salmon may be glazed with aspic jelly and garnished with cucumber slices, following the techniques explained at the beginning of the chapter on Pastes, Pâtés and Cold Platters (page 172).

1(1.6-3.25 kg/3½-7 lb) salmon
about 3.5 litres/6 pints Court Bouillon
(page 28)

Cut the fins from the fish, remove the scales and thoroughly wash the body cavity. Tie the mouth of the fish shut. Tie the body of the fish loosely to keep it in shape during cooking – two or three bands of string around the fish to prevent the body cavity from gaping are usually sufficient. Weigh the fish and calculate the cooking time. Allow 5 minutes per 450 g/1 lb for salmon up to 2.25 kg/5 lb in weight; 4 minutes per 450 g/1 lb plus 5 minutes for salmon up to 3.25 kg/7 lb.

Put the fish in a fish kettle and pour over the court bouillon. Bring the liquid gently to just below boiling point, lower the heat and simmer for the required cooking time. The court bouillon should barely show signs of simmering; if the liquid is allowed to bubble then it may damage the delicate salmon flesh. If serving the salmon cold, simmer for 5 minutes only, then leave the fish to cool in the cooking liquid.

Drain the salmon well and untie the body. Slide the salmon on to a large, heated platter. Slit the skin around the body immediately below the head and just above the tail of the fish. Carefully peel back the skin from the head towards the tail. Carefully turn the fish over and remove the skin from the second side. Untie the mouth.

Garnish the salmon with lemon slices and parsley sprigs. Freshly cooked vegetables (new potatoes and baby carrots) may be arranged around the fish. Serve at once.

SERVINGS FROM SALMON

Hot salmon served as a main course will yield the servings below. If the fish is served cold and dressed, as part of a buffet with other main dishes, then it will yield about 2 extra portions.

1.6 kg/3½ lb salmon – 4 portions
2.25 kg/5 lb salmon – 6 portions
3.25 kg/7 lb salmon – 10 portions

MICROWAVE TIP Provided it can be curled into a circular dish that will fit into your microwave, salmon may be cooked by this method. Prepare the fish, tuck 2 bay leaves, some peppercorns and a small sprig of parsley into the body cavity, then curl the fish into the dish (a 25 cm/10 inch quiche dish works well). Cover fish and dish with two layers of microwave film to hold the fish securely and prevent it from losing its shape. Cook on High. A 2.25 kg/5 lb salmon will take about 12 minutes. If you do not have a turntable, turn the dish three times while cooking. Allow to stand, covered, for 5 minutes. To serve hot, drain, remove the herbs from the body cavity and skin as suggested above. Allow to cool in the wrapping if serving cold.

ANGEVIN SALMON TROUT

fat for greasing
1(1 kg/2¼ lb) salmon trout
1 onion, finely chopped
375 ml/13 fl oz rosé wine
15 g/½ oz butter
15 ml/1 tbsp plain flour
30 ml/2 tbsp double cream
salt and pepper
125 ml/4 fl oz Hollandaise Sauce (page 42)

GARNISH
puff pastry fleurons (page 45)
watercress sprigs

Generously butter a fairly deep oven-proof dish large enough to hold the whole fish. Set the oven at 160°C/325°F/gas 3.

Cut the fins from the fish and thoroughly wash the body cavity. Put the fish in the dish, curling it round if necessary. Add the onion. Mix the wine with 100 ml/3½ fl oz water and pour over the fish. Oven-poach for 30 minutes.

Using a slotted spoon and a fish slice, carefully transfer the fish to a wooden board. Remove the skin and keep the fish hot. Strain the cooking liquid into a saucepan and boil until reduced by one third.

Melt the butter in a clean saucepan, add the flour and cook for 1 minute, stirring constantly. Gradually add the reduced cooking liquid, stirring all the time until the mixture comes to the boil. Remove from the heat and add the cream, with salt and pepper to taste. Beat in the hollandaise sauce.

Fillet the fish, placing the fillets on a warmed serving dish. Coat with half the sauce, pouring the rest into a sauceboat.

Garnish with the pastry fleurons and the watercress and serve the fish at once, with the remaining sauce.

SERVES 4

TWEED KETTLE

575 g/1¼ lb middle cut salmon
500 ml/17 fl oz Basic Fish Stock (page 27)
250 ml/8 fl oz dry white wine
pinch of ground mace
salt and pepper
25 g/1 oz chopped shallots or snipped chives
5 ml/1 tsp chopped parsley
25 g/1 oz butter
25 g/1 oz plain flour

Put the salmon in a saucepan with the fish stock, wine and mace. Add salt and pepper to taste. Bring the liquid to simmering point and simmer gently for 10-15 minutes or until the fish is just cooked through.

Using a slotted spoon and a fish slice, transfer the fish to a large plate. Remove the skin and bones and return them to the stock in the saucepan. Transfer the skinned fish to a warmed serving dish and keep hot.

Simmer the stock and fish trimmings for 10 minutes, then strain into a clean pan. Simmer gently, uncovered, until reduced by half. Stir in the shallots or chives and the parsley and remove from the heat.

In a small bowl, blend the butter with the flour. Gradually add small pieces of the mixture to the stock, whisking thoroughly after each addition. Return to the heat and simmer for 5 minutes, stirring. Pour the sauce over the fish and serve at once.

SERVES 4

POACHED TROUT WITH PRAWN SAUCE

Illustrated on page 39

125 ml/4 fl oz red wine
1 clove
1 bay leaf
4 trout, cleaned, heads left on
salt and pepper
25 g/1 oz butter
25 g/1 oz plain flour
125 ml/4 fl oz milk
100 g/4 oz peeled cooked prawns
45 ml/3 tbsp double cream

GARNISH
  parsley sprigs
  lemon wedges

Set the oven at 160°C/325°F/gas 3. Combine the red wine, clove and bay leaf in a shallow ovenproof dish large enough to hold all the trout in a single layer. Add the fish, with salt and pepper to taste. Cover tightly with foil to keep in all the moisture and place in the oven for 15-20 minutes, or until cooked. The fish poach in the wine and moisture in the gentle oven heat.

Using a slotted spoon and a fish slice, carefully transfer the fish one at a time to a platter or board. Remove the skin, then put the fish on a warmed serving dish, cover and keep hot. Strain the cooking liquid.

Melt the butter in a clean saucepan, add the flour and cook for 1 minute, stirring constantly. Gradually add the cooking liquid, stirring all the time until the mixture begins to thicken, then gradually add the milk, still stirring and bring to the boil. Lower the heat and simmer for 2-3 minutes, stirring occasionally.

Remove the sauce from the heat and stir in the prawns and cream. Pour the hot sauce over the fish, garnish and serve.

SERVES 4

☀ **MICROWAVE TIP**   The trout may be cooked in the microwave. Arrange them in alternate directions in a shallow dish. Pour over the wine and add the clove and bay leaf. Cover loosely and cook on High for 12 minutes, turning once. Strain off the cooking liquid as suggested above. Make the sauce in a large bowl by whisking the cooking liquid into the flour, then adding the milk and finally the butter. Cook on High for 10 minutes, whisking twice during cooking. Whisk again and stir in the prawns and cream. Reheat the fish for 1 minute on High if necessary, pour over the sauce, garnish and serve.

TROUT HOLLANDAISE

6 trout, cleaned, heads left on
1 litre/1¾ pints Court Bouillon (page 28)
chopped parsley to garnish
250 ml/8 fl oz Hollandaise Sauce
  (page 42), to serve

Put the trout in a saucepan large enough to hold them in a single layer. Add the court bouillon, bring to simmering point and poach the fish gently for 15 minutes.

Carefully remove the fish from the stock and arrange on a heated serving dish. Garnish with parsley and serve at once, with the sauce.

SERVES 6

PIKE QUENELLES

Illustrated on page 39

450 g/1 lb pike fillets, skinned and finely
    diced
4-5 egg whites
500 ml/17 fl oz double cream
salt and pepper
pinch of grated nutmeg
1 litre/1¾ pints Court Bouillon (page 28)

Purée the fish with the egg whites in a blender or food processor, then rub the mixture through a sieve into a bowl.

In a clean bowl, whip the cream to the same consistency as the fish purée. Fold the cream into the puréed fish lightly but thoroughly. Season the mixture with salt, pepper and nutmeg, cover the bowl and chill for several hours.

The chilled quenelle mixture is shaped and cooked in one operation. Prepare a large saucepan of hot water and place a large dinner plate on top of it: this will be used to keep the quenelles hot as they are cooked and before they are served. As soon as the first quenelle is placed on the hot plate, turn the heat off under the saucepan to prevent further cooking.

Heat the court bouillon in a large saucepan until just simmering: the surface should just quiver. Using 2 rounded dessertspoons shape the chilled mixture into ovals, and gently lower these into the liquid. To obtain a neat oval, scoop a portion of mixture cleanly from the bowl. Use the second spoon to cup the top of the portion, then slide the spoon over the mixture to scoop it from the first spoon. This technique of passing the mixture from one spoon to another makes the oval shape.

Simmer the quenelles for 8-10 minutes, then carefully remove with a slotted spoon.

Transfer the quenelles to the plate over the saucepan of hot water as they are cooked. Cover loosely with foil to keep hot until all the mixture is cooked.

Serve the quenelles immediately, with Fresh Tomato Sauce (page 43).

SERVES 4 TO 6

BRAISED PIKE

40 g/1½ oz butter
225 g/8 oz rindless streaky bacon rashers,
    cut into small squares
1 (1 kg/2¼ lb) pike, cleaned, trimmed,
    filleted and cut into 5 cm/2 inch cubes
250 ml/8 fl oz Basic Fish Stock (page 27)
10 ml/2 tsp lemon juice
salt and pepper
1 tablespoon plain flour
chopped parsley to garnish

Melt 25 g/1 oz of the butter in a saucepan and add the bacon. Fry until crisp, then add the fish cubes, turning until well coated in butter and bacon fat. Pour the stock and lemon juice into the pan and add plenty of salt and pepper. Bring to simmering point, cover the pan and poach the fish for 15 minutes.

Using a slotted spoon, transfer the fish and bacon to a warmed serving dish. Keep hot. Strain the cooking liquid into a clean saucepan.

In a small bowl, blend the remaining butter with the flour. Gradually add small pieces of the mixture to the stock, whisking thoroughly after each addition. Return the pan to the heat and simmer until the sauce thickens. Pour the sauce over the fish, garnish with parsley and serve at once.

SERVES 4

CARP WITH MUSHROOMS

Illustrated on page 40

butter for greasing
1.25 kg/2¾ lb carp fillets, skinned and cut
    into large pieces
salt and pepper
150 ml/¼ pint dry white wine
50 g/2 oz butter
1 onion, finely chopped
150 g/5 oz mushrooms, sliced
15 ml/1 tbsp chopped parsley
15 g/½ oz plain flour
150 ml/¼ pint double cream

Grease a large ovenproof dish. Set the oven at 160°C/325°F/gas 3. Arrange the fish fillets in the dish. Sprinkle with salt and pepper, add the wine and cover with a sheet of buttered greaseproof paper. Oven-poach for 25-35 minutes.

Using a slotted spoon and a fish slice, transfer the fish to a serving dish and keep hot. Reserve the cooking liquid.

Melt the butter in a frying pan, add the onion and fry gently for 3-4 minutes until transparent. Add the mushrooms and fry gently for 3 minutes, then add the parsley. Sprinkle in the flour, stir well and cook for 1 minute. Gradually add the reserved poaching liquid, mixing well. Simmer the sauce for 3-4 minutes until thick, then stir in the cream. Heat gently, but do not boil.

Taste the sauce, add salt and pepper, then pour it over the fish. Serve at once.

SERVES 6

MRS BEETON'S TIP Quickly toss a few small, whole button mushrooms in hot butter and sprinkle them with chopped parsley. Use to garnish the carp.

STUFFED CARP

1(1.4 kg/3 lb) carp, cleaned
salt and pepper

STUFFING
50 g/2 oz butter
1 onion, diced
15 ml/1 tbsp chopped parsley
5 ml/1 tsp snipped chives
100 g/4 oz fresh white breadcrumbs
3 eggs, beaten
350 g/12 oz mushrooms, chopped
about 75 ml/3 fl oz red wine (optional)

GARNISH
lemon wedges
parsley sprigs

Scale the fish, cut off the fins and thoroughly wash the body cavity. Sprinkle with salt and pepper and set aside.

Make the stuffing. Melt the butter in a saucepan, add the onion and fry gently for 3-4 minutes until soft. Remove from the heat and add the herbs and breadcrumbs, with the beaten eggs. Set aside for 10 minutes. Stir in the mushrooms and moisten with the red wine, if necessary. Add plenty of salt and pepper, and stir well. Do not leave the stuffing to stand or the mushrooms will weep and make it too soft.

Stuff the cavity of the fish, secure the opening with a skewer to keep it closed and wrap the fish securely in greased foil. Place in a fish kettle, large flameproof casserole or deep roasting tin and add water to cover. Bring to just below boiling point, lower the heat, cover and simmer for 25 minutes.

Lift out the fish, remove the foil and transfer to a warmed serving dish. Garnish with lemon wedges and parsley sprigs and serve at once. If preferred, the well-drained foil package may be laid on a board or platter for serving. Open the foil and turn it back, crumpling it down neatly. Add plenty of parsley to disguise the slightly discoloured foil.

SERVES 4

> MRS BEETON'S TIP   To cut up a small amount of parsley, place the sprigs in a cup or mug and snip downwards with clean kitchen scissors, turning the cup with your free hand.

---

*P*RAWN CELESTE

50 g/2 oz butter
100 g/4 oz mushrooms, sliced
1 tablespoon plain flour
salt and pepper
125 ml/4 fl oz milk
125 ml/4 fl oz single cream
225 g/8 oz peeled cooked prawns
15 ml/1 tbsp dry sherry
chopped parsley to garnish
4 slices toast, cut in triangles to serve

Melt the butter in a saucepan, add the mushrooms and cook over moderate heat for 3-4 minutes. Stir in the flour, with salt and pepper to taste and cook gently for 3 minutes. Gradually add the milk and cream, stirring constantly until the sauce thickens. Add the prawns and sherry. Spoon into a warmed serving dish, garnish with the chopped parsley and serve with the toast triangles.

SERVES 4

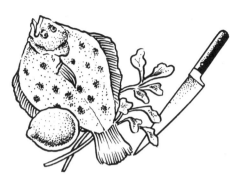

*P*RAWN CURRY

Illustrated on page 73

15 ml/1 tbsp ground coriander
2.5 ml/½ tsp ground cumin
2.5 ml/½ tsp chilli powder
2.5 ml/½ tsp turmeric
1 garlic clove, crushed
250 ml/8 fl oz Basic Fish Stock (page 27)
30 ml/2 tbsp oil
1 large onion, finely chopped
45 ml/3 tbsp tomato purée
2 tomatoes, peeled, seeded and chopped
450 g/1 lb peeled cooked prawns
juice of ½ lemon
10 ml/2 tsp coconut cream (optional)
coriander sprigs to garnish

Mix all the spices in a small bowl. Add the garlic and mix to a paste with a little of the stock. Set aside.

Heat the oil in a frying pan, add the onion and fry for 4-5 minutes until golden brown. Add the tomato purée and spice mixture, then cook for 1-2 minutes. Stir in the remaining stock and tomatoes, cover the pan and simmer gently for 20 minutes.

Add the prawns and lemon juice to the pan, with the coconut cream, if used. Stir until the coconut cream dissolves, then simmer for 5 minutes more. Garnish with coriander sprigs and serve with basmati rice.

SERVES 4

SWEET AND SOUR PRAWNS

225 g/8 oz peeled cooked prawns
15 ml/1 tbsp medium-dry sherry
salt and pepper
30 ml/2 tbsp oil
2 onions, sliced in rings
2 green peppers, seeded and sliced in
    rings
125 ml/4 fl oz chicken or vegetable stock
1(227 g/8 oz) can pineapple cubes,
    drained
15 ml/1 tbsp cornflour
30 ml/2 tbsp soy sauce
125 ml/4 fl oz white wine vinegar
75 g/3 oz sugar
whole cooked prawns to garnish

Spread out the prawns on a large shallow dish. Sprinkle with the sherry, salt and pepper, cover and set aside to marinate for 30 minutes.

Towards the end of the marinating time, heat the oil in a frying pan or wok. Add the onions and peppers and fry gently for 5-7 minutes. Add the stock and pineapple cubes. Cover and cook for 3-5 minutes.

In a small bowl, blend the cornflour, soy sauce, vinegar and sugar together. Stir the mixture into the pan or wok and bring to the boil, stirring, then simmer for 2 minutes until thickened. Lower the heat, add the prawns with the marinating liquid and heat for 1 minute.

Serve hot on a bed of rice, if liked. Garnish with the whole cooked prawns, in their shells.

SERVES 4

SCAMPI IN PAPRIKA CREAM

25 g/1 oz butter
15 ml/1 tbsp finely chopped onion
5 ml/1 tsp paprika
100 ml/3½ fl oz medium-dry sherry
450 g/1 lb peeled cooked scampi tails
3 egg yolks
200 ml/7 fl oz double cream
4 small tomatoes, peeled, seeded and cut
    in quarters
salt and pepper

Melt the butter in a saucepan, add the onion and cook gently for 8-10 minutes, stirring often, until the onion is softened but not browned.

Add the paprika and sherry to the onion and butter. Stir in and boil, uncovered, until reduced by half. Stir in the scampi tails, lower the heat and heat gently for 5 minutes.

Beat the egg yolks and cream in a small bowl. Stir in a little of the hot sauce and mix well. Add the contents of the bowl to the scampi and sauce mixture and heat gently, stirring. Do not allow the sauce to boil. Stir in the tomatoes and heat through gently, then spoon the mixture into a warmed serving dish. Serve at once, with boiled rice or chunks of French bread.

SERVES 4

SPANISH LOBSTER

Canned or frozen lobster meat may be used for this recipe.

30 ml/2 tbsp oil
1 large onion, chopped
4 tomatoes, peeled, seeded and chopped
125 ml/4 fl oz medium-dry sherry
salt and pepper
125 ml/4 fl oz Basic Fish Stock (page 27)
350 g/12 oz lobster meat, roughly diced
1 small bunch of chives, snipped
juice of ½ lemon

Heat the oil in a large frying pan. Add the onion and fry gently for 15-20 minutes until softened but not browned. Add the tomatoes and sherry, with plenty of salt and pepper. Cook over moderate heat until soft, stirring occasionally.

Pour in the stock and heat until just boiling. Cook at a fast simmer, stirring occasionally, until the mixture is reduced and thickened. This will take 15-20 minutes. The larger the pan, the quicker the extra liquid will evaporate, so take care not to allow the mixture to become too dry.

Add the lobster meat and stir it with the sauce. Heat gently for about 5 minutes, until the lobster is hot, then stir in the chives and lemon juice.

Serve at once with boiled rice or noodles, if liked.

SERVES 3 TO 4

LOBSTER THERMIDOR

Illustrated on page 74

45 ml/3 tbsp butter
2 shallots, finely chopped
150 ml/¼ pint dry white wine
5 ml/1 tsp chopped fresh tarragon
5 ml/1 tsp chopped fresh chervil
200 ml/7 fl oz Béchamel Sauce (page 41)
125 ml/4 fl oz double cream
30 ml/2 tbsp French mustard
30 ml/2 tbsp grated Parmesan cheese
salt and pepper
2 cooked lobsters

GARNISH
watercress sprigs
lemon slices

Set the oven at 200°C/400°F/gas 6. Melt the butter in a saucepan, add the shallots and fry gently for 5 minutes until soft. Add the wine and herbs, raise the heat and boil the mixture until reduced by half.

Stir the Béchamel sauce into the shallot mixture and remove from the heat. Add the cream and mustard, with half the cheese and salt and pepper to taste. Mix well. Set about 60 ml/4 tbsp of the sauce aside.

Twist off the lobster claws. Split the lobsters in half lengthways. Carefully remove the meat from the claws and body, keeping the lobster shells intact (see page 23). Chop the lobster meat coarsely and mix it with the sauce in the pan. Return the sauced lobster meat to the clean shells.

Place the filled shells on an ovenproof serving platter and spoon the reserved sauce over the top. Sprinkle with the remaining cheese. Brown in the oven for 10-15 minutes, garnish and serve very hot.

SERVES 4

QUEENS OF THE SEA

Queens are small scallops. They have good texture and flavour and are well worth looking for. They are usually sold shelled, as small round nuggets of meat.

75 g/3 oz butter
30 ml/2 tbsp dry white wine
16 queen scallops
30 ml/2 tbsp plain flour
pinch of paprika
250 ml/8 fl oz milk
salt and pepper
4 hard-boiled eggs
1 egg yolk
15 ml/1 tbsp double cream

Melt half the butter in a large frying pan. Add the wine and scallops and cook very gently for 3 minutes or until just cooked. Do not boil. Set the pan aside.

Melt the remaining butter in a saucepan, add the flour and paprika and cook for 1 minute, stirring constantly. Gradually add the milk, stirring, and bring to the boil. Simmer for 2 minutes until the sauce thickens. Add salt and pepper.

Spoon 60 ml/4 tbsp of the sauce into a shallow dish. Add the remaining sauce to the scallop mixture and heat gently, shaking the pan to blend the ingredients. Cut each of the eggs into 8 segments and arrange them on the sauce in the dish.

Beat the egg yolk and cream in a small bowl. Add to the scallops in sauce and heat gently, stirring. Do not allow the sauce to boil. As soon as the sauce has heated through, pour it over the hard-boiled eggs and place under a hot grill to brown slightly. Serve at once.

SERVES 4

COQUILLES ST JACQUES MORNAY

Illustrated on page 75

Great care must be taken not to overcook the scallops. Their delectable flavour and texture is easily spoiled by high heat.

fat for greasing
450 g/1 lb potatoes, halved
salt and pepper
50 g/2 oz butter
90 ml/6 tbsp single cream
8-12 large scallops, shelled, with corals
1 small onion, sliced
1 bay leaf
45 ml/3 tbsp dry white wine
juice of ½ lemon
25 g/1 oz plain flour
125 ml/4 fl oz milk
75 ml/5 tbsp single cream
45 ml/3 tbsp dry white breadcrumbs
60 ml/4 tbsp grated Parmesan cheese
watercress sprigs to garnish

Cook the potatoes in a saucepan of salted boiling water for about 30 minutes or until tender. Drain thoroughly and mash with a potato masher, or beat with a hand-held electric whisk until smooth. Beat in 25 g/1 oz of the butter and 15 ml/1 tbsp of the cream to make a creamy piping consistency.

Grease 4 scallop shells or shallow individual ovenproof dishes. Spoon the creamed potato into a piping bag fitted with a large star nozzle and pipe a border of mashed potato around the edge of each shell. Set the oven at 200°C/400°F/gas 6.

Combine the scallops, onion, bay leaf, wine and lemon juice in a saucepan. Add 75 ml/5 tbsp water. Bring to simmering point and poach the scallops gently for 5 minutes. Using a slotted spoon remove the scallops and cut into slices. Strain the cooking liquid into a jug.

Melt the remaining butter in a saucepan, add the flour and cook for 1 minute, stirring constantly. Gradually add the reserved cooking liquid, stirring all the time, until the sauce starts to thicken. Add salt and pepper to taste and stir in the milk. Bring to the boil, stirring, then lower the heat and simmer for 2-3 minutes. Remove from the heat and stir in the cream.

Divide the sliced scallops between the prepared scallop shells or dishes. Coat with the sauce and sprinkle lightly with the breadcrumbs and Parmesan.

Stand the scallop shells or dishes on a large baking sheet and bake for 10 minutes until the breadcrumbs are crisp and the potatoes browned. Garnish with the watercress sprigs and serve at once.

SERVES 4

STUFFED SQUID

8 squid, cleaned and trimmed
25 g/1 oz butter
1 small onion, finely chopped
1 garlic clove, crushed
grated rind and juice of ½ lemon
50 g/2 oz mushrooms, diced
50 g/2 oz fresh white breadcrumbs
30 ml/2 tbsp chopped parsley
5 ml/1 tsp dried marjoram
salt and pepper
a little oil for brushing
Fresh Tomato Sauce (page 43)
lemon wedges to garnish

Rinse the squid well, drain and dry on absorbent kitchen paper. Set aside. Melt the butter in a frying pan, add the onion and garlic and cook, stirring occasionally, until the onion is soft but not browned.

And the grated lemon rind and mushrooms to the pan and continue to cook until the mushrooms have reduced and most of the liquid has evaporated – this takes some time but is important to avoid making the stuffing too moist.

Remove the pan from the heat and stir in the breadcrumbs and herbs, with salt and pepper to taste. Add lemon juice to taste but avoid making the stuffing too moist.

Use a teaspoon to fill the squid pouches with stuffing – they should not be too full as the breadcrumb mixture expands on heating. Thread a small meat skewer through the open end of each squid to keep the stuffing enclosed, then pass the skewer through the pointed end of the body.

Brush the squid with oil and grill under moderate heat, turning occasionally, until they are golden brown all over. This will take about 15 minutes. Do not let the squid cook too quickly or the stuffing will not be cooked.

Heat the tomato sauce if necessary, then pour it into a serving dish. Arrange the squid in it and add lemon wedges for garnish. Any remaining lemon juice may be drizzled over the squid. Offer a mill of black pepper with the squid.

SERVES 4

GRILLED AND FRIED FISH

Grilling and frying are probably the most familiar and popular methods of cooking fish. This chapter offers some alternative ideas as well as all the basic information on how to achieve perfection using simple techniques.

GRILLING

Grilling is a quick cooking method, particularly well suited to oily fish, such as mackerel and herring.

FISH FOR GRILLING
The practicalities of grilling as a cooking method mean that the choice of fish is limited to the more sturdy cuts and varieties. Thus cod fillet is more suitable than plaice fillets which tend to break more easily, and cod steaks are even better since they are thicker and less likely to break up.

Fillets should be firm and fairly thick for cooking on the grill rack; otherwise they may be grilled in a flameproof dish. All fish steaks are ideal for grilling. Similarly, small whole fish cook well by this method but larger fish may not cook through sufficiently. Chunks of firm fish (monkfish, huss, thick end of cod fillet) may be skewered.

Shellfish such as Mediterranean prawns and lobster are good grilled; other varieties – scallops, mussels and oysters – need protection. Grilled small squid can be delicious.

MARINATING
Marinating is the process of soaking food before cooking. Its purpose is to flavour and to moisten food, also to tenderise meat. Fish is marinated before cooking principally for flavour, but also to moisten certain types.

Swordfish, tuna, shark, halibut and turbot all benefit from being marinated before grilling. Cubed monkfish and peeled uncooked prawns may also be marinated to keep them moist when skewered.

Oil is an important ingredient in marinades for fish – sunflower, grapeseed and groundnut oils are all light; olive oil contributes its own distinctive flavour. Fresh herbs, garlic, grated citrus rind, grated fresh root ginger, ground coriander, cumin and other curry spices may be used. Tomatoes, chopped onion, olives and capers are also worth remembering.

Unlike meat, fish does not require lengthy marinating for tenderising. A couple of hours is usually sufficient.

TURNING AND BASTING
During cooking the fish should be basted to keep it moist. A marinade may be drained and used for this purpose; otherwise oil may be used. Melted butter is another option but it tends to burn easily so should be reserved for seafood such as boiled lobster which grills very quickly. A mixture of melted butter and oil may be used.

Handle fish carefully to prevent it from breaking up. Check the cooking progress often and regulate the heat so that the fish is only turned once. Use a fish slice and palette knife or slotted spoon, or two slices to avoid the fish breaking. Turn skewered fish carefully.

USING FOIL
Fish often benefits from being cooked on foil. Fillets stay moist, but it is wise to be aware of the possible danger of flaming. Using foil to support the fish, but pricking holes all over the foil to drain the fat, is a good compromise.

TOPPINGS FOR GRILLED FISH
Flavoured butters are by far the easiest topping – have neat pats ready to place on each portion of cooked fish.

Other toppings can be placed on the fish before cooking. Here are a few ideas.

Cheese   One of the simplest toppings and delicious on cod steaks. Cook the steaks on one side in a flameproof dish. Turn them over and partially cook the second side, then top each steak with a slice of cheese such as creamy mozzarella. Cook under moderate heat until golden.

Tomatoes   Sliced peeled tomatoes are good under cheese. If they are added on their own, place them on top towards the end of grilling and baste them with oil.

Peppers   Thin rings of red or green pepper ar tasty and colourful – good with olive oil, garlic and chopped marjoram on meaty fish.

Breadcrumbs – gratin style   Fresh breadcrumbs may be added to make a gratin topping on fish which is almost cooked. Trickle melted butter over or mix the crumbs with grated cheese first – Parmesan is robust. Chopped walnuts and herbs are other tasty additions.

FRYING FISH

All three methods of frying may be used for seafood – deep, shallow and stir frying.

DEEP FRYING
Fish for frying must be coated, either in breadcrumbs, flour or batter. It is important to follow the rules of frying if results are to be crisp and light.

Temperature   Vegetable oil used for frying should be heated to 180°C/350°F. Check the temperature by using a sugar thermometer or by dropping a small cube of bread into the oil. The bread should brown in 30-60 seconds. If the oil is hot enough, it seals the coating on the food rapidly to give crisp, light results. If the oil is too cool, some of it is absorbed by the food before the outside becomes crisp and sealed. If the oil is too hot the outside will brown before the inside of the food is cooked.

When the oil is heated and the food added, the heat should be kept at a fairly high level for a about a minute before it is reduced to prevent the oil from overheating. The cold food cools down the oil when it is added and a common mistake is to reduce the heat under the pan at this stage. The time taken for the oil to come back to temperature will, of course, vary with the amount of food added.

By far the best way to deep fry is in an electric deep-fat fryer which automatically controls the temperature of the oil.

Draining   Once fried, the food should be lifted from the pan and held over it for a few moments so that excess oil drips off. Then it should be placed on a plate or dish covered with a double thickness of absorbent kitchen paper. The paper absorbs the excess oil, leaving the fried food crisp. Deep fried food should be served freshly cooked.

If you must keep fried fish hot for a short time, perhaps while cooking subsequent batches, place it on a thick pad of absorbent kitchen paper under a grill on low heat.

Choice of Seafood   Options include thick fish fillets coated in batter, cooked mussels or prawns in batter, squid rings in batter, whitebait coated in seasoned flour, fish cakes or croquettes in egg and breadcrumbs and white fish fillets coated in egg and breadcrumbs.

Oily fish, such as mackerel, herring and sardines, are not at their best when deep fried.

SHALLOW FRYING

Most fish may be cooked by this method but the choice of cooking fat is important.

Fat There are two options: either the cooking fat is discarded or it is served with the fish. For example, fish cooked in shallow oil is drained before serving, whereas butter used for cooking may be poured over the fish as an accompaniment. Although it is not practical to check the exact temperature of the fat before adding the fish, it is important that it is hot enough to prevent absorption. Remember that butter overheats at a lower temperature than oil. A combination of oil and butter may be used for flavour, as when olive oil and butter is used as a basis for a sauce to accompany the fish.

Turning and Draining The fish should be turned once during shallow frying. A large spatula or slice should be used along with a palette knife, fork or slotted spoon to prevent the fish from breaking.

Choice of Fish and Coating Small whole fish (trout, mackerel, red mullet and sardines), fillets or portions of fillets, steaks and cutlets are all suitable for shallow frying. Batter is not a good coating as it should be submerged completely in hot oil for successful cooking. Egg and breadcrumbs or seasoned flour are both suitable coatings.

Draining and Serving Fish coated in egg and breadcrumbs should be drained on absorbent kitchen paper. Fish coated in seasoned flour should be drained over the pan and absorbent kitchen paper used if it

is very crisp. Butter used in cooking may be flavoured with lemon juice, herbs or chopped capers and poured over the fish.

STIR FRYING

This is a quick method of moving food around in a large pan containing a small amount of very hot oil. All the ingredients should be cut to a similar size and should be of a type that will cook quickly.

Fish is usually stir fried with vegetables. Onions, carrots and celery, for example, should quickly be stirred around before the fish is added.

Choice of Fish Strips of whiting, plaice and other thin fillets are suitable. You might also like to try shellfish or squid. If using strips of fish, avoid stirring them so vigorously that they disintegrate.

COATING FOR FRYING

EGG AND BREADCRUMBS

The fish or seafood should be trimmed and dry. Coat it first in seasoned flour, then in beaten egg and lastly in fine, dry, white breadcrumbs. Use two forks to lift the food. Make sure the egg is in a wide dish which allows room to hold the fish. The breadcrumbs are best placed in a thick layer on a sheet of greaseproof paper or foil. The paper can be lifted and used to tease the crumbs over the egg-coated fish. Press a thick layer of crumbs on the fish, then gently shake off any excess.

BATTER

The batter should be freshly made. The fish or seafood is first coated in seasoned flour, then dipped in the batter just before being submerged in the hot oil. Use two forks to turn the food in the batter, taking care not to knock the air out of a very light mixture. Have the container near the pan, then lift the food and allow excess batter to drip off. Give the food a twist to catch drips of batter, then lower it carefully into the hot oil.

COATING BATTER

This is a firm batter, suitable for cod fillets and other large fish portions.

100 g/4 oz plain flour
pinch of salt
1 egg
125 ml/4 fl oz milk

Sift the flour and salt into a bowl and make a well in the centre.

Add the egg and a little milk, then beat well, gradually incorporating the flour and the remaining milk to make a smooth batter.

MAKES ABOUT 150 ML/¼ PINT

LIGHT BATTER

This light, thin batter is ideal for seafood such as mussels, prawns, oysters and squid rings.

100 g/4 oz plain flour
pinch of salt
15 ml/1 tbsp oil
2 egg whites

Sift the flour and salt into a bowl and make a well in the centre.

Pour 125 ml/4 fl oz cold water into the well in the flour and add the oil. Gradually beat the liquid into the flour to make a smooth, thick batter. Beat really well so that the batter is light.

Just before the batter is to be used, whisk the egg whites until stiff in a clean dry bowl. Fold the egg whites into the batter and use at once.

MAKES ABOUT 175 ML/6 FL OZ

GOLDEN GRILLED COD

Illustrated on page 40

margarine or butter for greasing
4 cod cutlets or steaks, about 2 cm/¾ inch thick
4 small tomatoes, halved
chopped parsley to garnish (optional)

TOPPING
25 g/1 oz margarine or butter
50 g/2 oz mild Cheddar or Gruyère cheese, finely grated
30 ml/2 tbsp milk (optional)
salt and pepper

Grease a shallow flameproof dish with margarine or butter, then arrange the fish in the dish. Grill under moderate heat for 2-3 minutes on one side only.

Meanwhile make the topping. Cream the margarine or butter with the grated cheese in a small bowl. Work in the milk, a few drops at a time, if using, and add salt and pepper to taste.

Turn the fish cutlets or steaks over, spread the topping on the uncooked side and return them to the grill. Lower the heat slightly and grill for 12-15 minutes until the fish is cooked through and the topping is golden brown. Arrange the tomatoes around the fish about 5 minutes before the end of the cooking time.

Serve the fish piping hot with the lightly grilled tomatoes. A little chopped parsley may be sprinkled over the fish for colour and flavour, if liked.

SERVES 4

COD CUTLETS WITH SHRIMP STUFFING

Illustrated on page 76

4 cod cutlets
15 ml/1 tbsp oil

STUFFING
25 g/1 oz butter
1 onion, chopped
50 g/2 oz fresh white breadcrumbs
15 ml/1 tbsp chopped parsley
150 g/5 oz peeled cooked shrimps or
    prawns, chopped
juice of ½ lemon
salt and pepper

GARNISH
lemon twists (page 45)
watercress sprigs
whole prawns

Make the stuffing. Melt the butter, add the onion and fry gently for 10 minutes until soft but not browned. Remove from the heat and stir in the breadcrumbs and parsley, with the shrimps or prawns and lemon juice. Add salt and pepper to taste.

Rinse the fish cutlets, pat them dry with absorbent kitchen paper and remove their bones. Arrange the fish neatly on a flame-proof platter or baking sheet and fill the centre spaces with the stuffing.

Sprinkle the oil over the stuffed fish and cook under a moderate grill for 15-20 minutes or until the fish is cooked through. If the stuffing begins to brown too fiercely before the fish is cooked, then reduce the heat. Garnish with lemon twists, watercress sprigs and whole prawns, and serve at once.

SERVES 4

BACALAO DOURADO

Bacalao – salt cod – looks like a skateboard but tastes delicous when properly soaked and cooked. Skimping on the soaking time leads to disaster, so plan ahead when cooking salt cod.

450 g/1 lb salt cod
125 ml/4 fl oz olive oil
2 onions, finely chopped
450 g/1 lb potatoes, very finely sliced
6 eggs, lightly beaten
salt and pepper
10 ml/2 tsp chopped parsley to garnish

Place the cod in a large bowl, cover with cold water and leave to soak for 24 hours in a cold place, changing the water occasionally.

Drain the fish and put it in a large saucepan with fresh water to cover. Bring to the boil, then drain again. Skin the fish, remove the bones and flake the flesh finely.

Heat 30 ml/2 tbsp of the olive oil in a large frying pan. Add the onions and fry over medium heat until golden – this will take 20-30 minutes depending on the type of pan and the heat. Do not be tempted to increase the heat under the pan so as to save time; this results in burning not browning. Add the flaked fish, cook for 3 minutes more, then pour off any excess oil. Set the pan aside.

Heat the remaining oil in a saucepan or second frying pan, add the sliced potatoes and fry gently for 10-15 minutes until tender but not crisp. Remove the slices from the oil with a slotted spoon, drain on absorbent kitchen paper and add to the flaked fish. Mix thoroughly.

Return the pan to moderate heat and cook, stirring lightly so as not to break up the potatoes, until heated through. Add the beaten eggs with salt and pepper to taste and continue cooking until the eggs have the consistency of creamy scrambled egg.

Turn the mixture out on to a heated serving dish, sprinkle with chopped parsley and serve at once.

SERVES 4 TO 6

SPICY FISH SLICES

Illustrated on page 73

675 g/1½ lb cod or hake fillets
7.5 ml/1½ tsp salt
5 ml/1 tsp turmeric
5 ml/1 tsp chilli powder
90 ml/6 tbsp oil
coriander sprigs to garnish

Cut the fish into 2 cm/¾ inch slices and spread it out in a shallow dish large enough to hold all the slices in a single layer. Mix the salt and spices in a bowl. Stir in enough water to make a thick paste. Rub the paste into the fish, cover and leave to marinate for 1 hour.

Heat the oil in a large frying pan. Add as much of the spiced fish as possible, but do not overfill the pan. Fry the fish for 5-10 minutes, until golden-brown all over, then remove from the pan with a slotted spoon. Drain on absorbent kitchen paper and keep hot while cooking the rest of the fish.

Garnish and serve hot, with rice or a small salad, if liked.

SERVES 4 TO 5

JAMAICAN FRIED FISH

225 g/8 oz fish bones and trimmings
3 green peppers, seeded and sliced
3 onions, sliced
3 carrots, sliced
2 bay leaves, split in half
2 cm/¾ inch fresh root ginger, peeled
    and finely chopped
8 peppercorns
1 blade of mace
salt
30 ml/2 tbsp groundnut oil
90 ml/6 tbsp malt vinegar
45 ml/3 tbsp sunflower or corn oil
1 kg/2¼ lb white fish fillets

Put the fish bones and trimmings in a large saucepan with the peppers, onions, carrots, bay leaves and ginger. Add the peppercorns and mace, with salt to taste. Pour in 350 ml/12 fl oz water, bring to the boil and simmer uncovered for 35 minutes. Add the groundnut oil and vinegar and simmer for 2 minutes more. Strain the stock, reserving the vegetables as accompaniments for the fish, if liked. Keep hot.

Heat the sunflower or corn oil in a large frying pan, add the fish fillets and fry for 7-8 minutes, turning once, until just browned. Remove the fish from the oil with a slotted spoon and drain on absorbent kitchen paper.

Place the fish fillets in a warmed serving dish, pour the reserved stock over and serve at once, with the reserved vegetables.

SERVES 6

VARIATION

JAMAICAN FISH SALAD Cook as suggested above, but let the fish fillets cool down in the stock. Chill. Garnish with olives and strips of pepper before serving.

HADDOCK AND FENNEL FLAMBE

1 kg/2¼ lb haddock or hake fillets
salt and pepper
15 ml/1 tbsp chopped fresh fennel
225 g/8 oz butter
60 ml/4 tbsp brandy
dried fennel stalks (see method)
lemon wedges to garnish

Have ready a metal serving dish large enough to accommodate the rack of your grill pan. Pile dried fennel leaves on the dish to a depth of 5 cm/2 inches. Melt 200 g/7 oz of the butter in a small saucepan. Keep it warm over a candle burner at the table. Have the brandy ready in a small jug. You will also need an all-metal soup ladle and a long match or taper.

Place the fish, skin side up, on the rack of the grill pan. Grill under moderate heat for 5 minutes, then carefully remove the skin. Turn the fillets over carefully, using a fish slice. Sprinkle with salt, pepper and chopped fennel, and dot with the remaining butter. Grill for 10 minutes more.

Place the rack containing the cooked fish over the fennel and carry it to the table. Pour the brandy into the soup ladle and warm it over the candle burner. Pour the warm brandy over the fish, then light the brandy and dried fennel.

When the flames have died down, transfer the fish to individual plates. Garnish with the lemon wedges. Serve with the melted butter.

SERVES 4

VARIATIONS

MACKEREL FLAMBE Slash the sides of 4 mackerel and tuck a few fennel leaves inside each. Season the fish, grill for 10-12 minutes, then flambé as suggested above.

 **MICROWAVE TIP** Melt the butter in a suitable jug for 2-3 minutes on High.

HERRINGS WITH MUSTARD SAUCE

4 herrings
10 ml/2 tsp lemon juice
salt and pepper
10 ml/2 tsp mustard powder
2 egg yolks
50 g/2 oz butter
30 ml/2 tbsp double cream
15 ml/1 tbsp chopped capers
15 ml/1 tbsp chopped gherkin

Scale the herrings, cut off the heads and remove the bones. Sprinkle the flesh with the lemon juice and season with plenty of salt and pepper. Grill under moderate heat for 3-5 minutes on each side. Transfer to a warmed serving dish and keep hot.

Combine the mustard and egg yolks in the top of a double saucepan, place over hot water and whisk until creamy. Add the butter, a small piece at a time, whisking well after each addition.

When the sauce thickens, remove the pan from the heat and stir in the cream, capers and gherkin. Add salt and pepper to taste, pour into a sauceboat and serve with the fish.

SERVES 4

GRILLED SMOKED HADDOCK

450-575 g/1-1¼ lb smoked haddock fillet,
trimmed and cut into serving portions
melted butter or oil for brushing
4 pats of Herb Butter (page 44), to serve

Place the fish in a large frying pan and pour in boiling water to cover. Leave to stand for 5 minutes. Carefully remove each portion with a fish slice, drain well and arrange, skin side up, in a grill pan.

Grill under moderate heat for 3-5 minutes, depending on the thickness of the fish. Turn the fish over, brush the uncooked sides generously with melted butter or oil and grill for 4 minutes more or until tender.

Serve on individual warmed plates, topping each portion with a pat of chilled herb butter.

SERVES 4

FRENCH FRIED HADDOCK

1 kg/2¼ lb haddock fillets, skinned
250 ml/8 fl oz milk
100 g/4 oz plain flour
salt and pepper
oil for deep frying
lemon wedges to serve

Cut the fish into 4-5 portions. Pour the milk into a shallow bowl. Spread out the flour in a second bowl; season with salt and pepper. Dip the pieces of fish first into milk and then into flour, shaking off the excess.

Put the oil for frying into a deep wide saucepan to a depth of at least 7.5 cm/ 3 inches. Heat the oil to 180-190°C/350-375°F or until a cube of bread added to the oil browns in 30 seconds. If using a deep-fat fryer, follow the manufacturer's instructions.

Carefully lower the fish into the hot oil and fry for 3-5 minutes until evenly browned. Drain on absorbent kitchen paper and serve on a warmed platter, with lemon wedges.

SERVES 4 TO 5

MRS BEETON'S TIP The fish should be of uniform thickness for frying. Any thin pieces, such as tail ends, should be folded double before flouring.

GRILLED KIPPERS

Illustrated on page 77

4 kippers
20 ml/4 tsp butter
4 pats of butter, chilled to serve
chopped parsley to garnish

Lay the kippers flat, skin side up, in the base of the grill pan. Do not place on a rack. Grill under moderate heat for 3 minutes.

Turn the kippers over, dot each one with 5 ml/1 tsp butter and grill for 3 minutes more.

Serve on individual warmed plates, topping each portion with a pat of chilled butter and a sprinkling of chopped parsley.

SERVES 4

FRIED WHITING

25-50 g/1-2 oz plain flour
salt and pepper
2 eggs
50 g/2 oz dry white breadcrumbs for
    coating
12 small whiting fillets
oil for deep frying

TARTARE SAUCE
125 ml/4 fl oz Mayonnaise (page 32)
5 ml/1 tsp chopped gherkin
5 ml/1 tsp chopped olives
5 ml/1 tsp chopped capers
5 ml/1 tsp chopped parsley
5 ml/1 tsp snipped chives
1.25 ml/¼ tsp French mustard
10 ml/2 tsp wine vinegar or lemon juice

Make the tartare sauce by mixing all the ingredients together in a small bowl. Cover and leave to stand for at least 1 hour before serving, to allow the flavours to blend.

Mix the flour with seasoning on a large plate. Beat the eggs in a shallow bowl. Spread out the breadcrumbs on a sheet of foil. Coat each whiting fillet first in flour, then in egg and finally in breadcrumbs. Roll up the fillets and keep in shape with a skewer or wooden cocktail stick.

Put the oil for frying into a deep wide saucepan to a depth of at least 7.5 cm/3 inches. Heat the oil to 180-190°C/350-375°F or until a cube of bread added to the oil browns in 30 seconds.

Carefully lower the whiting rolls into the hot oil and fry for 3-5 minutes. Drain on absorbent kitchen paper and serve on a warmed platter. Hand the tartare sauce separately.

SERVES 6

GOUJONS OF PLAICE

Illustrated on page 77

12(100 g/4 oz) plaice fillets
50 g/2 oz plain flour
salt and pepper
100 ml/3½ fl oz milk
oil for deep frying
Tartare Sauce (left) to serve

GARNISH
lemon wedges
parsley sprigs

Cut the fish fillets lengthways into short strips about 4 cm/1½ inches wide. Spread out the flour in a shallow bowl; season with salt and pepper. Pour the milk into a second bowl. Coat the strips of plaice first in milk and then in seasoned flour, shaking off any excess.

Put the oil for frying into a deep wide saucepan to a depth of at least 7.5 cm/3 inches. Heat the oil to 180-190°C/350-375°F or until a cube of bread added to the oil browns in 30 seconds. If you are using a deep-fat fryer, follow the manufacturer's instructions.

Carefully add the strips of fish, a few at a time, to the hot oil. Fry for 2-3 minutes until golden brown. Drain on absorbent kitchen paper and keep hot on a warmed dish. Reheat the oil before putting in each fresh batch of goujons. Garnish and serve with tartare sauce.

SERVES 6

FILLETS OF SOLE ORLY

Fresh Tomato Sauce (page 43) is the perfect accompaniment for this dish.

6 (175 g/6 oz) lemon sole fillets
oil for deep frying
lemon wedges to serve

MARINADE
  30 ml/2 tbsp chopped parsley
  30 ml/2 tbsp chopped onion
  salt and pepper
  15 ml/1 tbsp lemon juice
  15 ml/1 tbsp corn oil

BATTER
  50 g/2 oz plain flour
  salt
  15 ml/1 tbsp corn oil
  1 egg white

Mix all the ingredients for the marinade in a shallow bowl large enough to hold all the sole fillets in a single layer (see Mrs Beeton's Tip, right). Add the fish, cover and marinate for 1 hour. Drain the fish and pat dry on absorbent kitchen paper.

Make the batter. Mix the flour and salt in a bowl. Make a well in the centre, add 60 ml/4 tbsp water and the oil. Mix well, gradually incorporating the flour to make a smooth batter. In a clean, dry bowl whisk the egg white until stiff. Fold it into the batter.

Put the oil for frying into a deep wide saucepan to a depth of at least 7.5 cm/3 inches. Heat the oil to 180-190°C/350-375°F or until a cube of bread added to the oil browns in 30 seconds. If using a deep-fat fryer, follow the manufacturer's instructions.

Dip the fish fillets in the batter, carefully lower them into the hot oil and fry for 3-5 minutes until golden-brown. Drain on absorbent kitchen paper, arrange on a warmed platter and serve with lemon wedges.

SERVES 6

> **MRS BEETON'S TIP** A lasagne dish may be used for marinating the fish. Alternatively, line a roasting tin with foil.

SOLE MEUNIERE

50 g/2 oz plain flour
salt and pepper
4 large sole fillets
75 g/3 oz butter
30 ml/2 tbsp chopped parsley
juice of 1 lemon
lemon wedges to garnish

Spread the flour in a shallow bowl and season with salt and pepper. Lightly coat the fish fillets in the seasoned flour.

Melt the butter in a frying pan and fry the fillets over moderate heat for about 7 minutes, turning once, until golden-brown.

Using a slotted spoon and a fish slice, carefully transfer the fish to a warmed serving dish and keep hot. Continue heating the butter until it is nut-brown. Add the parsley.

Pour the butter over the fish, sprinkle with lemon juice and serve at once, garnished with lemon wedges.

SERVES 4

SOLE COLBERT

Illustrated on page 78

200 g/7 oz Maître d'Hôtel butter (page 44)
10 ml/2 tsp finely chopped fresh tarragon
6 Dover soles
100 g/4 oz plain flour
salt and pepper
2 eggs, lightly beaten
50 g/2 oz fresh white breadcrumbs
oil for deep frying

GARNISH
    lemon wedges
    tarragon sprigs

Mix the maître d'hôtel butter and tarragon. Remove the dark skin of the fish. Cut down the backbone on the skinned side and slice under the flesh, following the bones to make a pocket on each side (see page 19). Cut the backbone in three places with sharp scissors, to allow removal after cooking.

Spread the flour in a shallow bowl and season with salt and pepper. Put the beaten eggs in a second shallow bowl and spread out the breadcrumbs on a sheet of foil. Coat each fish first in flour, then in egg and breadcrumbs.

Put the oil for frying into a deep wide saucepan to a depth of at least 7.5 cm/3 inches. Heat the oil to 180-190°C/350-375°F or until a cube of bread added to the oil browns in 30 seconds. If using a deep-fat fryer, follow the manufacturer's instructions. Deep fry the fish, one at a time, until golden brown, reheating the oil as necessary.

Drain the fish on absorbent kitchen paper, remove the bone where cut and arrange on a warmed serving dish. Fill the pockets of the fish with the tarragon-flavoured butter and serve immediately, garnished with lemon and tarragon.

SERVES 6

SOLE ANTHONY

100 g/4 oz butter
225 g/8 oz dry white breadcrumbs
6(150 g/5 oz) Dover sole fillets
6 slices fresh or canned pineapple
25 g/1 oz sugar
parsley sprigs to garnish

SAUCE
    50 g/2 oz butter
    25 g/1 oz plain flour
    300 ml/½ pint Basic Fish Stock (page 27)
    60 ml/4 tbsp dry white wine
    2 egg yolks
    juice of ½ lemon
    salt and pepper
    75 g/3 oz mushrooms, chopped

Make the sauce. Melt 25 g/1 oz of the butter in a saucepan. Stir in the flour and cook over low heat for 2-3 minutes, without allowing the mixture to colour. Gradually add the fish stock, stirring constantly.

Increase the heat to moderate and cook, stirring, until the mixture boils and thickens to a coating consistency. Stir in the wine, lower the heat and simmer for 10 minutes.

Heat the sauce to just below boiling point and whisk in the remaining butter, a little at a time. Remove the pan from the heat.

Beat the egg yolks and lemon juice in a small bowl. Add a little of the sauce and mix well. Add the contents of the bowl to the sauce and heat gently, stirring. Do not allow the sauce to boil. Season with salt and pepper and add the mushrooms. Cover the sauce closely with damp greaseproof paper and keep warm.

Melt the butter in a small saucepan. Use some of it to grease a shallow flameproof dish. Pour the rest into a shallow bowl. Spread the breadcrumbs on a sheet of foil. Coat the fish in melted butter and then in breadcrumbs. Arrange in the prepared dish.

Grill the fish for 3 minutes on each side. Brush the pineapple slices with melted butter, sprinkle with sugar and brown under the grill.

Spoon the sauce into a flameproof serving dish. Arrange the fish on top and place a slice of pineapple on each. Grill for 5 minutes. Serve very hot, garnished with parsley sprigs.

SERVES 6

*F*RITTO MISTO

50 g/2 oz plain flour
salt and pepper
225 g/8 oz fresh sardines or sprats,
　cleaned
oil for deep frying
225 g/8 oz scampi tails, thawed if frozen
100 g/4 oz cauliflower sprigs, parboiled
　for 5 minutes and drained
2 courgettes
1 large onion, cut in thin rings
lemon wedges to serve

BATTER
　1 egg
　30 ml/2 tbsp corn oil
　100 g/4 oz plain flour
　pinch of salt
　15 ml/1 tbsp chopped parsley
　1 garlic clove, crushed

Make the batter. Combine the egg and oil in a 600 ml/1 pint jug. Add 300 ml/½

pint water and mix well. Mix the flour and salt in a bowl. Make a well in the centre, add the egg mixture and mix well, gradually incorporating the flour to make a smooth batter. Leave to stand for 15 minutes, then add the parsley and garlic.

Season the flour with salt and pepper and spread some of it out in a shallow bowl. Coat the sardines or sprats in the seasoned flour.

Put the oil for frying into a deep wide saucepan to a depth of at least 7.5 cm/3 inches. Heat the oil to 180-190°C/350-375°F or until a cube of bread added to the oil browns in 30 seconds. If using a deep-fat fryer, follow the manufacturer's instructions.

Carefully add the fish to the hot oil and fry for 1-2 minutes. Drain on absorbent kitchen paper and keep hot in a warmed dish. Reheat the oil. Dry the scampi and coat in seasoned flour. Dip in the batter, a few at a time, and deep fry for 3-4 minutes until crisp. Drain and keep hot with the fish. Reheat the oil.

Coat the cauliflower sprigs in seasoned flour, dip in the batter and deep-fry for 2-3 minutes. Drain and keep hot.

Using a canelle knife, score the skin of the courgettes deeply. Cut them in half across, then lengthways into quarters. Coat in seasoned flour, dip in batter and deep fry as for the cauliflower. Drain and keep hot with the fish. Repeat the procedure with the onion rings, reheating the oil as necessary.

Pile the mixture of fritters on a serving platter, sprinkle with salt and garnish with lemon wedges. Serve at once.

SERVES 6

FISH CAKES

Illustrated on page 79

Tasty, nutritious, easy to make and popular with children, home-made fish cakes are perfect for midweek family meals.

350 g/12 oz cooked white fish, flaked
450 g/1 lb potatoes
25 g/1 oz butter
30 ml/2 tbsp single cream or milk
15 ml/1 tbsp finely chopped parsley
salt and pepper
50 g/2 oz plain flour
oil for shallow frying

Remove any bones from the fish. Cook the potatoes in a saucepan of salted boiling water for about 30 minutes or until tender. Drain thoroughly and mash with a potato masher, or beat with a hand-held electric whisk until smooth. Beat in the butter and cream or milk. Add the flaked fish and parsley, with salt and pepper to taste. Set aside until cold.

Form the fish mixture into 8 portions, shaping each to a flat round cake. Spread out the flour in a shallow bowl, add salt and pepper and use to coat the fish cakes.

Heat the oil in a frying pan, add the fish cakes and fry for 6-8 minutes, turning once. Drain on absorbent kitchen paper, arrange on a warmed serving dish and serve.

SERVES 4

MRS BEETON'S TIP For extra flavour, try adding chopped anchovy fillets, fried finely chopped onion, grated Cheddar cheese or crumbled fried bacon to the basic mixture above.

MRS BEETON'S DRESSED WHITEBAIT

Illustrated on page 79

50 g/2 oz plain flour
salt and pepper
125 ml/4 fl oz milk
100 g/4 oz whitebait
oil for deep frying
cayenne pepper

GARNISH
  parsley sprigs
  lemon wedges

Mix the flour, salt and pepper in a sturdy polythene bag. Pour the milk into a shallow bowl. Dip the whitebait into the milk, then toss them in the seasoned flour in the bag. Shake off excess flour and make sure that all the fish are separate.

Put the oil for frying into a deep wide saucepan to a depth of at least 7.5 cm/3 inches. Heat the oil to 180-190°C/350-375°F or until a cube of bread added to the oil browns in 30 seconds. If using a deep-fat fryer, follow the manufacturer's instructions.

Carefully add the fish, a few at a time, to the hot oil in a chip basket and fry for 30 seconds to 1 minute. Drain on absorbent kitchen paper and keep hot in a warmed dish. Reheat the oil before putting in each fresh batch of fish.

When all the fish are fried, pile them on a serving platter, sprinkle with salt and cayenne and serve at once, garnished with parsley and lemon wedges.

SERVES 3 TO 4

FRIED SMELTS

Small silvery fish, related to salmon, smelts are too often overlooked.

200 g/7 oz plain flour
salt
15 ml/1 tbsp olive oil
1 egg, separated
30-45 ml/2-3 tbsp milk
oil for deep frying
18 smelts, cleaned, heads removed
watercress to garnish

Mix the flour and salt in a bowl. Make a well in the centre, add the oil, egg yolk and 30 ml/2 tbsp of the milk. Mix well, gradually incorporating the flour to make a stiff batter. Add the extra 15 ml/1 tbsp milk if necessary. Cover the batter and let it stand for 15 minutes.

In a clean, dry bowl whisk the egg white until stiff. Fold it into the batter.

Put the oil for frying into a deep wide saucepan to a depth of at least 7.5 cm/3 inches. Heat the oil to 180-190°C/350-375°F or until a cube of bread added to the oil browns in 30 seconds. If using a deep-fat fryer, follow the manufacturer's instructions.

Dip the fish in the batter, a few at a time, and deep fry for 1-2 minutes until crisp. Drain on absorbent kitchen paper and keep hot in a warmed dish. Reheat the oil before putting in each fresh batch of fish.

When all the fish are fried, pile them on a serving platter, garnish with watercress and serve at once.

SERVES 6

MONKFISH AND BACON KEBABS

Illustrated on page 114

125 ml/4 fl oz olive oil
1 garlic clove, crushed
5 ml/1 tsp lemon juice
5 ml/1 tsp dried oregano
800 g/1¾ lb monkfish, cleaned, trimmed and cut in 2 cm/¾ inch cubes
225 g/8 oz rindless streaky bacon rashers
200 g/7 oz small mushrooms
salt and pepper

Combine the olive oil, garlic, lemon juice and oregano in a shallow bowl large enough to hold all the monkfish cubes in a single layer. Mix well, add the fish, and marinate for 15 minutes. Drain the monkfish, reserving the marinade.

Thread a piece of bacon on to a kebab skewer. Add a cube of fish, then a mushroom, weaving the bacon between them. Continue to add the fish and mushrooms, each time interweaving the bacon, until the skewer is full. Add a second rasher of bacon if necessary. Fill five more skewers in the same way. Sprinkle with salt and pepper.

Grill the monkfish kebabs under moderate heat for 10-15 minutes, basting frequently with the reserved marinade.

SERVES 6

☀ **MICROWAVE TIP** Thread the mixture on wooden skewers. Put the skewers on a large plate. Spoon a little of the marinade over each kebab and cook on High for 8 minutes, turning and rearranging the kebabs once during cooking.

MACKEREL WITH GOOSEBERRY SAUCE

Gooseberry sauce is such a classic accompaniment to mackerel that in France the fruit is known as groseille à maquereau.

50 g/2 oz plain flour
salt and pepper
8 mackerel fillets
50 g/2 oz butter
juice of 1 lemon
45 ml/3 tbsp chopped parsley

SAUCE
450 g/1 lb gooseberries, topped and tailed
45 ml/3 tbsp dry still cider
25 g/1 oz butter
15 ml/1 tbsp caster sugar

Make the sauce by combining the gooseberries, cider and butter in a small pan. Bring the liquid to simmering point and poach the fruit, stirring occasionally, until soft. Purée the mixture by passing it through a sieve set over a small saucepan. Stir in the sugar.

Spread the flour in a shallow bowl, season with salt and pepper, and coat the fish lightly all over.

Melt the butter in a large frying pan, add the fish and fry gently for 5-7 minutes or until browned, turning once. Using a slotted spoon and a fish slice, transfer the fish to a warmed serving dish and keep hot.

Heat the gooseberry sauce. Continue to heat the butter in the frying pan until it becomes light brown. Stir in the lemon juice and parsley and pour over the fish. Pour the gooseberry sauce into a jug or sauceboat and serve at once, with the fish.

SERVES 4

☀ **MICROWAVE TIP** The gooseberries (left) can be cooked in the microwave. Combine the cider and butter in a mixing bowl and heat for 1 minute on High. Add the fruit, stir, cover the bowl and cook for 5-7 minutes or until soft. Stir once or twice during cooking.

SABO-NO-TERIYAKI

This dish can also be made with herring, salmon or bream.

150 ml/¼ pint soy sauce
45 ml/3 tbsp mirin (see Mrs Beeton's Tip)
pinch of chilli powder
15 ml/1 tbsp grated fresh root ginger
2 garlic cloves, crushed
4 mackerel fillets

Mix the soy sauce, mirin, chilli powder, ginger and garlic in a bowl. Stir well. Arrange the mackerel fillets in a shallow dish large enough to hold them all in a single layer. Pour the soy sauce mixture over, cover the dish and marinate for 2 hours.

Drain the fish, reserving the marinade. Cook under a hot grill for 5-10 minutes brushing the fish several times with the reserved marinade during cooking. Serve at once.

SERVES 4

🥣 **MRS BEETON'S TIP** If you cannot obtain mirin, which is a sweet Japanese rice wine, use a mixture of 45 ml/3 tbsp dry sherry and 10 ml/2 tsp sugar.

MARINATED FRIED HERRINGS

Serve as a starter with brown bread and butter.
Soured cream makes a good accompaniment.

8 herrings
2.5 ml/½ tsp salt
2.5 ml/½ tsp pepper
30 ml/2 tbsp plain flour
butter for shallow frying

MARINADE
300 ml/½ pint cider vinegar
90 g/3½ oz sugar
1 onion, thinly sliced
1 bay leaf
6 peppercorns

Make the marinade by combining the vinegar and sugar in a saucepan. Add 300 ml/½ pint water and bring to the boil, stirring until the sugar has dissolved. Set aside to cool.

Split the herrings and remove the backbones. Spread the flour in a shallow bowl, season with salt and pepper, and coat the fish lightly all over.

Melt the butter in a large frying pan, add the fish and fry for 7-8 minutes or until golden-brown, turning once. Using a slotted spoon and a fish slice, transfer the herrings to a dish large enough to hold them all in a single layer.

Tuck the onion slices, bay leaf and peppercorns around the mackerel and pour the cold vinegar mixture over. Cover the dish and set aside in a cool place for about 6 hours. Serve with brown bread and butter, if liked.

SERVES 4

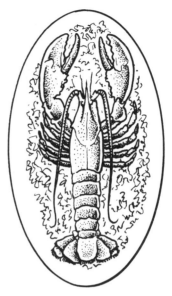

FRIED SKATE

Illustrated on page 113

50 g/2 oz plain flour
salt and pepper
1 egg, lightly beaten
50 g/2 oz dry white breadcrumbs
4 skate wings, total weight about
    575 g/1¼ lb
75 g/3 oz butter
Tartare Sauce (see Fried Whiting,
    page 100)

GARNISH
lemon slices
watercress sprigs

Spread the flour in a shallow bowl and season with salt and pepper. Put the egg in a second bowl and spread the breadcrumbs on a sheet of foil. Coat each skate wing first in seasoned flour, then in egg and finally in breadcrumbs.

Melt the butter in a large frying pan, add the fish and fry gently for 5 minutes on each side or until golden and cooked through. Garnish and serve with tartare sauce.

SERVES 4

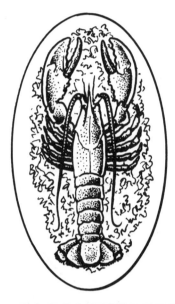

*T*ROUT MEUNIERE

4 trout
50 g/2 oz plain flour
salt and pepper
50 g/2 oz butter
juice of ½ lemon
10 ml/2 tsp chopped parsley
lemon twists (page 45) to garnish

Dry the fish well with absorbent kitchen paper. Spread the flour in a shallow bowl and add salt and pepper to taste. Add the fish and coat well on all sides.

Melt the butter in a large frying pan. When it foams, add the trout. Fry gently for 6-7 minutes on each side or until the skin is golden and crisp.

Using a slotted spoon and a fish slice, transfer the fish to a warmed serving dish. Keep hot. Season the butter remaining in the pan with salt and pepper and heat until it is nut-brown. Add the lemon juice and chopped parsley and pour over the trout. Garnish with lemon twists and serve at once.

SERVES 4

*T*ROUT WITH ALMONDS

100 g/4 oz butter
4 trout, cleaned and trimmed
salt and pepper
juice of ½ lemon
50 g/2 oz flaked almonds
125 ml/4 fl oz double cream
3 egg yolks

Melt the butter in a grill pan under moderate heat. Lay the trout in the pan and sprinkle with salt and pepper and lemon juice. Grill for 5 minutes.

Carefully turn the trout over. Sprinkle most of the almonds over the fish, spreading the rest at the side of the pan. Grill for 3-5 minutes more until the trout are tender and the almonds browned (see Mrs Beeton's Tip). Using a fish slice and slotted spoon, transfer the trout and almonds to absorbent kitchen paper to drain. Tip the grill pan juices into a small saucepan. Arrange the trout on a warmed serving platter and keep hot. Set the browned almonds aside.

Add the cream and egg yolks to the pan juices and mix well. Heat gently, stirring constantly until the sauce thickens. Do not let the mixture boil. Spoon the sauce over the trout, garnish with the reserved almonds and serve at once.

SERVES 4

> **MRS BEETON'S TIP** Watch the trout carefully after the almonds have been added. Almonds scorch very quickly; if necessary lower the grill pan or turn down the heat.

SALMON STEAKS WITH AVOCADO BUTTER

Illustrated on page 114

6 (175 g/6 oz) salmon steaks

MARINADE
    1 garlic clove, thinly sliced
    1 small onion, thinly sliced
    125 ml/4 fl oz olive oil
    45 ml/3 tbsp lemon juice
    15 ml/1 tbsp Worcestershire sauce
    salt and pepper

AVOCADO BUTTER
    2 ripe avocados
    15 ml/1 tbsp lemon juice
    100 g/4 oz unsalted butter, softened
    1 garlic clove, crushed
    15 ml/1 tbsp Worcestershire sauce
    dash of Tabasco sauce
    salt and pepper

GARNISH
    lemon slices
    dill sprigs

Make the marinade by mixing all the ingredients in a shallow dish large enough to hold the salmon steaks in a single layer. Add the salmon, turning them until well coated in the marinade. Cover and refrigerate for at least 6 hours.

Fifteen minutes before cooking, drain the salmon steaks, discarding the marinade. Make the avocado butter by mashing the avocado flesh with the lemon juice. Cream in the butter, blending throughly. Add the garlic, Worcestershire sauce and Tabasco sauce, with salt and pepper to taste. Mix well, then spoon into a serving dish.

Grill the salmon steaks under moderate heat for 4-5 minutes on each side. Garnish and serve at once, with the avocado butter.

SERVES 6

> **MRS BEETON'S TIP** When preparing the avocados (for the recipe, left), save one of the stones and add it to the bowl of avocado butter. It will help to prevent discoloration. Spoon it out just before serving.

MARINATED MACKEREL

6 mackerel
parsley sprigs to garnish

MARINADE
    100 ml/3½ fl oz olive oil
    juice of 1 lemon
    fresh thyme sprigs
    2 bay leaves
    parsley stalks
    salt and pepper

Rinse the fish inside and out and pat dry on absorbent kitchen paper. Make 3 diagonal slashes in the flesh on both sides of each fish.

Mix all the ingredients for the marinade in a shallow dish large enough to hold all the fish in a single layer. Add the mackerel, turning to coat them evenly in the marinade. Cover the dish and marinate the fish for 1 hour.

Drain the fish, reserving the marinade, and place on a rack over a grill pan. Grill under moderate heat for 5-7 minutes each side, turning once and basting frequently with the reserved marinade. Serve very hot, garnished with parsley sprigs.

SERVES 6

FRIED PERCH

12 perch fillets
30 ml/2 tbsp plain flour
salt and pepper
2 eggs, beaten
100 g/4 oz dry breadcrumbs
100 g/4 oz butter
45 ml/3 tbsp cooking oil
lemon wedges to garnish

MARINADE
1 spring onion, chopped
90-120 ml/6-8 tbsp olive oil
juice of 1 lemon
salt and pepper

Make the marinade by combining all the ingredients in a shallow dish large enough to hold all the fish fillets in a single layer or just overlapping. Add the fillets, cover the dish and marinate for at least 1 hour.

Spread out the flour in a shallow bowl and season with salt and pepper. Put the beaten egg in a second bowl and the breadcrumbs on a sheet of foil. Drain the perch fillets, discarding the marinade. Coat the fish in flour, then in egg, and finally in breadcrumbs.

Melt the butter in the oil in a frying pan, add the fish and fry gently for 6-8 minutes, turning once, until evenly browned on both sides. Using a slotted spoon and a fish slice, transfer the fish to a warmed serving platter, garnish with lemon wedges and serve at once.

SERVES 6

FRIED EELS

1-2 eels, total weight about 800 g/1¾ lb,
    skinned
25-50 g/1-2 oz plain flour
salt and pepper
1 egg, beaten
50 g/2 oz fresh white breadcrumbs
oil for shallow frying
fried parsley (page 45) or whole capers to
    garnish

Wash and dry the eels. Cut into 5 cm/2 inch pieces. Spread out the flour in a shallow bowl and season with salt and pepper. Put the beaten egg in a second bowl and the breadcrumbs on a sheet of foil. Coat the pieces of eel in flour, then in egg, and finally in breadcrumbs.

Heat the oil in a frying pan, add the eels and fry for 15-20 minutes or until brown. Drain well on absorbent kitchen paper, pile on a warmed serving dish and garnish with fried parsley or capers. Serve at once.

SERVES 5 TO 6

> **MRS BEETON'S TIP** Most fishmongers sell eels live but will prepare them for you. Ask to have the eels cut up into 5 cm/2 inch pieces.

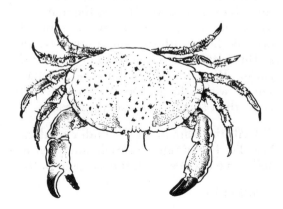

RED MULLET WITH HERBS

Illustrated on page 116

4 red mullet, trimmed and cleaned
50 g/2 oz butter
60 ml/4 tbsp oil
60 ml/4 tbsp red wine vinegar
2 shallots, finely chopped
6 peppercorns
15 ml/1 tbsp chopped parsley
15 ml/1 tbsp shredded fresh basil

MUSTARD SAUCE
25 g/1 oz butter
25 g/1 oz plain flour
150 ml/¼ pint milk
150 ml/¼ pint Basic Fish Stock (page 27)
2 egg yolks
10 ml/2 tsp French mustard
few drops of lemon juice
salt and pepper

Make the sauce. Melt the butter in a saucepan. Stir in the flour and cook over low heat for 2-3 minutes, without allowing the mixture to colour. Gradually add the liquid, stirring constantly. Raise the heat to moderate, stirring the mixture until it boils and thickens. Remove from the heat and cool slightly.

Beat the egg yolks and mustard in a small bowl. Add a little of the sauce and mix well. Add the contents of the bowl to the sauce and heat gently, stirring. Do not allow the sauce to boil. Stir in the lemon juice, with salt and pepper to taste. Cover the surface of the sauce closely with damp greaseproof paper and set aside until required.

Make 3 diagonal slashes in the flesh on both sides of each fish. Cut four squares of foil, each large enough to enclose one fish, and butter them generously.

Make a marinade by combining the oil, vinegar, shallots, peppercorns and herbs in a shallow dish large enough to hold all the mullet in a single layer. Add the fish, turning to coat them evenly in the marinade. Cover the dish and marinate the fish for 2 hours, basting frequently.

Drain the fish, discarding the marinade, and pack each in foil, wrapping each square around the fish to make a loose parcel. Grill the packages under high heat for 10-15 minutes.

Reheat the sauce gently. When all the fish are cooked (see Mrs Beeton's Tip), remove the foil and place them on a heated dish. Serve at once, with the sauce.

SERVES 4

 MRS BEETON'S TIP   To test the fish, remove the foil from one package and pierce the fish with a fine skewer. It should be tender right through.

GRILLED SALMON STEAKS

50 g/2 oz clarified butter
4 (175 g/6 oz) salmon steaks
salt and pepper
Maître d'Hôtel Butter (page 44) to
   garnish

Warm the clarified butter in a small saucepan. Season the salmon steaks with salt and pepper. Brush liberally with clarified butter. Grill under moderate heat for 4-5 minutes on each side, turning once. Garnish each portion with a pat of maître d'hôtel butter.

SERVES 4

FRIED SCAMPI TAILS

50 g/2 oz plain flour
salt and pepper
450 g/1 lb peeled scampi tails
oil for deep frying
lemon wedges to garnish
Tartare Sauce (see Fried Whiting, page
    100) to serve

BATTER
225 g/8 oz plain flour
salt
2 eggs, separated
30 ml/2 tbsp oil
60-90 ml/4-6 tbsp milk

Mix the flour, salt and pepper in a sturdy polythene bag. Add the scampi tails and toss until well coated. Shake off excess flour.

Make the batter. Mix the flour and salt in a bowl. Make a well in the centre, add the egg yolks, oil and 60 ml/4 tbsp of the milk. Mix well, gradually incorporating the flour to make a stiff batter. Add the extra 30 ml/2 tbsp milk if necessary. Cover the batter and let it stand for 15 minutes.

In a clean, dry bowl whisk the egg whites until stiff. Fold them into the batter.

Put the oil for frying into a deep wide saucepan to a depth of at least 7.5 cm/3 inches. Heat the oil to 180-190°C/350-375°F or until a cube of bread added to the oil browns in 30 seconds. If using a deep-fat fryer, follow the manufacturer's instructions.

Dip the floured scampi in the batter, a few at a time, and deep fry for 2-3 minutes until crisp. Drain on absorbent kitchen paper and keep hot in a warmed dish. Reheat the oil before putting in each fresh batch of scampi.

When all the scampi are fried, pile them on a serving platter, garnish with lemon and serve at once with tartare sauce.

SERVES 4

SPANISH PRAWNS

Illustrated on page 114

Supply paper napkins and fingerbowls for this dish – and don't forget a plate for the prawn shells.

75 ml/5 tbsp olive oil
1 garlic clove, crushed
1 small bunch of chives, snipped
450 g/1 lb whole cooked prawns
30 ml/2 tbsp dry sherry
salt and pepper
chives to garnish

Heat the oil in a large frying pan. Stir in the garlic and chives. Add the prawns and sherry, with salt and pepper to taste.

Cover the pan and cook over moderate heat for 3-5 minutes, turning the prawns over once. Serve in small bowls, garnished with chives, with crusty French bread, if liked.

SERVES 4

Fried Skate (page 107)

Salmon Steaks with Avocado Butter (page 109) and Spanish Prawns (page 112)

Red Mullet with Herbs (page 111) and Baked Herrings (page 130)

Kipper and Tomato Bake (page 132) and Sole with Prawns (page 137)

Baked Grey Mullet (page 138)

Crab Soufflé (page 151)

Creamed Salmon in Pastry (page 146)

Kedgeree (page 166)

OYSTER FRITTERS

10 small oysters
5 rindless back bacon rashers, each
    rasher cut into 4 pieces
10 ml/2 tsp lemon juice
cayenne pepper
oil for deep frying

BATTER
    100 g/4 oz plain flour
    1.25 ml/¼ tsp salt
    1 egg, beaten
    125 ml/4 fl oz milk
    5 ml/1 tsp grated onion
    10 ml/2 tsp chopped parsley

TO SERVE
    5 slices white bread
    50 g/2 oz Herb Butter (page 44)

Make the batter. Mix the flour and salt in a bowl. Make a well in the centre, and add the beaten egg and 60 ml/4 tbsp of the milk. Mix well, gradually incorporating the flour. Beat until smooth, then stir in the remaining milk, with the onion and parsley.

Open the oyster shells (see page 25), remove the oysters and dry gently on absorbent kitchen paper. Season an oyster with lemon juice and cayenne. Place between 2 bacon squares and press together firmly. Repeat with remaining oysters and bacon.

Put the oil for frying into a deep wide saucepan to a depth of at least 7.5 cm/ 3 inches. Heat the oil to 180-190°C/350- 375°F or until a cube of bread added to the oil browns in 30 seconds. If using a deep-fat fryer, follow the manufacturer's instructions.

Dip the bacon and oyster fritters in the batter, a few at a time, and deep fry for 2-3 minutes until golden brown. Drain on ab-sorbent kitchen paper and keep hot in a warmed dish. Reheat the oil before putting in each fresh batch of fritters.

Toast the bread. Using a biscuit cutter, cut each slice into 2 rounds and spread with parsley butter. Serve 1 fritter on each toast round.

MAKES 10 SMALL SAVOURIES

SCALLOPS ON SKEWERS

12 shallots or small onions, peeled
2 courgettes, cut in 2 cm/¾ inch cubes
8 rindless streaky bacon rashers
16 scallops
12 button mushrooms
40 g/1½ oz butter, melted
salt and pepper

Put the shallots or onions in a small saucepan with water to cover. Bring to the boil, lower the heat and simmer for 4 minutes. Add the courgettes and simmer for 2 minutes more. Drain thoroughly.

Stretch the bacon over the back of a knife and cut each rasher in half. Wrap half a rasher around each scallop. Thread the onions, courgettes, mushrooms and bacon-wrapped scallops alternately on 4 skewers.

Melt the butter and brush it over the kebabs. Sprinkle with salt and pepper to taste. Grill under moderate heat for 5-7 minutes, turning frequently.

SERVES 4

BAKED FISH DISHES

Baking is an easy, versatile cooking method, as this chapter shows. Most types of seafood may be baked in some way or other. To list all the possibilities would fill a separate book. Fish may be baked very simply, with herbs and lemon juice. It may be mixed with a sauce, layered with vegetables topped with breadcrumbs or made into a pie. The options are innumerable. Baking is one of the easiest cooking methods because, to a large extent, it takes care of itself. As with other methods, it is important to avoid overcooking the fish. Here are a few simple suggestions.

BAKING IN FOIL

Individual portions of fish cook well in closed foil packages. Steaks and small whole fish are ideal for baking by this method, and portions of thick fillet (from cod or monk-fish) are also suitable.

Cut pieces of foil large enough to hold the fish. Brush the middle of the foil with oil or melted butter and place the fish on it. Add herb sprigs – parsley, thyme or bay – and a trickle of oil or knob of butter. Season the fish and close or fold the foil around it. Fold the edges of the foil over to seal in the fish, then place the package on a baking sheet. To check whether the fish is cooked open a very small gap in the foil and test with a thin skewer.

Serve the foil packages on individual plates to be opened at the table.

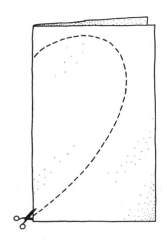

COOKING EN PAPILLOTTE

A traditional method of baking in paper, this works well for fish. Cut neat pieces of double thick greaseproof paper, large enough to hold the fish. The paper may be cut in various ways; oblong or square shapes, circles or heart-shaped pieces may be used.

Brush the paper with oil or melted butter and lay the fish in the middle. Bring the paper up over the fish and crumple the edges together firmly to seal in the contents. The edges of the paper must be closed over the top of the fish so that the package may be opened easily on the plate, revealing the contents ready to eat. Once cooked the paper becomes very brittle.

Non-stick baking parchment may be used instead of greaseproof paper for strength.

COOKING IN FILM

Roasting bags and film may be used for enclosing fish in sealed packages for baking. The large bags make practical containers for larger whole fish – redfish, grey mullet or a curved salmon trout. Several smaller fish (red mullet or mackerel) may be arranged in the same bag placed in a dish or roasting tin. This is useful if you do not have a suitable baking dish large enough to hold the fish.

BAKING IN SHELLS

Scrubbed scallop shells may be used for baking fish and seafood in sauce or with gratin toppings. The deep shells should be saved, thoroughly scrubbed, boiled, rinsed and dried (see also page 24). Some fishmongers sell the cleaned shells.

Smaller shells are also useful. Mussels may be 'stuffed' in their shells. Larger, deep oyster shells and clam shells are suitable both for holding fish and seafood during baking and as attractive serving vessels, particularly for appetisers.

FLAVOURING BAKED FISH

Whether the fish is enclosed in a package or placed in a covered dish, the choice of seasonings and flavourings is important.

Herbs, pared or grated lemon rind and cloves of garlic (whole, chopped or crushed) are typical additions. A moistening agent of some kind is usually added. This may be butter or margarine, a little oil or a squeeze of lemon juice. A couple of spoonfuls of milk may be used with white fish fillets, while a little white wine, dry cider or dry white vermouth can contribute flavour and moisture.

Vegetables should be selected with care. Onion added to a sauce can taste raw even after baking unless it is quickly cooked in oil or butter first. Carrots and celery also benefit from brief pre-cooking before being baked with fish. Cooked chopped spinach makes an excellent base on which to bake skinned fish fillets or steaks.

TOPPINGS

Baked fish is often finished off with a gratin topping of breadcrumbs. Chopped parsley, grated cheese (Cheddar or Parmesan) and a little melted butter may be mixed with the crumbs.

Other toppings include chopped nuts mixed with breadcrumbs, sliced boiled potatoes, diced boiled potatoes tossed with melted butter or sliced mozzarella cheese.

Creamy mixtures of yogurt or fromage frais with beaten egg also make good toppings but care must be taken not to bake these mixtures at too high a temperature or for too long or they may curdle.

The stage at which the topping is added depends on the ingredients and the cooking time. Fish and seafood which bakes very quickly may be topped when first placed in the oven. If the main part of the dish requires slightly longer, and the topping is light, as when a sprinkling of breadcrumbs is added, it is often best to add the topping halfway through cooking.

COD AU GRATIN

fat for greasing
4(100 g/4 oz) portions of cod fillet
25 g/1 oz butter
2 large onions, finely chopped
100 g/4 oz mushrooms, sliced
salt and pepper
1 green pepper, seeded and diced
450 g/1 lb tomatoes, peeled, seeded and
    sliced
50 g/2 oz Cheddar cheese, grated
75 g/3 oz fresh white breadcrumbs

Grease a fairly deep ovenproof dish. Set the oven at 190°C/375°F/gas 5. Arrange the cod portions on the base of the dish.

Melt the butter in a frying pan, add the onions and fry gently for 4-5 minutes until slightly softened. Remove the onions with a slotted spoon and place on top of the fish. Cook the mushrooms in the same way.

Meanwhile bring a small saucepan of salted water to the boil, add the diced green pepper and blanch for 2 minutes. Drain and add to the fish, followed by the mushrooms. Top with the tomato slices, generously sprinkled with salt and pepper.

Combine the cheese and breadcrumbs in a bowl, mix well, then sprinkle over the fish and vegetables. Bake for 30 minutes. Serve at once.

SERVES 4

SMOKED COD AND CORN CASSEROLE

1(326 g/11½ oz) can sweetcorn kernels,
    drained
450 g/1 lb smoked cod fillet, skinned and
    cut in 1 cm/½ inch strips
pepper
25 g/1 oz butter
125 ml/4 fl oz single cream

Set the oven at 180°C/350°F/gas 4. Drain the corn and spread a layer on the base of an ovenproof dish. Add a layer of cod strips. Season with pepper and dot with butter.

Repeat the layers until all the corn and cod have been used, then pour over the cream. Cover and bake for 25 minutes. Serve at once.

SERVES 3 TO 4

VARIATION

CORN 'N COD   Poach the smoked cod fillets, then drain and flake. Make a white sauce, using 50 g/2 oz each of butter and plain flour and 600 ml/1 pint milk (or milk mixed with the drained liquid from the can of sweetcorn). Add salt and pepper to taste and stir in the flaked cod and the corn. Spoon into a dish, top with grated Cheddar cheese and bake for 15-20 minutes at 180°C/350°F/gas 4.

———————◆———————

COLEY PROVENÇALE

fat for greasing
15 ml/1 tbsp oil
2 onions, chopped
1 green pepper, seeded and chopped
3 large tomatoes, peeled, seeded and
    chopped
2 garlic cloves, crushed
salt and pepper
575 g/1¼ lb coley fillet, skinned and cut
    into 2 cm/¾ inch cubes
8 green olives, stoned
8 black olives, stoned, to garnish

Grease a shallow ovenproof dish. Set the oven at 180°C/350°F/gas 4.

Heat the oil in a large frying pan, add the onions and pepper and fry gently for 5 minutes, stirring frequently. Add the tomatoes and garlic, lower the heat and simmer for 10 minutes, stirring occasionally. Remove from the heat and add salt and pepper to taste.

Put the fish cubes in the prepared dish. Add the green olives, then pour the tomato mixture over the top. Cover loosely with greased greaseproof paper or foil and bake for 30 minutes. Garnish with the black olives and serve at once.

SERVES 4 TO 5

MRS BEETON'S TIP The finest green olives generally come from Spain. They should be large and firm, with a good colour. Greek black olives are considered to be the best, but it is always worth buying loose olives rather than the canned or bottled variety, so that you can try before you buy.

BAKED MURRAY COD

oil for greasing
4 portions of cod fillet, total weight about
    450 g/1 lb, skinned
2 rindless fat back bacon rashers,
    chopped
1 large onion, finely chopped
250-350 ml/8-12 fl oz milk
1 bay leaf
salt and pepper
25 g/1 oz dry white breadcrumbs

Grease an ovenproof baking dish just large enough to hold all the fish in a single layer. Set the oven at 230°C/450°F/gas 7. Cook the bacon and onion together in a heavy-based pan until the fat runs from the bacon and the onion is slightly softened. Spread the mixture out in the dish. Top with the fish.

Pour the milk into a saucepan, add the bay leaf and bring to the boil. Remove the bay leaf, add salt and pepper to taste and pour the hot milk into the dish to the depth of the fish. The tops of the fish fillets should be exposed.

Cover the fish thickly with the breadcrumbs. Bake for 20 minutes or until the fish is tender and the topping browned. Serve piping hot with peas or spinach.

SERVES 4

HADDOCK IN CIDER

fat for greasing
575 g/1¼ lb haddock fillet, skinned and
    cubed
225 g/8 oz tomatoes, peeled and sliced
150 g/5 oz mushrooms, sliced
125 ml/4 fl oz dry cider
salt and pepper
30 ml/2 tbsp chopped parsley
25 g/1 oz Cheddar cheese, grated
30 ml/2 tbsp fresh white breadcrumbs

Grease a large ovenproof baking dish.
Set the oven at 230°C/450°F/gas 8. Spread
out the fish cubes in an even layer on the
base of the dish and top with the tomatoes
and mushrooms.

Pour the cider over the fish and sprinkle
with salt and pepper. Mix the parsley,
cheese and breadcrumbs together in a small
bowl. Scatter over the fish and bake for
20-25 minutes. Serve at once.

SERVES 4

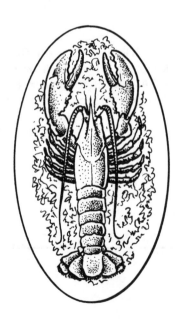

HADDOCK WITH SOURED CREAM

margarine or butter for greasing
25 g/1 oz butter
1 lemon, thinly sliced
575 g/1¼ lb haddock fillet, skinned and
    cut into serving portions
salt and pepper
125 ml/4 fl oz soured cream
paprika

GARNISH
    2 hard-boiled eggs, chopped
    30 ml/2 tbsp chopped parsley

Grease an ovenproof baking dish large
enough to hold all the fish. Set the oven at
200°C/400°F/gas 6.

Melt the butter in a large frying pan. Add
the lemon slices and cook them for about 3
minutes on each side, until just beginning
to brown. Remove from the heat.

Spread out the lemon slices and their
cooking liquor on the base of the dish, top
with the fish and sprinkle with salt and
pepper. Cover the dish with foil and bake
for 20-25 minutes.

Remove the foil and pour the soured
cream over the fish. Sprinkle with salt and
paprika and place under a moderate grill
until lightly browned on top. Garnish with
eggs and parsley and serve at once.

SERVES 4

 **MRS BEETON'S TIP** If
commercially soured cream is not
available, stir 5 ml/1 tsp lemon juice into
125 ml/4 fl oz single cream. Set aside for
10-15 minutes before use.

BAKED HADDOCK FILLETS

fat for greasing
1 onion, finely chopped
150 g/5 oz mushrooms, sliced
15 ml/1 tbsp chopped parsley
800 g/1¾ lb haddock fillets, skinned and
    cut into 4 portions
100 ml/3½ fl oz dry white wine
50 g/2 oz fresh white breadcrumbs
50 g/2 oz butter

Grease an ovenproof dish. Set the oven at 190°C/375°F/gas 5. Spread the onion and mushrooms over the base of the prepared dish. Sprinkle with the parsley and top with the fish.

Pour the wine into the dish, sprinkle the fish with the breadcrumbs and dot with butter. Bake for 30-35 minutes. Serve at once.

SERVES 4

BRILL AND POTATO MORNAY

800 g/1¾ lb potatoes
75 g/3 oz butter
575 g/1¼ lb brill fillets, skinned
salt and pepper
juice of 1 lemon
50 g/2 oz Cheddar cheese, grated

SAUCE
50 g/2 oz butter
50 g/2 oz plain flour
600 ml/1 pint milk, Basic Fish Stock
    (page 27) or a mixture
salt and pepper
50 g/2 oz Cheddar cheese, grated

Boil the potatoes in their skins in a large saucepan of salted water for 20-30 minutes, until tender. Drain and keep hot (see Mrs Beeton's Tip). Set the oven at 180°C/350°F/gas 4.

Make the sauce. Melt the butter in a saucepan. Stir in the flour and cook over low heat for 2-3 minutes, without allowing the mixture to colour. Remove the pan from the heat and gradually add the liquid, stirring constantly.

Return the pan to moderate heat, stirring until the mixture boils and thickens. Stir in the grated cheese. Cover the surface of the sauce with damp greaseproof paper and set aside until required.

Use a little of the butter to grease a shallow ovenproof baking dish and a sheet of greaseproof paper. Lay the fish in the dish. Add salt and pepper to taste, dot with the remaining butter and sprinkle with lemon juice. Cover the dish with the sheet of buttered greaseproof paper and bake for 15 minutes.

Meanwhile peel the potatoes and cut them into rounds. Reheat the cheese sauce, stirring constantly. Overlap the potato rounds to make a decorative topping for the fish. Pour the cheese sauce over the top, top with the grated cheese and brown under a hot grill.

SERVES 6

> **MRS BEETON'S TIP** An easy way to keep the potatoes warm is to drain off the water, cover the potatoes with crumpled absorbent kitchen paper and replace the saucepan lid. This method also works well for boiled peeled potatoes, which will then become perfectly dry.

*B*AKED WHITING

50 g/2 oz butter
4 whiting, cleaned and trimmed
salt and pepper
75 g/3 oz dry white breadcrumbs
lemon twists (page 45)

Use a little of the butter to grease an ovenproof baking dish. Melt the remaining butter in a small saucepan. Set the oven at 190°C/375°F/gas 5.

Brush the whiting all over with melted butter, season with salt and pepper and sprinkle liberally with breadcrumbs. Place in the prepared dish and bake for 20 minutes. Garnish with lemon twists and serve.

SERVES 4

*I*RISH BAKE

A simple supper dish that goes down well with the younger members of the family

butter or margarine for greasing
450 g/1 lb potatoes, thinly sliced
450 g/1 lb firm white fish fillet, skinned
    and cut in 2 cm/¾ inch cubes
1 small onion, grated
50 g/2 oz mushrooms, sliced
salt and pepper
1(298 g/11 oz) can ready-to-serve tomato
    soup
chopped parsley to garnish

Grease a shallow ovenproof dish. Set the oven at 200°C/400°F/gas 6. Cook the potatoes in boiling salted water for 10 minutes, then drain well.

Lay the fish in the prepared dish. Top with the grated onion and mushrooms, then add a layer of sliced potatoes. Pour the soup over the potatoes, then bake for 25-30 minutes, or until the fish is cooked and the mixture is bubbling hot.

Sprinkle with chopped parsley and serve.

SERVES 4

*J*OHN DORY AU GRATIN

fat for greasing
8 John Dory fillets
salt and pepper
60 ml/4 tbsp milk
50 g/2 oz Gruyère cheese, grated
100 g/4 oz dry white breadcrumbs
25 g/1 oz butter

Grease an ovenproof baking dish. Set the oven at 190°C/375°F/gas 5.

Roll up the fish fillets and place them in the prepared dish. Sprinkle with salt and pepper and pour over the milk. Mix the cheese and breadcrumbs in a bowl and sprinkle the mixture over the fish.

Dot with butter and bake for 20 minutes. Serve at once.

SERVES 3 TO 4

BAKED GRAYLING

Grayling are freshwater members of the salmon family (see page 11). They have firm white flesh and a flavour similar to, though not as pronounced as trout.

2(450 g/1 lb) grayling
25 g/1 oz butter
2 large onions, thinly sliced
30 ml/2 tbsp chopped parsley
salt and pepper
250 ml/8 fl oz dry white wine
250 ml/8 fl oz double cream
juice of ½ lemon
watercress sprigs to garnish

Clean the fish and remove the heads and fins. Use half the butter to generously grease a large ovenproof dish. Set the oven at 200°C/400°F/gas 6.

Cover the base of the prepared dish with the onions. Sprinkle with parsley, salt and pepper. Lay the fish side by side in the dish.

Melt the remaining butter in a small saucepan. Brush it over the fish and bake for 10 minutes. Add the wine to the dish, baste the fish and bake for 15 minutes more.

Pour the cream into the dish and bake for a further 5 minutes. Squeeze the lemon juice over the fish, garnish with watercress sprigs and serve at once.

SERVES 2

BAKED MULLET

25 g/1 oz butter
225 g/8 oz onions, thinly sliced
225 g/8 oz tomatoes, peeled, seeded and sliced
4(225 g/8 oz) grey mullet, cleaned and trimmed
100 ml/3½ fl oz dry white wine
salt and pepper
15 ml/1 tbsp chopped fresh tarragon or 5 ml/1 tsp dried tarragon
1 lemon, sliced
sippets (see Mrs Beeton's Tip) to garnish

Use the butter to grease a shallow oven-proof baking dish and a sheet of greaseproof paper. Set the oven at 190°C/375°F/gas 5.

Spread out the onion rings on the base of the dish and top with the sliced tomatoes. Lay the fish on top of the vegetables and pour the wine over. Sprinkle with salt, pepper and tarragon.

Arrange the lemon slices on top of the fish and cover loosely with the buttered greaseproof paper. Bake for 30 minutes. Garnish with sippets and serve from the dish.

SERVES 4

> 🥄 **MRS BEETON'S TIP** To make sippets, toast white or granary bread until golden. Cut into triangles, cubes or fancy shapes.

RED MULLET WITH MUSHROOMS

25 g/1 oz butter
6 small red mullet, cleaned and trimmed

STUFFING
25 g/1 oz butter
1 large onion, chopped
225 g/8 oz mushrooms, finely chopped
50 g/2 oz fresh white breadcrumbs
25 g/1 oz parsley, chopped
salt and pepper

GARNISH
baby tomatoes
watercress sprigs

Use the butter to grease an ovenproof baking dish large enough to hold all the fish in a single layer. Set the oven at 190°C/375°F/gas 5.

Make the stuffing. Melt the butter in a small saucepan and fry the onion for 3-4 minutes or until soft. Transfer to a bowl and add the chopped mushrooms, breadcrumbs and parsley, with salt and pepper to taste. Stuff the fish with this mixture.

Place the stuffed fish in the prepared baking dish, cover and bake for 30 minutes. Garnish with baby tomatoes and watercress sprigs and serve at once.

SERVES 6

RED MULLET BAKED IN FOIL

6 red mullet, cleaned and trimmed
50 g/2 oz butter
salt and pepper
juice of ½ lemon

GARNISH
lemon wedges
parsley sprigs

Set the oven at 190°C/375°F/gas 5. Lay each mullet on a piece of foil large enough to enclose it completely. Dot with butter, sprinkle with salt and pepper and add a little lemon juice. Fasten the packages by folding the edges of the foil firmly together over the fish.

Put the fish packages on a baking sheet and bake for 20-30 minutes. Remove from the foil, taking care to save the cooking juices. Transfer the fish to a warmed platter, pour over the cooking juices and serve at once, garnished with lemon and parsley.

SERVES 6

BAKED HERRINGS

Illustrated on page 115

butter for greasing
4 herrings, cleaned and scaled
salt and pepper
25 g/1 oz butter
2 onions, finely sliced
450 g/1 lb tomatoes, peeled and sliced
30 ml/2 tbsp malt vinegar
parsley to garnish

Grease an ovenproof baking dish. Set the oven at 190°C/375°F/gas 5. Make 3 shallow cuts on either side of each herring and sprinkle with salt and pepper.

Melt half the butter in a frying pan. Add the onions and fry gently for 5 minutes. Place the tomato slices on the base of the prepared dish. Add the onions and sprinkle with salt and pepper, and the vinegar.

Arrange the fish on top and dot with the remaining butter. Cover and bake for 45 minutes. Garnish with parsley.

SERVES 4

*H*ERRINGS STUFFED WITH SHRIMPS

4 herrings
salt and pepper
1 egg, beaten
toasted breadcrumbs
25 g/1 oz butter

STUFFING
15 ml/1 tbsp fresh white breadcrumbs
15 ml/1 tbsp milk
50 g/2 oz peeled cooked shrimps, chopped
cayenne pepper
few drops of anchovy essence

Set the oven at 190°C/375°C/gas 5. Scale the herrings, cut off the heads and remove the bones without breaking the skin. Sprinkle with plenty of salt and pepper.

Make the stuffing by combining all the ingredients in a small bowl. Mix well. Spread the filling on the flesh side of the fillets and roll up tightly. Fasten each with a small skewer.

Pack the herrings tightly in an ovenproof dish. Brush with the egg, sprinkle with the browned breadcrumbs, dot with the butter and bake for 30-35 minutes. Serve at once.

SERVES 4

*S*TUFFED HERRINGS

butter for greasing
4 large herrings

STUFFING
50 g/2 oz butter
225 g/8 oz onions, finely chopped
225 g/8 oz cooking apples
15 ml/1 tbsp cider or white wine vinegar
salt and pepper

Grease a flat ovenproof dish and a piece of foil large enough to cover it. Set the oven at 190°C/375°F/gas 5. Scale the herrings, cut off the heads and·remove the bones without breaking the skin.

Make the stuffing. Melt the butter in a large frying pan, add the onions and fry gently for about 10 minutes until soft. Peel, core and grate the apples and add them to the pan. Mix well, then add the vinegar, with salt and pepper to taste.

Divide the stuffing between the herrings, filling the cavities and then reshaping the fish. Lay them on the prepared dish, cover loosely with the foil and bake for 25 minutes. Serve at once.

SERVES 4

☀ **MICROWAVE TIP** Arrange the stuffed herrings in alternate directions in a suitable dish. Cover with microwave film and cook on High for 7-8 minutes.

HERRINGS TAILS-IN-AIR

4 herrings with roes
50 g/2 oz fresh white breadcrumbs
1 tomato, peeled, seeded and chopped
2 small onions
10 ml/2 tsp chopped parsley
salt and pepper
milk (see method)
1 green pepper, seeded and sliced in
    rings
150 ml/¼ pint canned ready-to-serve
    tomato soup

Scale the herrings. Cut off the heads but leave the tails on, trimming them neatly. Cut off the fins and remove the bones. Chop the roes and set them aside in a bowl. Set the oven at 200°C/400°F/gas 6.

Add the breadcrumbs to the roes, together with the tomato. Grate 1 onion and add it to the mixture with the parsley. Add salt and pepper to taste and bind with a little milk, if required.

Lay the herrings on a board. Put 15 ml/ 1 tbsp of the breadcrumb mixture on the head end of each and roll up towards the tail. Place the rolled herrings in an ovenproof dish with the tails sticking up in the centre.

Cut the second onion into rings. Scatter the onion and green pepper rings over the fish. Pour the soup over the top, cover and bake for 20-30 minutes.

SERVES 4

KIPPER AND TOMATO BAKE

Illustrated on page 116

fat for greasing
250 ml/8 fl oz milk
4 kippers
45 ml/3 tbsp chopped parsley
15 ml/1 tbsp fresh white breadcrumbs
50 g/2 oz butter, softened
lemon juice
salt and pepper
225 g/8 oz tomatoes, sliced
chopped parsley to garnish

Grease a shallow ovenproof dish. Set the oven at 160°C/325°F/gas 3. Heat the milk in a large frying pan, add the kippers and poach over gentle heat for 3 minutes. Remove the pan from the heat, cover and leave to stand for 5 minutes. Remove the kippers from the pan, reserving 30 ml/2 tbsp of the poaching liquid. Skin and bone the kippers and flake the flesh.

In a bowl, mix the flaked kippers, the reserved poaching liquid, parsley, breadcrumbs and butter. Add a little lemon juice and salt and pepper to taste.

Spread the mixture in the prepared dish, top with tomato slices and bake for 20 minutes. Sprinkle with chopped parsley before serving.

SERVES 4

  MRS BEETON'S TIP Try to find oak smoked kippers. The flavour is infinitely better than that of kippers that have been artificially dyed to an unnatural dark brown.

*B*AKED MACKEREL PARCELS

25 g/1 oz butter
4 small mackerel, cleaned and trimmed
150 g/5 oz Mushroom Stuffing (page 30)
salt and pepper
juice of 1 lemon
8 grilled button mushrooms to garnish

Use most of the butter to grease 4 pieces of foil, each large enough to enclose one mackerel. Set the oven at 200°C/400°F/gas 6. Pat the fish dry. Fill the cavities with the mushroom stuffing.

Lay a fish on each piece of foil and dot with the remaining butter. Sprinkle lightly with salt, pepper and lemon juice and bring up the foil to make 4 loose parcels.

Support the parcels on a baking sheet and bake for 20 minutes. Open one parcel and test the fish with a fine skewer. It should be tender all the way through. Serve the mackerel in the parcels, each opened just enough to show the tops of the fish. Place two grilled mushrooms on each.

SERVES 4

*M*ACKEREL WITH SOURED CREAM SAUCE

fat for greasing
30 ml/2 tbsp plain flour
8(50 g/2 oz) mackerel fillets
45 ml/3 tbsp chopped parsley
50 g/2 oz butter
salt and pepper
2 egg yolks
125 ml/4 fl oz milk
125 ml/4 fl oz soured cream

Grease an ovenproof dish and a piece of foil large enough to cover it. Set the oven at 190°C/375°F/gas 5. Spread out the flour in a shallow bowl, add the mackerel fillets and coat well on all sides. Shake off excess flour.

Arrange the floured fish in the prepared dish and sprinkle with the parsley. Dot with the butter and sprinkle with salt and pepper. Cover loosely with the greased foil and bake for 20 minutes.

Using a slotted spoon and a fish slice, carefully transfer the fish to a warmed serving dish and keep hot. Tip the cooking liquid into a small saucepan.

Mix the egg yolks, milk and soured cream together and add to the cooking liquid in the pan. Heat very gently, stirring until the mixture thickens. Do not allow it to boil. Pour the sauce over the fish and serve at once.

SERVES 4

———————— ◆ ————————

PLAICE PORTUGAISE

fat for greasing
25 g/1 oz butter
2 shallots, sliced
4 tomatoes, peeled, seeded and chopped
100 g/4 oz mushrooms, halved if large
8(75 g/3 oz) plaice fillets
100 ml/3½ fl oz dry white wine
salt and pepper

Grease a shallow ovenproof baking dish and a piece of foil large enough to cover it. Set the oven at 190°C/375°F/gas 5.

Melt the butter in a frying pan, add the shallots and fry for 2-3 minutes until slightly softened. Stir in the tomatoes and mushrooms and fry for 3-4 minutes. Spread the mixture in the prepared dish.

Fold each fillet into 3, skin side in, and arrange on the tomato mixture. Pour the wine over the fish, sprinkle with salt and pepper to taste and cover loosely with the foil. Bake for 25 minutes. Spoon the sauce mixture over the fish and serve at once.

SERVES 4

> **MRS BEETON'S TIP** If you grow fresh herbs, add a few chopped leaves of marjoram, basil or oregano to the tomato mixture for extra flavour.

PLAICE STUFFED WITH PRAWNS

fat for greasing
8(75 g/3 oz) plaice fillets, skinned
100 ml/3½ fl oz white wine
250 ml/8 fl oz Basic Fish Stock (page 27)
25 g/1 oz butter
100 g/4 oz button mushrooms, halved if large
25 g/1 oz plain flour
juice of 1 lemon
salt and pepper
100 ml/3½ fl oz double cream
puff pastry fleurons (page 45)
chopped parsley

STUFFING
50 g/2 oz fresh white breadcrumbs
50 g/2 oz butter, softened
50 g/2 oz peeled cooked prawns, chopped

Grease a shallow ovenproof baking dish and a piece of foil large enough to cover it. Set the oven at 190°C/375°F/gas 5. Make the stuffing by mixing all the ingredients together in a bowl.

Spread the stuffing over the plaice and roll up. Place the plaice rolls in the prepared dish and pour the wine and fish stock over. Cover loosely with the foil and bake for 20 minutes. Using a slotted spoon, transfer the fish to a warmed serving dish. Keep hot. Tip the cooking liquid into a jug.

Meanwhile melt the butter in a saucepan. Add the mushrooms and fry gently for 3-4 minutes. Stir in the flour and cook for 1 minute. Gradually add the cooking liquid, stirring constantly until the mixture boils and thickens. Lower the heat and stir in the lemon juice, with salt and pepper to taste.

Remove the pan from the heat, cool slightly, then stir in the cream. Pour the sauce over the fish, decorate with the pastry fleurons and sprinkle with chopped parsley. Serve at once.

SERVES 4

> ☀ **MICROWAVE TIP** The sauce can be made in the microwave. Slice the mushrooms. Put the butter and flour in a bowl. Whisk in the cooking liquid, then cook on High for 6 minutes, whisking thoroughly once during cooking and again when cooking is complete. Add the mushrooms and lemon juice and cook for 2-3 minutes more. Remove from the microwave, cool slightly, then stir in the cream.

*D*UNWICH PLAICE

25 g/1 oz butter
4(275 g/10 oz) plaice, cleaned and trimmed

STUFFING
 100 g/4 oz mild Cheddar cheese, grated
 50 g/2 oz fresh white breadcrumbs
 5 ml/1 tsp mustard powder
 salt and pepper
 10 ml/2 tsp shredded fresh basil or 5 ml/ 1 tsp dried basil
 juice of ½ lemon
 30 ml/2 tbsp beaten egg

GARNISH
 2 Vandyke tomatoes (see Mrs Beeton's Tip)
 4 rolled anchovies

Use most of the butter to grease a shallow ovenproof baking dish and a piece

of foil large enough to cover it. Set the oven at 190°C/375°F/gas 5. Make a cut down the entire length of each fish as though for filleting. Remove the bone to make a pouch (see page 19).

Make the stuffing by mixing all the ingredients together in a small bowl. Lift the 2 loose flaps on one of the fish and fill the pouch with a quarter of the stuffing. Repeat with the remaining fish.

Place the fish in the prepared dish, dot with the remaining butter, cover with the foil and bake for 20-30 minutes. Decorate each portion with half a Vandyke tomato and a rolled anchovy. Serve at once.

SERVES 4

> 🥣 **MRS BEETON'S TIP** Vandyke tomatoes are easy to cut and they look very effective. Using a sharp-pointed knife, make a zig-zag cut around the circumference of each tomato, from the skin to the centre. Gently pull the two halves apart.

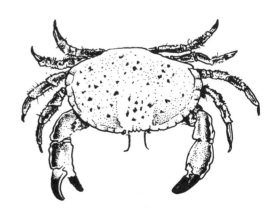

SOLE DIEPPOISE

In this classic dish, the sole is poached in white wine with mussels and shrimps.

fat for greasing
1 (800 g/1¾ lb) sole, cleaned and trimmed
1 small onion, thinly sliced
1 bouquet garni
150 ml/¼ pint dry white wine
12 mussels, scrubbed and bearded
15 ml/1 tbsp white wine vinegar
12 peeled cooked prawns or shrimps
15 ml/1 tbsp butter
15 ml/1 tbsp plain flour
1 egg yolk
90 ml/6 tbsp single cream
salt and pepper
pinch of grated nutmeg
juice of ½ lemon
pinch of cayenne pepper or paprika

Grease a shallow ovenproof baking dish and a piece of foil large enough to cover it. Set the oven at 190°C/375°F/gas 5.

Skin and fillet the sole. Put the bones, skin and head in a saucepan with the onion, bouquet garni and white wine. Put the mussels into the pan, bring to the boil, lower the heat and simmer for 6 minutes.

Using a slotted spoon, remove the mussels. Discard any that remain shut. Shell the mussels and set them aside. Add 150 ml/¼ pint water to the pan and stir in the vinegar. Reduce the liquid by boiling gently for 15 minutes, uncovered, then strain into a jug.

Fold each fillet in half and place in a single layer in the prepared dish. Pour in the reserved cooking liquid and arrange the shelled mussels and prawns or shrimps around the fish. Cover with the foil and bake for 20 minutes.

Drain the stock from the fish into a saucepan and heat to simmering point. Keep the fish and shellfish hot. In a small bowl, cream the butter to a paste with the flour.

Add the butter and flour paste to the fish stock, a little at a time, whisking after each addition. Raise the heat and bring the sauce to the boil, whisking constantly. Boil for 10 minutes. Lower the heat.

Mix the egg yolk and cream in a bowl and stir in about 100 ml/3½ fl oz of the thickened sauce. Add the contents of the bowl to the sauce and bring the mixture to just below boiling point. Add salt, pepper and nutmeg and pour the sauce evenly over the fish and shellfish. Sprinkle with the lemon juice and dust with the cayenne or paprika. Serve at once.

SERVES 4

FILLETS OF SOLE BONNE FEMME

fat for greasing
16 lemon sole fillets
275 g/10 oz mushrooms
50 g/2 oz butter
12 black peppercorns
2-3 parsley stalks
25 g/1 oz plain flour
300 ml/½ pint Basic Fish Stock (page 27)
salt and pepper
lemon juice
2 shallots, sliced
15 ml/1 tbsp chopped parsley
250 ml/8 fl oz dry white wine

Grease a shallow ovenproof baking dish and a piece of foil large enough to cover it. Arrange the sole fillets on the base. Set the oven at 180°C/350°F/gas 4. Cut off the mushroom stems and set them aside. Slice the mushrooms caps and scatter them over the fish.

Melt 25 g/1 oz of the butter in a saucepan, add the mushroom stems, peppercorns and parsley stalks. Cook over gentle heat for 10 minutes. Add the flour and cook over low heat for 2-3 minutes, without allowing the mixture to colour. Gradually add the stock and simmer, stirring, for 3-4 minutes. Rub the sauce through a sieve into a clean saucepan. Add salt, pepper and lemon juice to taste. Cover the surface with damp greaseproof paper and set aside.

Sprinkle the shallots and parsley over the fish, sprinkle with salt and pepper and pour in the wine. Cover with the foil and bake for 20 minutes.

Using a slotted spoon and fish slice, transfer the fish to a warmed serving dish and keep hot. Strain the cooking liquid into a saucepan. Boil it rapidly until reduced by half.

Meanwhile return the sauce to a gentle heat and bring to simmering point. Stir the sauce into the reduced cooking liquid with the remaining butter. As soon as the butter has melted, pour the sauce over the fish. Place under a hot grill until lightly browned. Serve at once.

SERVES 8

SOLE WITH PRAWNS

Illustrated on page 116

100 g/4 oz peeled cooked prawns, finely chopped
50 g/2 oz fresh white breadcrumbs
1 egg
salt and pepper
12 Dover sole or lemon sole fillets
125 ml/4 fl oz dry white wine
125 ml/4 fl oz Basic Fish Stock (page 27)
50 g/2 oz butter
50 g/2 oz plain flour
250 ml/8 fl oz milk
salt and pepper

GARNISH
whole cooked prawns
parsley sprigs
lemon slices or wedges

Set the oven at 190°C/375°F/gas 5. Mix the prawns, breadcrumbs and egg in a bowl, with salt and pepper to taste. Spread the mixture over each fillet and roll up. Pour over the wine and stock and bake for 20 minutes.

Using a slotted spoon, transfer the stuffed fish rolls to a warmed serving dish and keep hot. Tip the cooking juices into a jug.

Melt the butter in a saucepan. Stir in the flour and cook over low heat for 2-3 minutes, without allowing the mixture to colour. Gradually add the reserved cooking juices and the milk, stirring constantly until the sauce boils and thickens. Add salt and pepper to taste.

Pour the sauce over the fish and garnish before serving.

SERVES 6

BAKED GREY MULLET

Illustrated on page 117

2(1 kg/2¼ lb) grey mullet, scaled,
  cleaned and trimmed
2-3 rindless streaky bacon rashers

FORCEMEAT
  50 g/2 oz margarine, melted
  100 g/4 oz fresh white breadcrumbs
  pinch of grated nutmeg
  15 ml/1 tbsp chopped parsley
  5 ml/1 tsp chopped mixed fresh herbs
  grated rind of ½ lemon
  salt and pepper
  1 egg, beaten

GARNISH
  lemon wedges
  fresh herb sprigs

Set the oven at 180°C/350°F/gas 4. Make the forcemeat by combining all the ingredients except the egg in a bowl. Mix well, adding enough of the egg to moisten. The forcemeat should not be sloppy.

Stuff the fish with the forcemeat and place them in an ovenproof dish or on a baking sheet. Lay the bacon rashers over the top of each and bake for 25-30 minutes.

Transfer to a warmed platter, garnish with the lemon wedges and fresh herb sprigs and serve at once.

SERVES 4

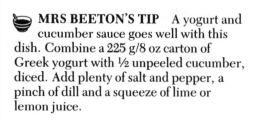

  🥣 **MRS BEETON'S TIP** A yogurt and cucumber sauce goes well with this dish. Combine a 225 g/8 oz carton of Greek yogurt with ½ unpeeled cucumber, diced. Add plenty of salt and pepper, a pinch of dill and a squeeze of lime or lemon juice.

BAKED SMELTS

12 smelts, cleaned and trimmed
100 g/4 oz dry white breadcrumbs
50 g/2 oz butter
salt
cayenne pepper
squeeze of lemon juice

GARNISH
  fried parsley (page 45)
  lemon wedges

Set the oven at 190°C/375°F/gas 5. Arrange the fish in a shallow ovenproof baking dish.

Cover the fish with the breadcrumbs and dot with the butter. Sprinkle with plenty of salt and cayenne and bake for 15 minutes.

Just before serving, add a squeeze of lemon juice. Serve garnished with fried parsley and lemon wedges.

SERVES 3

BAKED FRESH SARDINES

fat for greasing
45 ml/3 tbsp olive oil
2 large onions, finely chopped
45 ml/3 tbsp medium-dry white wine
225 g/8 oz tomatoes, peeled, seeded and
  chopped
salt and pepper
900 g/2 lb sardines, cleaned and trimmed
50 g/2 oz fresh white breadcrumbs
25 g/1 oz butter
watercress sprigs to garnish

Grease a shallow ovenproof baking dish. Set the oven at 180°C/350°F/gas 4.

Heat the oil in a small saucepan, add the onions and fry gently for about 5 minutes until lightly browned. Add the wine and boil until the volume is reduced by two thirds. Stir in the tomatoes, with salt and pepper to taste. Cook for 3-4 minutes.

Pour the tomato mixture into the prepared dish, arrange the sardines on top and sprinkle with the breadcrumbs. Dot with the butter and bake for 25 minutes. Serve hot, garnished with watercress.

SERVES 6

*B*AKED TURBOT

3 shallots, chopped
6(150 g/5 oz) turbot fillets
150 g/5 oz mushrooms, sliced
salt and pepper
250 ml/8 fl oz Basic Fish Stock (page 27)
juice of 1 lemon
250 ml/8 fl oz double cream
3 egg yolks
12 puff pastry fleurons (page 45)

Spread out the chopped shallots on the base of a shallow ovenproof baking dish. Arrange the fish on the top and add the mushrooms. Sprinkle with salt and pepper to taste and pour over the stock and lemon juice. Cover and bake for 30 minutes.

Using a slotted spoon, transfer the fish and mushrooms to a dish; keep hot. Tip the cooking juices into a clean saucepan.

Mix the cream and egg yolks in a bowl. Add to the cooking liquid and heat very gently until thickened, stirring constantly. Do not boil. Pour the sauce over the fish and top with the fleurons.

SERVES 6

*T*URBOT MARENGO

fat for greasing
4(1 cm/½ inch thick) turbot steaks
350 ml/12 fl oz Basic Fish Stock (page 27)
50 g/2 oz butter
1 onion, sliced
1 carrot, sliced
1 turnip, sliced
5 ml/1 tsp dried mixed herbs
25 g/1 oz plain flour
1(70 g/2½ oz) can tomato purée
salt and pepper

GARNISH
stuffed green olives
chopped parsley
lemon slices

Grease a shallow ovenproof baking dish. Set the oven at 180°C/350°F/gas 4. Arrange the fish in the dish, add 75 ml/5 tbsp of the fish stock and bake for 20 minutes.

Meanwhile melt 25 g/1 oz of the butter in a frying pan. Add the onion, carrot and turnip and fry gently for 5 minutes until soft. Sprinkle over the herbs, add the remaining stock and cover the pan. Simmer for 20 minutes. Strain the stock into a jug, discarding the solids in the strainer.

Melt the remaining butter in a saucepan, add the flour and cook for 1 minute. Gradually add the reserved cooking liquid, stirring constantly, then stir in the tomato purée and seasoning. Simmer the sauce, stirring occasionally, for 10 minutes.

When the fish is cooked, transfer it to warmed serving dish. Pour over the sauce, garnish with olives, parsley and lemon slices and serve at once.

SERVES 4

TURBOT DUGLERE

fat for greasing
1(1.5 kg/3¼ lb) turbot, cleaned and
    trimmed
40 g/1½ oz butter
30 ml/2 tbsp oil
1 small onion, finely chopped
225 g/8 oz tomatoes, peeled and chopped
30 ml/2 tbsp white wine vinegar
200 ml/7 fl oz dry white wine
salt and pepper
1 bouquet garni
10 ml/2 tsp plain flour

Skin and fillet the turbot, reserving the trimmings in a saucepan. Grease a shallow ovenproof baking dish. Set the oven at 190°C/375°F/gas 5.

Melt 25 g/1 oz of the butter in the oil in a frying pan. Add the onion and fry for 2-3 minutes until soft but not coloured. Add the chopped tomatoes, vinegar and white wine. Simmer for 10 minutes; set aside.

Lay the fish fillets in the prepared dish. Sprinkle with salt and pepper and pour over the tomato mixture. Cover the dish with a lid or foil and bake for 20 minutes.

Meanwhile add 300 ml/½ pint water and the bouquet garni to the fish trimmings. Bring to the boil, lower the heat and simmer for 15 minutes. Remove from the heat. Strain the liquid into a small saucepan. In a small bowl, cream the remaining butter to a paste with the flour.

Add the butter and flour paste to the fish stock, a little at a time, whisking after each addition. Return to the heat and bring the sauce to the boil, whisking constantly until the sauce thickens. Add salt and pepper to taste and pour the sauce over the fish.

SERVES 4

APRICOT-STUFFED TROUT

The apricots for the stuffing need to be soaked overnight, so start preparation the day before cooking – or use ready-to-eat fruit.

fat for greasing
6 trout, cleaned and trimmed
2 onions, finely chopped
salt and pepper
250 ml/8 fl oz dry white wine
75 g/3 oz butter
25 g/1 oz plain flour
250 ml/8 fl oz Basic Fish Stock (page 27)
60 ml/4 tbsp dry white wine
2 egg yolks
juice of ½ lemon
chopped parsley to garnish

STUFFING
75 g/3 oz dried apricots
75 g/3 oz fresh white breadcrumbs
pinch of dried thyme
pinch of ground mace
pinch of grated nutmeg
1 celery stick, finely chopped
25 g/1 oz butter

Make the stuffing. Soak the apricots overnight in a small bowl with water to cover. Next day, drain the fruit, reserving the soaking liquid, and chop finely, Mix the apricots in a bowl with the breadcrumbs, salt, pepper, herbs, spices and celery. Melt the butter in a small saucepan and stir it into the mixture. Moisten further with a little of the reserved soaking liquid (see Mrs Beeton's Tip).

Grease a shallow ovenproof baking dish. Set the oven at 180°C/350°F/gas 4. Fill the trout with the apricot stuffing. Spread out the onions on the base of the prepared dish, arrange the trout on top and sprinkle with plenty of salt and pepper. Pour the wine into the dish, dot the fish with 25 g/1 oz of the butter, cover and oven-poach for 25 minutes.

Meanwhile, melt 25 g/1 oz of the remaining butter in a saucepan. Stir in the flour and cook over low heat for 2-3 minutes, without allowing the mixture to colour. Gradually add the fish stock, stirring constantly until the sauce boils and thickens. Add salt and pepper to taste. Lower the heat, add the wine and simmer for 10 minutes.

Bring the sauce to just below boiling point and whisk in the remaining butter, a little at a time. Remove the pan from the heat. Blend the egg yolks and lemon juice in a small bowl, add a little of the hot sauce and mix well. Add the contents of the bowl to the sauce and mix well. Cover with damp greaseproof paper and set aside.

Using a slotted spoon and fish slice, carefully transfer the fish to a wooden board. Strain the cooking liquid into a saucepan. Skin the trout, then arrange them on a warmed flameproof serving dish and keep hot.

Boil the cooking liquid until it is reduced by a quarter, then add it to the white wine sauce. Place over moderate heat and warm through, stirring the sauce until it thickens. Do not allow it to boil. Pour the hot sauce over the fish. Place under a moderate grill for 4-5 minutes to brown lightly. Garnish with chopped parsley and serve at once.

SERVES 6

> **MRS BEETON'S TIP** If you use ready-to-eat dried apricots, moisten the stuffing with a little chicken stock.

BAKED TROUT WITH OLIVES AND TOMATOES

4(225 g/8 oz) trout
50 g/2 oz plain flour
salt and pepper
125 ml/4 fl oz oil
1 large onion, sliced
25 g/1 oz stuffed green olives, sliced
225 g/8 oz tomatoes, peeled, seeded and
  chopped
30 ml/2 tbsp white wine vinegar
juice of 1 lemon
15 ml/1 tbsp capers
25 g/1 oz butter
fresh herbs to garnish

Wash and scale the trout. Cut off the fins and wipe the fish with a cloth. Spread out the flour in a shallow bowl, season with salt and pepper and coat the trout well on all sides. Shake off excess flour.

Heat the oil in a large frying pan and brown the trout on both sides for 2-3 minutes. Using a slotted spoon and a fish slice, transfer the trout to a shallow ovenproof baking dish large enough to hold them all in a single layer. Set aside.

Add the onion and olives to the oil remaining in the pan and fry for 4 minutes until golden. Remove with a slotted spoon and spread over the fish. Top with the tomatoes. Sprinkle with the vinegar and lemon juice. Scatter the capers on top, add salt and pepper to taste and bake for 15 minutes.

Meanwhile melt the butter in a small frying pan until foaming. Pour it over the cooked fish, garnish with fresh herbs and serve at once.

SERVES 4

BAKED SALMON

800 g/1¾ lb middle cut salmon
salt and pepper
grated nutmeg
2 small shallots, chopped
15 ml/1 tbsp chopped parsley
25 g/1 oz butter
100 ml/3½ fl oz dry white wine

Set the oven at 190°C/375°F/gas 5. Wash and dry the fish and lay it on a sheet of heavy-duty foil large enough to enclose it completely. Lift the edges of the foil and pinch the corners together to make a shallow case. Sprinkle the fish with salt, pepper and a little grated nutmeg. Add the chopped shallots and sprinkle the parsley over the fish. Dot with the butter and pour over the wine.

Carefully lift the edges of the foil and pinch them together to enclose the fish and the wine. Carefully transfer the foil parcel to an ovenproof dish. Cook for 25 minutes.

Drain the fish and serve hot with Hollandaise Sauce (page 42) or leave to cool in the cooking juices, drain and serve with green salad, thinly sliced cucumber and Mayonnaise (page 32).

SERVES 6 TO 8

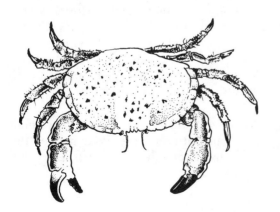

SALMON AURORE

50 g/2 oz butter
1 shallot, finely chopped
4 salmon steaks
salt and pepper
125 ml/4 fl oz dry white wine
125 ml/4 fl oz tomato juice
25 g/1 oz plain flour
125 ml/4 fl oz Hollandaise Sauce (page 42)
5 ml/1 tsp snipped chives
puff pastry fleurons (page 45) to garnish

Using 15 g/½ oz of the butter, grease an ovenproof dish (large enough to hold all the steaks in a single layer) and a piece of foil large enough to cover it. Set the oven at 190°C/375°F/gas 5.

Sprinkle the shallot over the base of the dish and add the salmon steaks. Season with salt and pepper and pour over the wine and tomato juice. Cover loosely with the foil and bake for 20 minutes.

Using a fish slice, transfer the salmon to a warmed serving dish. Cover loosely with the foil and keep hot. Strain the cooking liquid into a small pan, bring to the boil; cook for 10 minutes. Remove from the heat.

Meanwhile cream 25 g/1 oz of the remaining butter to a paste with the flour in a small bowl. Add the butter and flour paste to the reduced cooking liquid, a little at a time, whisking after each addition. Return the pan to the heat and heat the sauce, stirring constantly until it thickens.

Stir in the remaining butter, the Hollandaise sauce and the chives. Pour the sauce over the fish and serve at once, garnished with puff pastry fleurons.

SERVES 4

CAPE COD PIE

fat for greasing
450 g/1 lb potatoes, halved
salt and pepper
90 g/3½ oz butter
30-45 ml/2-3 tbsp single cream
25 g/1 oz plain flour
300 ml/½ pint milk
salt and pepper
450 g/1 lb cooked cod, skinned, boned and
    flaked
50 g/2 oz Cheddar cheese, grated
few grains of cayenne pepper
1 egg, beaten
pinch of grated nutmeg

Grease a 1 litre/1¾ pint pie dish. Cook the potatoes in a saucepan of salted boiling water for about 30 minutes or until tender. Drain thoroughly and mash with a potato masher, or beat with a hand-held electric whisk until smooth. Beat in 25 g/1 oz of the butter and the cream. Set aside until cold.

Set the oven at 190°C/375°F/gas 5. Melt 25 g/1 oz of the remaining butter in a saucepan. Stir in the flour and cook over low heat for 2-3 minutes, without allowing the mixture to colour. Gradually add the milk, stirring constantly until the sauce boils and thickens. Add salt and pepper to taste. Stir in the flaked cod, half the cheese and 15 g/½ oz of the remaining butter. Check the seasoning and add the cayenne. Remove from the heat.

Set aside about 10 ml/2 tsp of the beaten egg for glazing. Stir the remaining egg into the cold mashed potato. Melt the remaining butter and stir it into the potato with the nutmeg. Line the prepared dish with half the potato mixture.

Heat the fish mixture until it bubbles. Pour it into the lined pie dish and cover evenly with the rest of the potato. Press the edge with the tines of a fork. Glaze with the reserved egg and sprinkle with the remaining cheese. Bake for 8-12 minutes until well browned.

SERVES 4 TO 5

———————— ◈ ————————

OYSTERS ROCKEFELLER

24 oysters
3 shallots, finely chopped
100 g/4 oz fresh spinach, finely chopped
2 celery sticks, finely chopped
10 ml/2 tsp chopped thyme
15 ml/1 tbsp Worcestershire sauce
100 g/4 oz butter
30 ml/2 tbsp pastis or other aniseed-
    flavour liquor
50 g/2 oz fresh white breadcrumbs

Open the oysters (see page 25), reserving the liquor. Arrange the oysters, on the half shell, in an ovenproof dish. Set the oven at 220°C/450°F/gas 7.

Combine the chopped vegetables and thyme in a saucepan. Add the oyster liquor and 100 ml/3½ fl oz water. Boil for 5-7 minutes, then add the Worcestershire sauce and butter. Beat until the butter melts and the mixture is well blended, then add the pastis. Mix well.

Pour the sauce over the oysters, sprinkle with the breadcrumbs and bake for 5-10 minutes.

SERVES 2

*P*RAWN QUICHE

1 small onion, thickly sliced
1 small carrot, thickly sliced
½ celery stick, thickly sliced
300 ml/½ pint milk
1 bay leaf
1 parsley stalk
1 thyme sprig
4 white peppercorns
salt
25 g/1 oz butter
25 g/1 oz plain flour
30 ml/2 tbsp single cream
150 g/5 oz Cheddar cheese, grated
200 g/7 oz peeled cooked prawns
juice of ½ lemon

SHORT CRUST PASTRY
100 g/4 oz plain flour
1.25 ml/¼ tsp salt
50 g/2 oz margarine
flour for rolling out

Combine the onion, carrot, celery and milk in a saucepan. Add the herbs and spices, with salt to taste. Heat to simmering point, cover, turn off the heat and allow to stand for 30 minutes to infuse.

Set the oven at 200°C/400°F/gas 6. Make the pastry. Sift the flour and salt into a bowl, then rub in the margarine until the mixture resembles fine breadcrumbs. Add enough cold water to make a stiff dough. Press the dough together with your finger-tips.

Roll out the pastry on a lightly floured surface and use to line an 18 cm/7 inch flan tin or ring placed on a baking sheet. Line the pastry with greaseproof paper and fill with baking beans. Bake 'blind' for 20 minutes.

Meanwhile finish making the filling. Strain the flavoured milk into a measuring jug, discarding the solids in the strainer. Melt the butter in a saucepan. Stir in the flour and cook over low heat for 2-3 minutes without allowing the mixture to colour. Gradually add the flavoured milk, stirring constantly.

Raise the heat to moderate, stirring until the mixture thickens. Stir in the cream and half the cheese, then add the prawns. Mix well. Finally add the lemon juice.

Remove the flan tin from the oven, take out the paper and beans and return the flan shell to the oven for 5 minutes. Pour the prawn mixture into the flan shell, top with the remaining cheese and brown under a moderate grill. Serve hot.

SERVES 4

MRS BEETON'S TIP Ceramic baking beans for baking 'blind' may be purchased from cookware shops. Ordinary dried beans or peas may be used instead. These are sprinkled over the greaseproof paper to weight the pastry slightly. After use, the beans or peas are cooled and stored in an airtight container. They may be used again and again, but may not be cooked to be eaten in another recipe.

KOULIBIAC

Koulibiac is a large oblong pastry filled with a mixture of cooked rice and salmon. Smoked salmon offcuts or canned salmon may be used instead of fresh salmon. This is good either hot or cold and is therefore ideal for formal meals, buffets or picnics.

fat for greasing
450 g/1 lb salmon fillet or steaks
salt and pepper
juice of ½ lemon
175 g/6 oz long-grain rice
50 g/2 oz butter
1 onion, chopped
60 ml/4 tbsp chopped parsley
15 ml/1 tbsp chopped fresh tarragon
 (optional)
4 hard-boiled eggs, roughly chopped
450 g/1 lb puff pastry
1 egg, beaten, to glaze
150 ml/¼ pint soured cream to serve

Lay the salmon on a piece of greased foil large enough to enclose it completely. Sprinkle with salt, pepper and a little of the lemon juice, then wrap the foil around the fish, sealing the edges firmly.

Place the rice in a large saucepan and add 450 ml/¾ pint water. Bring to the boil, lower the heat and cover the pan. Simmer the rice for 10 minutes, then place the foil-wrapped fish on top of the rice. Cover the pan again and cook for about 10 minutes more or until the grains of rice are tender and all the water has been absorbed.

At the end of the cooking time, remove the foil-packed salmon from the pan. Transfer the fish to a board, reserving all the cooking juices, then discard the skin and any bones. Coarsely flake the flesh and set the fish aside. Tip the cooked rice into a bowl.

Melt half the butter in a small saucepan. Add the onion and cook over low heat for about 15 minutes until it is soft but not browned. Mix the cooked onion with the rice and add the salmon and parsley, with salt and pepper to taste. Put the chopped hard-boiled eggs in a bowl. Add the tarragon, if used. Melt the remaining butter and trickle it over the eggs.

Set the oven at 220°C/425°F/gas 7. Cut a large sheet of foil, at least 30 cm/12 inches long. On a floured board, roll out the pastry to a rectangle measuring about 50 × 25 cm/ 20 × 10 inches. Trim the pastry to 43 × 25 cm/17 × 10 inches. Cut the trimmings into long narrow strips. Set aside.

Lay the pastry on the foil. Spoon half the rice mixture lengthways down the middle of the pastry. Top with the egg mixture in an even layer, then mound the remaining rice mixture over the top. Fold one long side of pastry over the filling and brush the edge with beaten egg. Fold the other side over and press the long edge together firmly. Brush the inside of the pastry at the ends with egg and seal them firmly.

Use the foil to turn the koulibiac over so that the pastry seam is underneath, then lift it on to a baking sheet or roasting tin. Brush all over with beaten egg and arrange the reserved strips of pastry in a lattice pattern over the top. Brush these with egg too.

Bake the koulibiac for 30-40 minutes, until the pastry is well puffed and golden. Check after 25 minutes and if the pastry looks well browned tent a piece of foil over the top to prevent it from overcooking.

Serve a small dish of soured cream with the koulibiac, which should be cut into thick slices.

SERVES 8

CREAMED SALMON IN PASTRY

Illustrated on page 119

125 ml/4 fl oz white wine
1 bouquet garni
1 onion, sliced
salt and pepper
450 g/1 lb salmon pieces or steaks
50 g/2 oz butter
25 g/1 oz plain flour
150 g/5 oz mushrooms, sliced
75 ml/5 tbsp double cream
450 g/1 lb puff pastry, thawed if frozen
plain flour for rolling out
beaten egg to glaze

GARNISH
lemon wedges
dill sprigs

Put the wine in a saucepan with 125 ml/
4 fl oz water. Add the bouquet garni and
onion slices, with salt and pepper to taste.
Bring to the boil, lower the heat and
simmer for 5 minutes. Strain into a clean
pan, add the salmon and poach gently for
10-15 minutes or until cooked. Using a
slotted spoon, transfer the fish to a wooden
board. Remove the skin and any bones and
flake the flesh. Reserve the cooking liquid.

Melt half the butter in a saucepan. Stir in
the flour and cook over low heat for 2-3
minutes, without allowing the mixture to
colour. Gradually add the reserved cooking
liquid, stirring constantly until the sauce
boils and thickens. Lower the heat and
simmer for 3-4 minutes. Stir in the flaked
salmon and remove from the heat.

Melt the remaining butter in a frying
pan. Add the mushrooms and fry for 3-4
minutes. Using a slotted spoon, add the
mushrooms to the salmon mixture. Stir in
the cream, cover the surface of the mixture
with damp greaseproof paper and set aside.

Set the oven at 200°C/400°F/gas 6. Roll
out the pastry 3 mm/⅛ inch thick on a
floured surface. Cut to a 25 cm/10 inch
square, reserving the pastry trimmings.
Place the salmon mixture in the middle and
brush the edges of the pastry with beaten

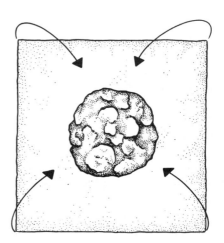

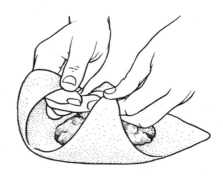

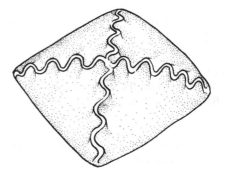

egg. Lift the corners of the pastry to the middle, enclosing the filling. Seal with beaten egg. Make leaf shapes from the trimmings and use to hide the seal on the top of the pastry envelope. Glaze with egg.

Place the pastry envelope on a baking sheet and bake for 15 minutes. Lower the temperature to 190°C/375°F/gas 5 and bake for 20 minutes more. Serve hot, garnished with lemon wedges and dill.

SERVES 4 TO 6

SALTBURN FISH PIE

Although haddock is traditionally used for this dish, cod or any other firm white fish is equally suitable.

butter for greasing
450 g/1 lb haddock fillet
60 ml/4 tbsp grated onion
salt and pepper
30 ml/2 tbsp lemon juice
2 gammon steaks, trimmed and cut into
    7.5 cm/3 inch squares
3 hard-boiled eggs, sliced
30 ml/2 tbsp chopped parsley

SHORT CRUST PASTRY
    150 g/5 oz plain flour
    1.25 ml/¼ tsp salt
    65 g/2½ oz margarine
    plain flour for rolling out

Grease a 750 ml/1¼ pint pie dish. Set the oven at 200°C/400°F/gas 6. Make the pastry. Sift the flour and salt into a bowl, then rub in the margarine until the mixture resembles fine breadcrumbs. Add enough cold water to make a stiff dough. Press the dough together with your fingertips, wrap in a polythene bag and chill until required.

Put the haddock in a large frying pan. Sprinkle the onion over the top, with salt and pepper to taste, and add the lemon juice. Pour enough water into the pan to almost cover the fish. Heat the liquid to simmering point and simmer for 8-15 minutes or until the fish is just tender. Using a fish slice and slotted spoon, transfer the fish to a wooden board. Remove any fins, bones or skin and flake the fish. Reserve the cooking liquid.

Put a layer of fish into the prepared pie dish. Cover with a layer of gammon, then a layer of sliced egg. Sprinkle with salt and parsley. Continue layering until all the ingredients have been used. Moisten with a little of the reserved cooking liquid.

Roll out the pastry on a lightly floured surface and use to make a crust for the pie. Dampen the edges of the dish, lay the pastry crust on the dish and press down firmly to seal. Bake for 25-30 minutes. Serve hot.

SERVES 4

 MRS BEETON'S TIP When the pastry has been rolled to a round large enough to cover the pie, place the rolling pin in the middle of the pastry, lop half the pastry over it, then use the rolling pin to lift the pastry into position.

STARGAZEY PIE

This is a wonderful old Cornish recipe. Its appearance may be a bit off-putting but it tastes delicious. The top crust is traditionally glazed with thick Cornish cream, but single cream or top-of-the-milk may be used instead.

6 even-sized pilchards or herring, scaled and cleaned
1 onion, finely chopped
1 small sharp cooking apple
90 ml/6 tbsp fresh white breadcrumbs
salt and pepper
150-175 ml/5-6 fl oz dry still cider
2 hard-boiled eggs
2 rindless back bacon rashers, finely chopped
10 ml/2 tsp cider vinegar
6 parsley sprigs to garnish

SHORT CRUST PASTRY
150 g/5 oz plain flour
1.25 ml/¼ tsp salt
65 g/2½ oz margarine
plain flour for rolling out
cream for glazing

Rinse in cold water a pie dish or ovenproof plate that will just hold two fish placed end to end across the centre, with their tails overlapping in the centre and their heads sticking over the edge. Turn the pie dish upside down to drain until required.

Make the pastry. Sift the flour and salt into a bowl, then rub in the margarine until the mixture resembles fine breadcrumbs. Add enough cold water to make a stiff dough. Press the dough together with your fingertips, wrap in a polythene bag and chill.

Set the oven at 160°C/325°F/gas 3. Split the fish, without removing the heads or tails, and ease out the backbones. Set 30 ml/2 tbsp of the chopped onion aside and put the rest in a bowl. Peel and grate the apple and add it to the bowl with the breadcrumbs. Add salt and pepper to taste and moisten the stuffing with 45-60 ml/3-4 tbsp of the cider. Stuff the fish with the mixture and reshape neatly. Reserve any leftover stuffing.

Roll out the pastry on a lightly floured surface and use just over half of it to line the chosen dish. Arrange the fish in a star shape with heads right on the edge of the dish and tails overlapping in the centre. Lift the tails and form them into an upright cluster, securing them with wooden cocktail sticks if necessary. Twist a piece of foil over and around them.

Fill the triangular spaces between the fish with egg, bacon, the reserved onion and any leftover stuffing. Sprinkle with the vinegar and pour the remaining cider into the dish.

Roll out the remaining pastry on a floured surface and make a crust for the pie. Make a hole in the centre of the crust large enough to fit around the fish tails. Dampen the edges of the pastry.

Very carefully lift the pastry on the rolling pin and lay it on the pie, with the fish tails sticking through the middle. Press the pastry crust between the fish heads, pushing it back slightly around the heads so that they stick out. Brush the top crust with cream and bake for 1 hour. Garnish with sprigs of parsley around the tails and serve very hot.

SERVES 6

SEAFOOD SUPPERS AND SNACKS

Fresh and frozen fish are quick and easy to cook, making these ingredients an ideal choice for speedy meals. For really snappy suppers there is a wide choice of canned seafood that is extremely versatile and just as tasty and healthy as the fresh food.

STORECUPBOARD STANDBYS

The following are some of the many canned and bottled fish and shellfish available, with notes on their use.

Anchovies Canned anchovy fillets in olive oil have a wide variety of uses: chop them and mix with cooked pasta, garlic and grated Parmesan cheese; add them to a plain pizza; pound them to a paste and mix with mayonnaise, fromage frais or yogurt to make a dip.

Brisling Smoked brisling or sprats are often sold as skippers. The tiny smoked fish are very tasty. Serve them with plenty of black pepper, lemon juice and crusty bread. Also try them on pizza, to top toast or flavour a quiche.

Cod Roe Both pressed and soft roes are available in cans. Pressed roe can be sliced, topped with cheese and grilled, or coated in egg and breadcrumbs, then fried. Soft roes stirred with a little hot butter, parsley and seasoning are good on toast. Soft roes may also be used to make a quick dip or paste. Mix them with mayonnaise, garlic, plenty of seasoning and lemon juice to taste.

Crab White crab meat is of good quality and therefore expensive. Serve in scallop shells or small dishes, baked in a creamy sauce inside a ring of piped mashed potato. Add canned crab meat to a suitable sauce for filling vols-au-vent or in any recipe that calls for fresh crab meat.

Dressed crab is the seasoned dark meat. Spread it on toast, use it to make tiny canapes or a sandwich filling. Added to a white sauce it may be used as a coating for hard-boiled eggs which should then be served with rice or pasta. It is good for stuffing boiled eggs too.

Herrings There is a wide choice, from ready-to-serve rollmops to canned herring fillets in various sauces.

Packets of plain herring fillets in oil are worth searching for – they are delicious in soured cream, with a garnish of chopped onion and parsley. Strips of herring make a terrific salad with apple and onion.

Mackerel Steaks, fillets and smoked mackerel are available canned in brine, oil or tomato sauce. Use to make fish cakes, flake into a tomato sauce seasoned with curry spices and serve on rice, or make into a pâté with lots of lemon rind added; both unsmoked and smoked fish are suitable. Mackerel also makes good fish pie or quiche filling when mixed with cheese sauce (page 42).

Pilchards As well as those in tomato sauce, look out for pilchards in brine. This product is another good candidate for flavouring with curry spices. Pilchards in tomato sauce make tasty fish cakes (or just make one big one in a shallow frying pan – no need to coat with crumbs – and cut it into wedges).

Salmon There are various types, including red and pink salmon. Serve plain with Mayonnaise (page 32), flake and use in fish cakes, soufflés or mousses. Add to white sauce as a filling for pancakes or pastries or a pasta sauce.

Sardines Delicious on toast, with slices of mozzarella on top. Use on a pizza; mash with soft cheese to make pâté; flake as a filling for omelettes or use with cooked potato and onion as a filling for pasties.

Shrimps and Prawns Choose frozen prawns for preference; canned ones tend to be tough.

Sild Lightly smoked, tiny fish canned in oil or tomato sauce. These may be served plain with lemon, on toast or grilled, flaked and mixed in salad. Sild are used for pâtés and spreads. Good on pizza too.

Smoked Mussels and Oysters The canned ones tend to be strong, oily and nothing like as good as freshly smoked shellfish; however, when drained they can be useful as a standby. Toss them with pasta and cream or serve them on canapés with lemon juice.

Tuna Steak and chunks are canned in brine or oil. Use to make dips, sauces, pâtés. Tuna is also tasty when served hot. Try it in white sauce, as the basis of delicious fish cakes, tossed with rice or pasta or used as a filling for omelettes.

FREEZER STANDBYS

There is a wide range of prepared fish dishes and products, too long to list and evaluate. The following notes may be helpful if you want to turn bought fish into a home-made supper.

Fish Fingers These have more potential than may seem possible. Grill until crisp, then serve hot or cold as dippers with garlic-flavoured mayonnaise. Cooked fish fingers may be used as a filling for quiche. Alternatively top with a mixture of fried peppers, onions and canned chopped tomatoes. Bake them from frozen on a plain cheese and tomato pizza too.

Boil-in-the-bag Fish Look out for kipper fillets with butter and cod in sauce as both are really versatile. Follow the packet instructions for cooking, then add the kippers to rice mixtures to make a kedgeree-style supper. They are also delicious served simply with a topping of poached eggs and plenty of crusty bread.

Cod in sauce (and similar products) can be cooked to make an instant base for a pie topped with mashed potato. Pop the pie under a moderate grill to brown. It is also an ideal pancake filling. Flaked and spread in a cooked pastry case, the cooked fish and sauce may be topped with cheese and breadcrumbs, then grilled to make a tasty flan.

Battered and Crumbed Bite-sized Portions Lots of different seafoods receive this treatment, from nuggets of cod to scampi. They all make good dippers. Alternatively, serve the cooked portions on rice, with a sweet and sour sauce poured over the top, or toss them with a good mixture of stir-fried vegetables.

OMELETTE ARNOLD BENNETT

Illustrated on page 159

150 g/5 oz smoked haddock
25 g/1 oz unsalted butter
60 ml/4 tbsp single cream
2 eggs, separated
salt and pepper
30 ml/2 tbsp grated Parmesan cheese
parsley sprigs to garnish

Bring a saucepan of water to simmering point, add the haddock and poach gently for 10 minutes. Using a slotted spoon transfer the fish to a large plate. Remove any skin or bones. Flake the fish into a large bowl and add half the butter and 15 ml/1 tbsp of the cream. Mix well.

In a separate bowl mix the egg yolks with 15 ml/1 tbsp of the remaining cream. Add salt and pepper to taste. Add to the fish mixture and stir in half the cheese.

In a clean dry bowl, whisk the egg whites until stiff. Fold them into the fish mixture.

Heat half the remaining butter in an omelette pan. Pour in half the fish mixture and cook quickly until golden brown underneath (see Mrs Beeton's Tip). Sprinkle over half the remaining cheese, spoon over 15 ml/1 tbsp of the remaining cream and brown quickly under a hot grill. Do not fold. Very quickly make a second omelette in the same way. Garnish and serve at once.

SERVES 2

🥣 MRS BEETON'S TIP Use a slim spatula to lift one side of the omelette in order to check the colour underneath.

CRAB SOUFFLE

Illustrated on page 118

fat for greasing
50 g/2 oz butter
45 ml/3 tbsp plain flour
250 ml/8 fl oz milk
salt and pepper
4 eggs, separated plus 1 white
200 g/7 oz flaked crab meat
2-3 drops Tabasco sauce
30 ml/2 tbsp dry white wine

Grease a 900 ml/1½ pint soufflé dish. Set the oven at 190°C/375°F/gas 5.

Melt the butter in a saucepan, stir in the flour and cook slowly for 2-3 minutes without colouring, stirring all the time. Add the milk gradually and beat until smooth. Cook for 1-2 minutes more, still stirring. Remove from the heat and beat hard until the sauce comes away cleanly from the sides of the pan. Cool slightly, put into a bowl and add salt and pepper to taste.

Beat the yolks into the flour mixture one by one. Stir in the crab meat and add the Tabasco sauce and wine.

In a clean, grease-free bowl, whisk all the egg whites until stiff. Using a metal spoon, stir 1 spoonful of the whites into the crab meat mixture to lighten it, then fold in the rest until evenly distributed.

Spoon into the prepared dish and bake for 30-35 minutes until well risen and browned. Serve immediately, with hot buttered toast if liked.

SERVES 4

*F*ISH SCRAMBLE

225 g/8 oz smoked haddock fillet
150 ml/¼ pint milk
salt and pepper
4 eggs
25 g/1 oz butter
4 slices buttered toast to serve

Put the haddock into a saucepan, pour over the milk and grind in some pepper. Bring to simmering point and poach gently for 10 minutes or until the fish flakes easily when pierced with the point of a knife. Using a slotted spoon transfer the fish to a large plate. Remove any skin or bones and flake the flesh. Reserve the milk used for cooking in a jug.

In a large bowl, beat the eggs with 60 ml/4 tbsp of the reserved milk. Add salt to taste. Melt the butter in a clean saucepan, add the haddock and stir over gentle heat until heated through. Pour the beaten eggs over the haddock. Lower the heat and cook gently, stirring constantly until the mixture is just set and creamy. Serve at once on buttered toast.

SERVES 4

VARIATION

WHITE FISH SCRAMBLE Substitute any white fish for the smoked haddock. This gives a dish with a more delicate flavour, suitable for anyone on a light diet.

*F*ISH CUSTARD

fat for greasing
450 g/1 lb sole or plaice fillets, skinned
500 ml/17 fl oz milk
4 eggs
2.5 ml/½ tsp grated lemon rind
salt and pepper

Grease a 750 ml/1¼ pint ovenproof dish. Set the oven at 150°C/300°F/gas 2. Arrange the fish fillets on the base of the dish.

Warm the milk in a saucepan, but do not allow it to approach boiling point. Beat the eggs, lemon rind, salt and pepper in a large bowl. Stir in the milk. Strain the custard into the dish.

Stand the dish in a roasting tin. Pour in enough boiling water to come halfway up the sides of the dish. Bake for 1½ hours or until the custard is set in the centre.

SERVES 4

VARIATION

SMOKED COD CUSTARD Bring the milk to simmering point in a saucepan, add 450 g/1 lb smoked cod and poach for 10 minutes. Drain, reserving the milk in a measuring jug. Remove any skin or bones from the fish and flake the flesh into the prepared dish. Make up the milk to 500 ml/17 fl oz if necessary. Use the warm (not hot) fish-flavoured milk to make the custard. Proceed as above.

Scampi Jambalaya (page 167)

Paella Valencia (page 168)

Smoked Mackerel Pâté (page 174) and Taramasalata (page 175)

Potted Shrimps or Prawns (page 176) and Gravad Lax (page 177)

Prawn Cocktail (page 177) and Moulded Salmon Salad (page 180)

Salad Niçoise and Bean Salad with Tuna (both on page 186)

Omelette Arnold Bennet (page 151)

Devilled Herring Roes (page 161) and Angels on Horseback (page 163)

SCALLOPED COD'S ROE

fat for greasing
400 g/14 oz smoked cod's roe, skinned
salt
white wine vinegar
45 ml/3 tbsp single cream
browned breadcrumbs

SAUCE
   25 g/1 oz butter
   25 g/1 oz plain flour
   300 ml/½ pint milk
   salt and pepper
   15 ml/1 tbsp chopped parsley

Make the sauce. Melt the butter in a saucepan. Stir in the flour and cook over low heat for 2-3 minutes, without allowing the mixture to colour. Gradually add the milk, stirring constantly until the sauce boils and thickens. Add salt and pepper to taste. Stir in the parsley. Cover the surface of the sauce with damp greaseproof paper and set aside.

Grease 4 scallop shells. Set the oven at 200°C/400°F/gas 6. Put the cod's roe in a saucepan with water to cover. Flavour the water with a little salt and vinegar and bring to simmering point. Poach the cod's roe for 10 minutes, remove with a slotted spoon and set aside on a plate until tepid; the roe will firm up.

Chop the cod's roe and add it to the parsley sauce with the cream. Mix lightly. Divide the cod's roe mixture between the prepared scallop shells, top with the browned breadcrumbs and place on a baking sheet. Bake for 2-3 minutes or until the sauce bubbles and the crumbs are crisp.

SERVES 4

DEVILLED HERRING ROES

Illustrated on page 160

200 g/7 oz soft herring roes
30 ml/2 tbsp plain flour
salt and pepper
clarified butter for shallow frying
50 g/2 oz butter, softened
3 anchovy fillets, mashed
lemon juice
4 slices of bread
cayenne pepper
paprika

Rinse the herring roes. Spread the flour in a shallow bowl, add salt and pepper to taste and roll the herring roes lightly in the seasoned flour until coated.

Melt the clarified butter in a frying pan, add the floured roes and fry for about 10 minutes until golden-brown all over. Drain on absorbent kitchen paper.

Mix half the softened butter with the anchovy fillets in a small bowl. Add a dash of lemon juice and a little black pepper to taste. Toast the bread and cut off the crusts. Cut each slice in half and spread with the anchovy butter. Arrange the roes on the buttered toast and place in a heated dish.

Melt the remaining butter in a frying pan until nut-brown and foaming. Add a squeeze of lemon juice and a pinch of cayenne. Pour the mixture over the roes, dust with paprika and serve very hot.

MAKES 8 SAVOURIES

SARDINE CASSOLETTES

3 large slices of stale bread, each about
    2 cm/¾ inch thick
oil for shallow frying
1 (65 g/2½ oz) can sardines in oil, drained
15 ml/1 tbsp Greek yogurt
1 tbsp tomato purée
salt and pepper
few drops of lemon juice
10 ml/2 tsp grated Parmesan cheese
watercress sprigs to garnish

Set the oven at 180°C/350°F/gas 4. Using a 5 cm/2 inch biscuit cutter, stamp out 8-10 rounds from the bread. Mark an inner circle on each bread round, using a 3.5 cm/1¼ inch cutter.

Heat the oil in a large frying pan, add the bread rounds and fry until lightly browned. Remove the rounds with a slotted spoon and drain on absorbent kitchen paper. With the point of a knife, lift out the inner ring on each round to form a hollow case. Put the cases on a baking sheet and place in the oven for a few minutes to crisp the insides. Cool completely.

Make the filling by mashing the sardines thoroughly and mixing them with the yogurt and tomato purée. Add salt and pepper to taste and stir in the lemon juice and Parmesan. Spoon into the prepared cases and garnish with watercress.

MAKES 8 TO 10 SAVOURIES

TUNA SAUCE

A real quickie to serve with cooked pasta or rice. It also goes well with mashed potato, particularly if the potato is arranged in a ring in a flameproof dish and grilled until brown before being filled with sauce. The sauce may also be ladled into split baked potatoes or into scooped-out crusty rolls.

25 g/1 oz butter or margarine
1 (200 g/7 oz) can tuna
1 onion, chopped
25 g/1 oz plain flour
450 ml/¾ pint milk
100 g/4 oz mushrooms, sliced
50 g/2 oz Cheddar cheese, grated
salt and pepper
30 ml/2 tbsp chopped parsley

Melt the butter in a saucepan. If the tuna is canned in oil, drain the oil into the pan with the butter. Drain and flake the tuna and set it aside. Add the onion and cook gently, stirring occasionally, for about 15 minutes or until soft. Stir in the flour and cook for 1 minute, then reduce the heat to low and slowly pour in the milk, stirring constantly. Bring to the boil, lower the heat again and simmer for 3 minutes.

Stir the mushrooms and cheese into the sauce with salt and pepper to taste. Cook over low heat until the cheese melts, then add the parsley and flaked drained tuna. Stir for 1-2 minutes until the tuna is hot, then serve at once.

SERVES 4

CRAB AU GRATIN

25 g/1 oz butter
25 g/1 oz plain flour
300 ml/½ pint milk
salt and pepper
400 g/14 oz white crab meat, flaked
100 g/4 oz Gruyère cheese, grated
50 g/2 oz fresh white breadcrumbs
30 ml/2 tbsp grated Parmesan cheese

GARNISH
    tomato slices
    parsley sprigs

Melt the butter in a saucepan. Stir in the flour and cook over low heat for 2-3 minutes, without allowing the mixture to colour. Gradually add the milk, stirring constantly until the sauce boils and thickens. Add salt and pepper to taste.

Stir the crab meat and Gruyère cheese into the sauce. Spoon into a flameproof dish, sprinkle with the breadcrumbs and Parmesan and brown under a moderate grill for 2-3 minutes. Garnish with tomato slices and parsley sprigs and serve at once.

SERVES 4

MRS BEETON'S TIP The crab meat mixture may be served in crab shells, if liked. Make sure the shells are scrupulously clean and dry. Give them an attractive gloss by buffing them with a piece of absorbent kitchen paper dipped in oil.

ANGELS ON HORSEBACK

Illustrated on page 160

8 large shelled oysters
8 rindless streaky bacon rashers
2-3 slices bread
butter for spreading

Wrap each oyster in a bacon rasher. Fasten the rolls with small poultry skewers, place in a grill pan and grill for 4-6 minutes.

Meanwhile toast the bread. Spread with butter and cut into small fingers. Remove the skewers and serve on toast fingers.

MAKES 8 SAVOURIES

SAUCY ANGELS

6 rindless streaky bacon rashers
5 ml/1 tsp finely chopped onion
2.5 ml/½ tsp chopped parsley
125 ml/4 fl oz thick White Sauce (page 41)
2.5 ml/½ tsp lemon juice
paprika ● salt
800 g/1¾ lb canned or bottled mussels, drained
12 small rounds fried bread

Set the oven at 180°C/350°F/gas 4. Using a rolling pin, stretch and flatten each rasher of bacon. Cut them in half. Stir the onion and parsley into the white sauce, add the lemon juice and season with paprika and a little salt. Stir in the mussels.

Spoon 2 or 3 mussels with sauce on to each piece of bacon. Roll up carefully, securing each bacon roll with a small skewer. Place on a baking sheet and bake for 7-8 minutes. Serve hot on fried bread.

MAKES 12 SAVOURIES

RICE AND PASTA SPECIALITIES

Quick-cooking rice and pasta combine well with all types of fish and seafood to make a wide variety of dishes, from traditional kedgeree to special dishes like crab-stuffed cannelloni. Use the recipes in this chapter as a basis for experimenting to expand your repertoire.

TYPES OF RICE

There are many types available in most good supermarkets and even more on offer in specialist stores.

Long-grain White Rice The most basic rice, found in the smallest shop. White rice has had all the outer husk removed to leave white grains. Price is a good indication of quality, with some very cheap packets holding broken grains.

Easy-cook Rice There are many brands of easy-cook rice, both white and brown. This type of rice has been treated and partially cooked. The grains cook quickly and remain separate and whole. Always follow the packet instructions closely.

Brown Rice Brown rice retains some of the outer covering on the grain. The types vary according to the brand; the cooking time varies too. Brown rice usually takes nominally longer to cook than white rice; however overcooking is a common fault with this grain. When cooked, brown rice should be nutty in flavour and slightly chewy (not soft). The grains should be separate – more so than with a fluffy white rice (such as basmati). Brown rice is over-cooked if the grains have burst and softened.

Basmati Rice Both brown and white are now available, the latter being more traditional and providing marginally more flavour. Most often served with Indian dishes, basmati rice is a delicious grain with a distinct, very delicate, aroma and flavour. Open a new packet of good basmati rice and take the trouble to smell the delicate scent of the grains. It is far superior to the easy-cook and plain types of rice and well worth buying. However, to overcook basmati is a crime because the flavour is diminished.

Risotto Rice Italian risotto rice has rounder, shorter grains than other types of rice used for savoury cooking. When cooked, the grains should be creamy, not separate. This type of rice is essential for making authentic risotto.

Convenience Types Frozen cooked rice, canned rice and a broad range of flavoured rice or rice mixtures are available (in cans, packets or frozen). The best advice is to sample and decide for yourself – frozen cooked rice and canned cooked rice are undeniably quick and easy, with grains that remain separate and dry, but rather mean on flavour.

Wild Rice Not a rice at all, but a species of aquatic grass, this consists of dark, long, thin grains (almost black in colour) which do not become soft on cooking but remain firm and chewy. Packets often contain a mixture of different types of wld rice, or wild rice mixed with brown, cultivated, grain. Wild rice is good when mixed with other ingredients (for example, in a stuffing) or scented with herbs and lemon as an accompaniment. Served solo, wild rice is satisfying; you will not need as much as if you were serving white or brown rice. A large base of wild rice can overpower fish and seafood in terms of texture.

PASTA

Dried pasta is available in many different shapes, sizes and colours, from tiny pieces for adding to soup (good in fish and seafood chowders) to large shells for stuffing.

Seafood sauces go well with all sorts of pasta, from spaghetti or tagliatelle to macaroni or rigatoni. Shells and other small, rounded shapes are suitable for mixing into fish sauces. Lasagne, cannelloni and large shells may be filled or layered with fish and seafood mixtures.

A Selection of Pasta Shapes

1 *spaghetti*
2 *cannelloni tubes*
3 *shells*
4 *long thin spirals* (fusilli)
5 *twists*
6 *lasagne sheet*
7 *cartwheels*
8 *bows*
9 *macaroni*
10 *elbow macaroni*
11 *tagliatelle*

ORIENTAL PASTA DISHES

Although pasta is usually associated with Italian cooking, remember that Chinese egg noodles are the basis for chow mein, a dish which is good made with prawns or crab meat. A nest of Chinese egg noodles is the perfect accompaniment for a dish like Sweet and Sour Prawns (page 88).

FRESH PASTA

Fresh pasta is now readily available. It cooks very quickly and tastes good. It also freezes well and cooks rapidly from frozen. Toss fresh pasta with some peeled cooked prawns and/or mussels, olive oil and garlic to make a memorable meal.

PASTA SALADS

Cold cooked pasta and seafood marry well in salads. Combined with vegetables and mixed with oil-based dressings or creamy sauces, a pasta and seafood salad makes a main meal, first course or splendid addition to a cold buffet.

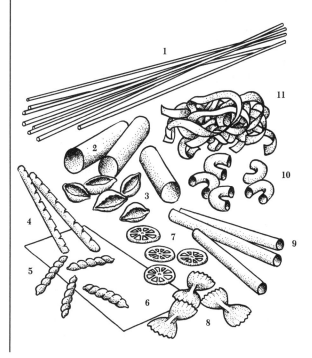

KEDGEREE

Illustrated on page 120

No Victorian country-house breakfast would have been complete without kedgeree. Hard-boiled egg and parsley are the traditional garnish, sometimes arranged in the shape of the cross of St. Andrew.

salt and pepper
150 g/5 oz long-grain rice
125 ml/4 fl oz milk
450 g/1 lb smoked haddock
50 g/2 oz butter
15 ml/1 tbsp curry powder
2 hard-boiled eggs, roughly chopped
cayenne pepper

GARNISH
15 g/½ oz butter
1 hard-boiled egg, white and yolk sieved
  separately
15 ml/1 tbsp chopped parsley

Bring a saucepan of salted water to the boil. Add the rice and cook for 12 minutes. Drain thoroughly, rinse under cold water and drain again. Place the strainer over a saucepan of simmering water to keep the rice warm.

Put the milk in a large shallow saucepan or frying pan with 125 ml/4 fl oz water. Bring to simmering point, add the fish and poach gently for 4 minutes. Using a slotted spoon and a fish slice, transfer the haddock to a wooden board. Discard the cooking liquid.

Remove the skin and any bones from the haddock and break up the flesh into fairly large flakes. Melt half the butter in a large saucepan. Blend in the curry powder and add the flaked fish. Warm the mixture through. Remove from the heat, lightly stir in the chopped egg and season with salt, pepper and cayenne.

Melt the remaining butter in a second pan, add the rice and toss until well coated. Season with salt, pepper and cayenne. Add the rice to the haddock mixture and mix well. Pile the kedgeree on to a warmed dish.

Dot the kedgeree with the butter, garnish with sieved hard-boiled egg yolk, egg white and parsley and serve at once.

SERVES 4

SHRIMP AND RICE STIR

salt and pepper
200 g/7 oz long-grain rice
100 g/4 oz butter
100 g/4 oz mushrooms, sliced
100 g/4 oz cooked ham, cut in thin strips
225 g/8 oz peeled cooked shrimps

Bring a saucepan of salted water to the boil. Add the rice and cook for 15 minutes. Drain thoroughly, rinse under cold water and drain again. Place the strainer over a saucepan of simmering water to keep the rice warm.

Melt the butter in a frying pan, add the mushrooms and fry for 3-4 minutes until golden. Stir in the rice and fry for 4 minutes, then add the ham and shrimps. Lower the heat and simmer for 2-3 minutes. Add salt and pepper to taste, pile on to a warmed serving dish and serve at once.

SERVES 4

SCAMPI JAMBALAYA

Illustrated on page 153

25 g/1 oz butter
15 ml/1 tbsp oil
2 onions, finely chopped
100 g/4 oz cooked ham, diced
3 tomatoes, peeled and chopped
1 green pepper, seeded and finely
    chopped
1 garlic clove, crushed
pinch of dried thyme
salt and pepper
cayenne pepper
5 ml/1 tsp Worcestershire sauce
225 g/8 oz long-grain rice
125 ml/4 fl oz hot chicken stock
450 g/1 lb peeled cooked scampi tails
100 g/4 oz shelled cooked mussels
    (optional)
30 ml/2 tbsp medium-dry sherry
thyme sprigs to garnish

Melt the butter in the oil in a deep frying pan. Add the onions and fry gently for 4-5 minutes until soft. Add the ham, tomatoes, green pepper and garlic, then stir in the thyme, with salt, pepper and cayenne to taste. Add the Worcestershire sauce and rice. Stir well. Pour in the hot chicken stock, cover the pan and cook for 12 minutes.

Add the scampi to the pan, with the mussels, if used. Lower the heat, cover and simmer for 5 minutes more or until the rice is perfectly cooked. Stir in the sherry, add the garnish and serve at once.

SERVES 4

FISH AND RICE SOUFFLE

fat for greasing
500 ml/17 fl oz milk
1 onion slice
6 peppercorns
1 small bay leaf
piece of lemon rind
450 g/1 lb cod or haddock fillets
50 g/2 oz cooked rice
salt and pepper
3 eggs, separated plus 1 egg white

Grease a 1 litre/1¾ pint soufflé dish. Set the oven at 190°C/375°F/gas 5.

Put the milk in a large shallow saucepan or frying pan with the onion, peppercorns, bay leaf and lemon rind. Bring to simmering point, add the fish and poach gently for about 15 minutes or until cooked. Using a slotted spoon and a fish slice, transfer the haddock to a wooden board. Strain the cooking liquid into a bowl and stir in the rice.

Remove the skin and any bones from the haddock. Flake the flesh finely and add it to the rice mixture with plenty of salt and pepper. Add the egg yolks one by one, stirring well after each addition.

In a clean, grease-free bowl, whisk all the egg whites until stiff. Using a metal spoon, fold the whites into the fish and rice. Spoon into the prepared dish and bake for 30-35 minutes until well risen and browned. Serve immediately.

SERVES 4

*P*AELLA VALENCIANA

Illustrated on page 154

1 kg/2¼ lb mussels, washed, scraped and
    bearded
30 ml/2 tbsp plain flour
1(1.5 kg/3¼ lb) roasting chicken, cut into
    portions
90 ml/6 tbsp olive oil
2 garlic cloves
675 g/1½ lb risotto rice
pinch of saffron threads
salt

GARNISH
    450 g/1 lb cooked shellfish (prawns,
        crayfish, lobster or crab)
    strips of canned pimiento
    green or black olives
    chopped parsley

Wash, scrape and beard the mussels, following the instructions on page 25. Put them in a large saucepan with 125 ml/4 fl oz water. Place over moderate heat and bring to the boil. As soon as the liquid bubbles up over the mussels, shake the pan 2 or 3 times, cover, lower the heat and simmer until the mussels have opened. Discard any that remain shut. Remove the mussels with a slotted spoon and shell them, retaining the best half shells. Strain the mussel liquid through muslin into a large measuring jug, add the cooking liquid and make up to 1.25 litres/2¼ pints with water. Set aside.

Put the flour in a stout polythene bag, add the chicken portions and shake until well coated. Heat 45 ml/3 tbsp of the olive oil in a large frying pan, add the chicken and fry until golden brown on all sides. Using tongs, transfer the chicken to a plate and set aside.

Heat the remaining oil in a large deep frying pan or paella pan. Slice half a garlic clove thinly and add the slices to the oil.

Fry until golden brown, then discard the garlic. Add the rice to the pan and fry very gently, turning frequently with a spatula. Crush the remaining garlic. Pound the saffron to a powder with a pestle in a mortar and sprinkle it over the rice with the garlic. Season with salt.

Add the reserved cooking liquid to the pan and heat to simmering point, stirring frequently. Cook for 5 minutes, still stirring. Add the chicken pieces, cooking them with the rice for 15-20 minutes until they are tender and the rice is cooked through.

Garnish with the shellfish, pimiento, olives and parsley. Replace the mussels in the half shells and arrange them on top of the rice mixture. Remove the pan from the heat, cover with a clean cloth and set aside for 10 minutes before serving. Serve from the pan.

SERVES 8

🥣 **MRS BEETON'S TIP**   Success depends upon correct cooking of the traditional risotto rice; the grains should be separate and not soggy

---

SPAGHETTI ALLA MARINARA

100 g/4 oz butter
1 garlic clove, crushed
10 ml/2 tsp chopped parsley
15 ml/1 tbsp shredded fresh basil or
    5 ml/1 tsp dried basil
salt and pepper
225 g/8 oz spaghetti, broken into short
    lengths
50 g/2 oz Parmesan cheese, grated
25 g/1 oz plain flour
225 g/8 oz peeled cooked scampi tails
30 ml/2 tbsp oil
pinch of grated nutmeg

SAUCE
45 ml/3 tbsp oil
2 rindless streaky bacon rashers,
    finely chopped
½ onion, finely chopped
1 garlic clove, crushed
½ red pepper, seeded and finely chopped
25 g/1 oz plain flour
50 g/2 oz tomato purée
4 large tomatoes, peeled, seeded and
    chopped or 1(397 g/14 oz) can chopped
    tomatoes
300 ml/½ pint chicken stock
salt and pepper
5 ml/1 tsp thick honey
15 ml/1 tbsp chopped fresh herbs
    (oregano, basil, rosemary, parsley)

Make the sauce. Heat the oil in a large saucepan, add the bacon and fry for 2 minutes. Add the onion, garlic and pepper and cook gently for 5 minutes, stirring occasionally. Stir in the flour and tomato purée and cook for 5 minutes more.

Add the chopped tomatoes and chicken stock. Bring to the boil, stirring occasion-ally, then lower the heat and simmer for 30 minutes. Add salt and pepper to taste, stir in the honey and herbs and keep warm.

Cream 50 g/2 oz of the butter with the garlic, parsley and basil in a small bowl. Set aside. Bring a large saucepan of salted water to the boil, add the spaghetti and boil for 10-12 minutes or until tender. Drain in a colander, rinse with hot water and drain again. Turn on to a sheet of greaseproof paper and pat dry.

Tip the spaghetti into a clean pan. Add the remaining butter and half the Parmesan. Season with plenty of salt and pepper and heat through. Transfer to a large shallow flameproof dish and keep warm.

Put the flour in a stout polythene bag with salt and pepper to taste. Add the scampi and toss until well coated. Shake off excess flour. Heat the oil in a large frying pan and shallow fry the scampi for 5 minutes. Drain off the oil and add the scampi to the spaghetti. Stir in the herb butter.

Spoon the tomato sauce over the pasta and shellfish, sprinkle with the remaining Parmesan and brown under a moderate grill for 3-5 minutes. Serve at once.

SERVES 4

MUSSEL RISOTTO

1.6 kg/3½ lb mussels
50 g/2 oz butter
30 ml/2 tbsp olive oil
1 onion, finely chopped
2 garlic cloves, crushed
225 g/8 oz risotto rice
grated rind of ½ lemon
1 bay leaf
300 ml/½ pint dry white wine
salt and pepper
300 ml/½ pint hot Basic Fish Stock
    (page 27) or water
75 g/3 oz Parmesan cheese, grated
60 ml/4 tbsp chopped parsley
8 lemon wedges to serve

Wash, scrape and beard the mussels following the instructions on page 25. Discard any that are open and do not shut when tapped. Put the mussels in a large saucepan. Add 125 ml/4 fl oz water and place over moderate heat to bring to the boil. As soon as the liquid boils, shake the pan and put a tight-fitting lid on it. Cook for about 5 minutes until all the mussels have opened, shaking the pan a couple of times.

Heat half the butter with the olive oil in a separate saucepan. Add the onion and garlic, then cook gently, stirring occasionally, for 10 minutes. Stir in the rice, lemon rind and bay leaf. Cook for a few minutes, stirring gently, until all the rice grains are coated in fat.

Pour in the wine, with salt and pepper to taste. Bring to the boil. Stir once, lower the heat and cover the pan tightly. Leave over low heat for 15 minutes.

Meanwhile, strain the mussels and reserve the cooking liquid. Discard any mussels that have not opened. Reserve a few mussels in shells for garnish and remove the others from their shells.

Pour the mussel cooking liquid and the hot stock or water into the rice mixture. Stir lightly, then cover the pan again. Continue to cook for 15-20 minutes more or until the rice is cooked, creamy and moist. Stir in the remaining butter and the cheese. Taste the risotto, adding more salt and pepper if required, then sprinkle in the parsley and place all the mussels on top. Cover the pan tightly and leave off the heat for 5 minutes.

Lightly fork the mussels and parsley into the risotto, turn it into 4 serving bowls and add a couple of lemon wedges to each. Garnish with the reserved mussels.

SERVES 4

CRAB-STUFFED CANNELLONI

fat for greasing
8 cannelloni tubes
salt and pepper
225 g/8 oz crab meat
25 g/1 oz fresh breadcrumbs
3 spring onions, chopped
225 g/8 oz ricotta cheese
600 ml/1 pint Fresh Tomato Sauce
    (page 43)
225 g/8 oz mozzarella cheese, sliced

Grease a large, shallow baking dish with butter. Alternatively, prepare 4 individual gratin dishes. Cook the cannelloni in boiling salted water for 10 minutes, until tender. Drain and rinse in cold water, then lay out to dry on a clean tea-towel.

Set the oven at 190°C/375°F/gas 5. Place the crab meat in a bowl and shred it with two forks. If using brown meat as well as white, add it after the white has been shredded. Mix in the breadcrumbs, spring onions and ricotta, with salt and pepper.

There are two ways of filling cannelloni: either put the crab mixture into a piping bag fitted with a large plain nozzle and force the mixture into the tubes, or use a tea-spoon to fill the tubes. For those who are confident about using a piping bag the former method is less messy.

Lay the filled cannelloni in the prepared baking dish or dishes. Pour the tomato sauce over. Top with the mozzarella and bake for about 40 minutes, until golden.

SERVES 4

SEAFOOD LASAGNE

butter for greasing
12 sheets lasagne
salt and pepper
25 g/1 oz butter
1 onion, chopped
1 celery stick, diced
1 bay leaf
25 g/1 oz plain flour
300 ml/½ pint red wine
45 ml/3 tbsp tomato purée
60 ml/4 tbsp chopped parsley
450 g/1 lb white fish fillet, skinned and cut
    into small pieces
225 g/8 oz peeled cooked prawns, thawed
    if frozen
225 g/8 oz shelled cooked mussels, thawed
    if frozen
100 g/4 oz mushrooms, sliced
600 ml/1 pint White Sauce (page 41)
100 g/4 oz mozzarella cheese, diced

Grease a large lasagne dish with butter. Cook the lasagne in a large saucepan of boiling salted water. Add the sheets in-dividually, bending them into the pan as they soften. When tender (after about 10 minutes), drain the lasagne and rinse them immediately in cold water. Lay the sheets out to dry on a clean tea-towel.

Melt the butter in a saucepan. Add the onion and celery, then cook, stirring oc-casionally, for 10 minutes. Stir in the bay leaf and flour, then gradually pour in the wine, stirring all the time. Add 125 ml/4 fl oz water and bring to the boil, stirring. Stir in the tomato purée and parsley, lower the heat and simmer for 5 minutes. Taste and season the sauce.

Set the oven at 180°C/350°F/gas 4. Re-move the wine sauce from the heat. Add the fish, prawns and mussels. Make sure that any frozen seafood is well drained. Lastly, stir in the mushrooms.

Place a layer of lasagne in the prepared dish, then top with half the seafood sauce. Lay half the remaining lasagne over the sauce, then pour on all the remaining sea-food mixture. Top with the rest of the lasagne. Stir the mozzarella into the white sauce, then pour this over the lasagne.

Bake for 50-60 minutes until golden brown and bubbling hot. If liked, serve with salad and crusty bread to mop up the sauce.

SERVES 6

PASTES, PATES AND COLD PLATTERS

Dressed salmon is one of the ultimate buffet dishes while many of the more humble cold seafood specialities are too easily dismissed. This chapter offers ideas for all occasions, from a simple sprat paste to an elaborate moulded salad.

DRESSING SALMON AND LARGE FISH

Although salmon is the most obvious choice for serving cold, carp, salmon trout and bass are equally well suited to this treatment. Also, it is worth remembering that dressed fish fillets or steaks are an excellent alternative to whole fish. Since the dressing of a whole fish often presents the cook with problems, the following techniques are worth noting.

BONING POACHED SALMON

Follow the recipe for Hot Poached Salmon (page 82). Cool the fish in the court bouillon, following the instructions for serving cold and removing the skin.

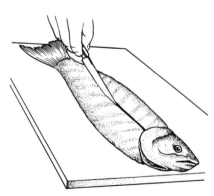

Using a sharp, pointed knife, cut the flesh around the head down to the bone.

Cut the flesh down to the bone around the tail. Make a cut into the flesh along the length of the fish as far as the bone (left).

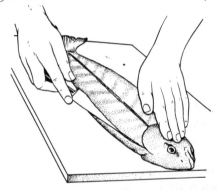

Cut horizontally into the flesh, along the backbone of the fish, from head to tail to loosen the top fillet.

Have a piece of foil on the work surface beside the fish ready to hold the fillets. You need a long palette knife or two fish slices to remove the fillet. Carefully slide the knife or slices under the fillet and lift it off in one piece. If the fish is large, cut the fillet in half or into three portions, then remove each piece neatly.

Carefully cut the flesh off the bone over the belly of the fish and lift it off, in one piece or several pieces, as before.

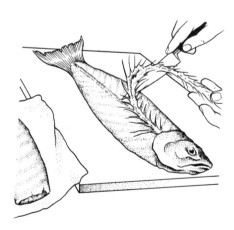

Now remove all the bones from the fish. If serving a salmon trout, snip the backbone at the head and tail end. The bones of salmon come away easily in sections.

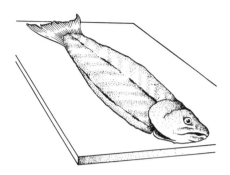

When all the bones have been removed, carefully replace the fillets in their original position. There will be small gaps and untidy-looking areas but these will be covered by the garnish.

GARNISHING SALMON

The final dressing: cut the finest possible slices of cucumber. Thick slices will not do – they have to be thin enough to curve to the shape of the fish. Dip each slice in fish Aspic Jelly (page 28) and lay it on the salmon. Start at the tail, overlapping each row of cucumber to mimic scales.

When the fish is completely covered with cucumber, use a teaspoon to lightly glaze it with more aspic. At this stage the salmon may be chilled for a few hours until just before serving, when the final garnish should be added.

Pipe stars or shells of Mayonnaise (page 32) around the tail and head of the fish, also along the top and base of the body if liked. Small triangles of lemon slices or sliced stuffed olives may be used to cover the eye of the fish. Sprigs of parsley may also be used as a garnish.

CURVED FISH

If the fish has been curved for cooking, it should be garnished with the bones in place.

SMOKED MACKEREL PATE

Illustrated on page 115

25 g/1 oz clarified butter plus extra for
    sealing
2 shallots, finely chopped
75 g/3 oz tomato purée
5 ml/1 tsp soft light brown sugar
juice of ½ lemon
8 crushed peppercorns
15 ml/1 tbsp shredded fresh basil
1.25 ml/¼ tsp dried tarragon
few drops of Tabasco sauce
450 g/1 lb smoked mackerel fillets,
    skinned
75 ml/5 tbsp double cream

Melt the clarified butter in a saucepan,
add the shallots and cook over gentle heat
for 2-3 minutes until soft. Add the tomato
purée, sugar, lemon juice, peppercorns and
herbs and cook gently for 4-5 minutes. Stir
in the Tabasco sauce, set aside to cool.

Roughly purée the shallot mixture,
mackerel and cream in a blender or food
processor. Turn into a suitable dish or
mould and cool. Cover with clarified butter
and chill until firm. Serve with toast.

MAKES ABOUT 450 G/1 LB

> **MRS BEETON'S TIP**   Serve this
> pâté in tomato shells. Cut small
> tomatoes in half and remove the pulp,
> setting it aside for use in a soup or sauce.
> Invert the tomato shells on absorbent
> kitchen paper to drain thoroughly, then
> fill each shell with the mackerel pâté. The
> pâté may be put in a piping bag fitted with
> a large star nozzle and piped into the
> shells, if preferred. Thin it down a little
> with additional cream, if necessary.

HERRING ROE PATE

100 g/4 oz soft herring roes
salt and pepper
75 g/3 oz butter
30 ml/2 tbsp lemon juice
15 ml/1 tbsp chopped parsley
chopped lettuce to garnish

Sprinkle the herring roes with salt and
pepper. Melt 25 g/1 oz of the butter in a
small frying pan, add the roes and fry gently
for 10 minutes. Process the roes to a smooth
paste in a blender or food processor, or
pound them in a mortar.

Soften the remaining butter and add it to
the roe mixture, with the lemon juice and
parsley. Turn into a small mould and chill
for 2 hours until set.

Turn out of the mould, garnish with the
chopped lettuce and serve with fingers of
hot dry toast or fresh brown bread.

MAKES ABOUT 175 G/6 OZ

VARIATION

HERRING ROE SAUCE   Cook the
herring as in the recipe above, frying 30
ml/2 tbsp finely chopped onion in the
butter before adding the roes. Process to a
paste, tip into a saucepan and add 250 ml/
8 fl oz double cream. Season to taste with
salt, pepper and lemon juice. Serve with
grilled white fish, garnished with a few
peeled cooked prawns for colour.

*T*ARAMASALATA

Illustrated on page 115

A food processor may be used to make taramasalata in a few seconds.

100 g/4 oz smoked cod's roe, skinned
1 garlic clove, halved
30 ml/2 tbsp lemon juice
60 ml/4 tbsp olive oil
black pepper

Pound the cod's roe and garlic in a mortar with the lemon juice until smooth. Add the olive oil and 30 ml/2 tbsp water alternately in small amounts, beating well after each addition, until the paste is smooth and completely blended. Grind in black pepper to taste and serve with warm pitta bread, lemon wedges and olives.

SERVES 4

☀ **MICROWAVE TIP** Warm the contents of a packet of pitta bread on several sheets of absorbent kitchen paper for 1-2 minutes on High.

---

*P*OTTED SALMON

450 g/1 lb cold cooked salmon, skinned
   and boned
salt and pepper
pinch of cayenne pepper
pinch of ground mace
anchovy essence
50 g/2 oz softened clarified butter plus
   extra for sealing

Pound the salmon flesh in a mortar or process roughly in a blender or food pro-

cessor. Add salt, pepper, cayenne, mace and anchovy essence to taste. Blend in the softened clarified butter.

Rub the mixture through a fine sieve into a bowl. Turn into small pots. Cover with a layer of clarified butter and refrigerate until the butter is firm.

MAKES ABOUT 450 G/1 LB

*P*OTTED LOBSTER

This rich mixture is delicious with crisp thin toast or with thin slices of rye bread. It also makes a luscious topping for canapes.

450 g/1 lb boiled lobster
125 ml/4 fl oz single cream
1.25 ml/¼ tsp ground white pepper
pinch of ground mace
pinch of cayenne pepper
salt
100 g/4 oz unsalted butter, melted

Pick the lobster meat from the shell and dice it finely. Put it in a bowl. Heat the cream, white pepper, mace and cayenne without boiling. Add salt to taste.

Pour the spiced cream over the lobster meat and mix well. Gradually stir in the melted butter. Turn the mixture into a large dish or 4 individual dishes. Refrigerate until firm.

MAKES ABOUT 575 G/1¼ LB

POTTED SHRIMPS OR PRAWNS

Illustrated on page 156

225 g/8 oz unsalted butter
450 g/1 lb peeled cooked shrimps or
 prawns
1.25 ml/¼ tsp ground white pepper
1.25 ml/¼ tsp ground mace
1.25 ml/¼ tsp ground cloves
dill sprigs to garnish

Melt the butter in a saucepan, add the shrimps or prawns and heat very gently, without boiling. Add the pepper, mace and cloves.

Using a slotted spoon, transfer the prawns to small pots. Pour a little of the hot spiced butter into each pot.

Set the remaining spiced butter aside until the residue has settled, then pour over the shrimps or prawns. Chill until the butter is firm. Store in a refrigerator for no more than 48 hours. Garnish with dill.

MAKES ABOUT 675 G/1½ LB

POTTED HERRING FILLETS

*This makes an excellent sandwich spread or
topping for cocktail biscuits.*

1(198 g/7 oz) can herring fillets in tomato
 sauce
25 g/1 oz butter
pinch of ground mace
salt and pepper
melted clarified butter

Mash the herring fillets with any sauce from the can. Melt the butter in a small saucepan. Add the mashed herrings, the mace and salt and pepper to taste. Stir until just heated through.

Cool slightly, then turn into small pots. Cover with a layer of clarified butter and refrigerate until the butter is firm.

MAKES ABOUT 200 G/7 OZ

SPRAT PASTE

*An inexpensive starter which also makes a good
toast topper or sandwich filler.*

450 g/1 lb sprats, cleaned
10 ml/2 tsp butter
pinch of cayenne pepper
black pepper
1.25 ml/¼ tsp ground mace
5 ml/1 tsp anchovy essence
15 ml/1 tbsp lemon juice
melted clarified butter for sealing

Set the oven at 180°C/350°F/gas 4. Place the sprats on a large sheet of foil supported on a baking sheet. Dot the fish with butter and fold the foil over to make a parcel. Bake for 10-15 minutes.

While still warm, remove the heads, tails, skin and backbones from the fish. Pound the flesh well in a mortar, then rub through a sieve into a bowl.

Add cayenne, black pepper and mace to taste, then beat in the anchovy essence and lemon juice. Turn into small pots. Cover with a layer of clarified butter and refrigerate until the butter is firm.

MAKES ABOUT 450 G/1 LB

*G*RAVAD LAX

Illustrated on page 156

2 unskinned salmon fillets, total weight
    about 1 kg/2¼ lb
200 g/7 oz salt
90 g/3½ oz caster sugar
50 g/2 oz white peppercorns, crushed
90 g/3½ oz fresh dill plus extra to garnish

Keep the salmon fillets separate. Cut each fillet into pieces, about 13 cm/5 inches square. Score the skin on each piece in 4 places. Mix the salt, sugar and peppercorns in a bowl.

Sprinkle a third of the salt mixture on the base of a shallow dish. Place the pieces from one salmon fillet, skin side down, on the mixture. Cover with a further third of the salt mixture and add half the dill. Arrange the pieces from the second fillet, skin side up, on top and cover with the remaining salt mixture and dill.

Place a heavy plate on top of the fish and weight it down. Leave at room temperature for 6 hours, then transfer to a refrigerator. Leave for 48 hours, during which time the salt mixture will become a brine solution. Drain off the brine before serving. Serve as for smoked salmon, garnished with fresh dill. Mayonnaise, flavoured lightly with French mustard, is a good accompaniment (see page 32).

SERVES 4 TO 6

*P*RAWN COCKTAIL

Illustrated on page 157

4 lettuce leaves, shredded
225 g/8 oz peeled cooked prawns
75 ml/5 tbsp Mayonnaise (page 32)
15 ml/1 tbsp tomato purée
few drops of Tabasco sauce
5 ml/1 tsp chilli vinegar or tarragon
    vinegar (optional)
4 whole cooked prawns to garnish

Place a little shredded lettuce on the base of 4 glass dishes. Put the prawns on top. Mix the mayonnaise with the tomato purée and add a few drops of Tabasco sauce. Stir in the vinegar, if liked. Spoon the mayonnaise mixture over the prawns and garnish each dish with a whole cooked prawn, preferably in the shell. Serve with brown bread and butter, if liked.

SERVES 4

VARIATIONS

AVOCADO RITZ Serve the prawns and mayonnaise on avocado halves. Cut the avocados in half and remove the stones just before topping and serving. If there is likely to be any delay, brush the avocado flesh with lemon juice to prevent discoloration.
PRAWN AND HORSERADISH COCK-TAIL Omit the Tabasco sauce and vinegar from the recipe above and add 5 ml/1 tsp grated fresh horseradish or 15 ml/1 tbsp creamed horseradish.

FRESH SALMON MOUSSE

oil for greasing
450 g/1 lb salmon fillet or steak (a tail
    piece may be used)
1 litre/1¾ pints Court Bouillon (page 28)
15 g/½ oz gelatine
50 g/2 oz butter, softened
45 ml/3 tbsp double cream, lightly
    whipped
15 ml/1 tbsp medium-dry sherry

BÉCHAMEL SAUCE
½ small onion
½ small carrot
1 small celery stick
300 ml/½ pint milk
1 bay leaf
few parsley stalks
1 sprig of thyme
1 clove
6 white peppercorns
1 blade of mace
salt
25 g/1 oz butter
25 g/1 oz plain flour

Brush a glass or metal fish mould with oil. Leave upside down to drain. Make the sauce. Combine the onion, carrot, celery and milk in a saucepan. Add the herbs and spices, with salt to taste. Heat to simmering point, cover, turn off the heat and allow to stand for 30 minutes to infuse. Strain into a measuring jug.

Melt the butter in a saucepan. Stir in the flour and cook over low heat for 2-3 minutes, without allowing the mixture to colour. Gradually add the flavoured milk, stirring constantly until the mixture boils and thickens. Remove the pan from the heat, cover the surface of the sauce with damp greaseproof paper and set aside until required.

Put the salmon in a large saucepan and cover with court bouillon. Bring to the boil, lower the heat and simmer for 15 minutes. Drain, cool and remove the skin and bones. Pound to a paste in a mortar or process in a blender or food processor until smooth.

Place 30 ml/2 tbsp water in a small bowl and sprinkle the gelatine on to the liquid. Stand the bowl over a saucepan of hot water and stir the gelatine until it has dissolved completely.

Tip the salmon into a large bowl and add the cold Béchamel sauce. Mix until thoroughly blended, then add the softened butter, whipped cream, sherry and dissolved gelatine. Mix well, then spoon into the prepared mould. Smooth the top, cover with cling film and chill for 2-3 hours until set. Turn out (see Mrs Beeton's Tip), garnish with cucumber and radish slices and serve.

SERVES 6 TO 8

MRS BEETON'S TIP   Rinse the serving platter in cold water, draining off the excess. Run the point of a sharp knife around the edge of the salmon mould to loosen it, then dip the mould in warm water. Invert the plate on top of the mould, then, holding mould and plate firmly, turn both right side up again. The mould should lift off easily. If necessary, move the mousse to the desired position on the platter – the skin of water remaining on the plate will make this possible. Repeat the process if the mousse does not come out first time, but avoid leaving it in the warm water for too long or the design on the mousse will be blurred.

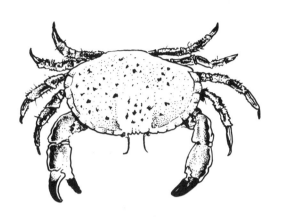

KIPPER MOUSSE

fat for greasing
75 g/3 oz butter
3 mushrooms or 8 mushroom stems,
    chopped
6 black peppercorns
1-2 parsley stalks
25 g/1 oz plain flour
250 ml/9 fl oz Basic Fish Stock (page 27) or
    chicken stock
salt and pepper
lemon juice
1 small onion, finely sliced
575 g/1¼ lb kipper fillets, skinned and cut
    into 2.5 cm/1 inch pieces
250 ml/8 fl oz Mayonnaise (page 32)
75 ml/5 tbsp dry white wine
15 g/½ oz gelatine
250 ml/8 fl oz double cream

GARNISH
    lemon slices
    parsley sprigs

Melt 25 g/1 oz of the butter in a sauce-pan, add the chopped mushrooms, pepper-corns and parsley stalks. Cook over gentle heat for 10 minutes. Add the flour and cook over low heat for 2-3 minutes, without allowing the mixture to colour. Gradually add the stock and simmer, stirring, for 3-4 minutes. Rub the sauce through a sieve into a clean saucepan. Add salt, pepper and lemon juice to taste. Cover the surface with damp greaseproof paper and set aside until cold.

Grease a soufflé dish or oval pâté mould. Melt the remaining butter in a frying pan, add the onion and fry gently for 2-3 minutes. Add the fish and fry gently for 7 minutes more. Tip the contents of the pan into a large bowl and stir in the cold sauce and the mayonnaise. Process the mixture in a blender or food processor or pound to a smooth paste in a mortar. Using a rubber spatula, scrape the purée into a large bowl.

Place the wine in a small bowl and sprinkle the gelatine on to the liquid. Stand the bowl over a saucepan of hot water and stir the gelatine until it has dissolved completely. Add it to the kipper purée and mix very thoroughly. Blend in the cream and add salt, pepper and a dash of lemon juice to taste.

Turn the mixture into the prepared dish or mould, cover with cling film and chill for at least 2 hours. Serve from the dish or turn out on to a serving dish (see Mrs Beeton's Tip, left). Garnish with lemon slices and parsley sprigs and serve.

SERVES 4 TO 6

☀ **MICROWAVE TIP** Dissolve the gelatine in the microwave if preferred. Stir into the wine in a small bowl, let stand until spongy, then cook on High for 30-45 seconds.

FISH TERRINE

450 g/1 lb plaice fillets, skinned
225 g/8 oz smoked salmon offcuts
600 ml/1 pint White Sauce (page 41)
6 eggs
30 ml/2 tbsp chopped parsley
30 ml/2 tbsp snipped chives
salt and pepper
Hollandaise Sauce (page 42) to serve

Set the oven at 160°C/325°F/gas 3. Prepare a bain marie: have a large roasting tin or dish and a kettle or boiling water ready. Base line and grease a 900 g/2 lb loaf tin.

Pick any tiny bones from the plaice and purée it in a food processor or blender. Transfer to a large bowl. Check that the smoked salmon offcuts are free of all bones and skin, then purée them and place in a separate, large bowl.

Add half the sauce to the plaice purée, the remainder to the smoked salmon. Beat 3 eggs and stir them into the plaice mixture; beat the remaining eggs and add to the smoked salmon mixture. Stir the parsley into the plaice, the chives into the smoked salmon. Add salt and pepper to taste to the plaice mixture; pepper only to the smoked salmon mixture.

Spoon half the plaice mixture into the prepared tin. Top with the salmon mixture, then the remaining plaice mixture. Cover with foil and stand the terrine in the roasting tin. Pour boiling water into the outer tin to come almost up to the rim. Bake the fish terrine in the bain marie for 1¼ hours, or until it feels firm to the touch. If the middle feels soft, continue cooking.

Leave the cooked terrine to stand for 5 minutes before turning it out. Invert the tin on to a warmed platter. Serve in slices with the hollandaise sauce. Alternatively, the terrine may be served cold with Mayonnaise (page 32) or soured cream and crisp Melba toast.

SERVES 8

———————— ◇ ————————

MOULDED SALMON SALAD

Illustrated on page 157

500 ml/17 fl oz White Wine Fish Stock
    (page 27)
25 g/1 oz gelatine
salt and pepper
½ unpeeled cucumber, sliced
2 firm tomatoes, sliced
225 g/8 oz cooked salmon or 1(397g/
    14 oz) can salmon, drained

Heat the stock in a saucepan, stir in the gelatine and stir briskly until completely dissolved. Add salt and pepper to taste. Set aside to cool but do not allow to set.

Cover the bottom of a 600 ml/1 pint mould with some cool fish stock. Chill until set. Arrange a few cucumber and tomato slices on the jelly-lined mould, then pour a little more stock over the top to keep the garnish in place. Chill again until set. Add a layer of salmon and another layer of stock, and chill again until set.

Repeat these layers until the mould is full, then cover with cling film and chill until required. Invert the mould on to a wetted plate (see Mrs Beeton's Tip, page 178) to serve.

SERVES 6 TO 8

CHOPPED HERRINGS

3 salted herrings, soaked in cold water
   overnight
1 large cooking apple
1 small mild onion
2 hard-boiled eggs, yolks and whites
   separated
1 slice white bread, crust removed
10-15 ml/2-3 tsp white wine vinegar
15-30 ml/1-2 tbsp caster sugar

Drain the herrings and remove the skin and bones. Rinse well and drain again. Quarter the apple and remove the skin and core.

Mince together the herrings, onion, apple, hard-boiled egg whites, 1 hard-boiled egg yolk and the bread. Turn the mixture into a bowl and stir in vinegar and sugar to taste. Mix well and spoon into a serving dish. Sieve the remaining egg yolk over the surface to serve.

SERVES 6 TO 8

> **MRS BEETON'S TIP** Herring fillets in oil may be used to this recipe. They are ready to use when drained and give delicious results.

HERRING ROLLS

25 g/1 oz butter, softened
2 hard-boiled eggs, yolks and whites
   separated and finely chopped
8 anchovy fillets, finely chopped
cayenne pepper
4 rollmop herrings, each divided into
   2 fillets
lemon juice

GARNISH
8 lemon slices
4-6 sliced gherkins
1 small diced beetroot
chopped parsley

Cream the butter in a bowl with the hard-boiled egg yolks and anchovies. Add a pinch of cayenne and mix well.

Spread most of the butter mixture on the rollmops and roll up firmly. Spread the remaining mixture thinly on the round ends of each roll and dip in the chopped egg white. Sprinkle the rolls with lemon juice and arrange on a plate, garnished with lemon slices, gherkins, beetroot and parsley.

SERVES 4

VARIATION

SALTED HERRING ROLLS Use salted herrings instead of rollmops. Soak them in cold water for several hours before use, then fillet, being careful to remove all the bones.

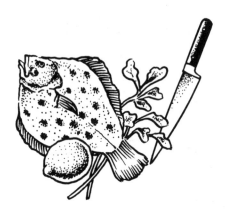

MATJES HERRINGS IN CREAM SAUCE

Allow plenty of time for making this dish: the herrings need to be soaked for 10-12 hours and the finished dish must be chilled for several hours before serving.

8 plain matjes herring fillets (not spiced), cleaned
milk for soaking
2-3 eating apples
lemon juice
½ large Spanish onion, sliced in wafer-thin rings

SAUCE
125 ml/4 fl oz soured cream
75 ml/5 tbsp double cream
salt and pepper
5 ml/1 tsp sugar

Remove any bones from the herrings. Pat dry with absorbent kitchen paper and lay in a shallow glass or enamel bowl. Pour over milk to cover, then cover the bowl tightly. Set aside for 10-12 hours in a cold place to draw out most of the saltiness from the fish.

Quarter, peel and core the apples. Slice very thinly into a bowl, sprinkle with the lemon juice and set aside. Drain the herring fillets and pat dry with absorbent kitchen paper. Reserve 2-3 onion rings for garnishing. Layer the rest with the fish and apple slices in a flat dish.

Make the sauce by beating the soured cream and double cream together until well blended and fairly thick. Add salt and pepper and sugar to taste. Pour the sauce over the fillets and garnish with the reserved onion rings. Cover and chill for several hours so that the flavours blend. Serve with brown bread.

SERVES 4 TO 8

SOUSED HERRINGS

Soused herrings make an excellent starter or summer main course. Serve them with potato salad and radicchio.

6 herrings, scaled, heads removed and boned
salt and pepper
150 ml/¼ pint malt vinegar
15 ml/1 tbsp pickling spice
4 bay leaves
2 small onions, sliced in rings

Set the oven at 150°C/300°F/gas 2. Season the herrings. Roll up the fillets, skin side in, from the tail end. Place neatly and fairly close together in an ovenproof baking dish.

In a jug, mix the vinegar with 100 ml/ 3½ fl oz water. Pour over the herrings, sprinkle with pickling spice and add the bay leaves. Lay the onion rings on top. Cover the dish loosely with foil and bake for 1½ hours. Remove from the oven and leave to cool completely.

SERVES 6

HERRING AND TOMATO SALAD

3 salted herrings, cleaned

MARINADE
2 onions, chopped
12 bay leaves
30 ml/2 tbsp caster sugar
60 ml/4 tbsp distilled vinegar
(see Mrs Beeton's Tip)
45 ml/3 tbsp tomato purée

Pat the herrings dry with absorbent kitchen paper. Lay them in a shallow glass or enamel bowl. Pour over cold water to cover, then cover the bowl tightly. Set aside for 6 hours in a cold place.

Make the marinade by combining all the ingredients in a large shallow dish. Add 15 ml/1 tbsp water and mix well.

Drain the herrings and pat dry with absorbent kitchen paper. Cut them into small pieces, discarding the bones. Add the herring pieces to the marinade and mix well. Cover the dish and marinate for 48 hours, stirring several times.

SERVES 6

> **MRS BEETON'S TIP** Vinegars vary considerably in the percentage of acetic acid they contain. Malt and cider vinegars are milder than wine vinegars. The strongest vinegars are labelled fortified or distilled. Distilled vinegar is usually made from malt. It is colourless. If you find it difficult to obtain, use pickling vinegar instead.

MACKEREL SALAD

500 ml/17 fl oz Court Bouillon (page 28)
8 mackerel fillets, cleaned
45 ml/3 tbsp cider vinegar
15 ml/1 tbsp gelatine
75 ml/5 tbsp Mayonnaise (page 32)

GARNISH
tarragon, chervil or parsley sprigs
tomato wedges
watercress sprigs

Bring the court bouillon to simmering point in a saucepan, add the mackerel and poach gently for 15 minutes. Using a slotted spoon, transfer the fish to a wooden board. When cool enough to handle, remove the skin neatly, then leave until cold.

Meanwhile place the vinegar in a small bowl and sprinkle the gelatine on top. Stand the bowl over a saucepan of hot water and stir the gelatine until it has dissolved completely. Alternatively, dissolve the gelatine in the microwave (see Mrs Beeton's Tip, page 179). Mix with the mayonnaise and chill until on the point of setting.

Arrange the mackerel fillets, skinned side up, on a serving dish. Coat each fish with the semi-set mayonnaise and garnish with fresh herb sprigs, tomato wedges and watercress.

SERVES 4

CAMARGUE MUSSELS

2 kg/4½ lb mussels
1 onion, sliced
2 garlic cloves, cut in slivers
1 carrot, sliced
1 celery stick, sliced
1 bouquet garni
125 ml/4 fl oz white wine
chopped parsley to serve

MAYONNAISE
  1 egg yolk
  5 ml/1 tsp French mustard
  salt
  cayenne
  5 ml/1 tsp white wine vinegar
  100 ml/3½ fl oz sunflower oil
  20 ml/4 tsp lemon juice

Wash, scrape and beard the mussels following the instructions on page 25. Put them in a large saucepan. Tuck the sliced vegetables among the mussels and add the bouquet garni.

Pour over the wine and add 125 ml/4 fl oz water. Place the pan over moderate heat and bring to the boil. As soon as the liquid bubbles up over the mussels, shake the pan several times, cover, lower the heat and simmer until the mussels have opened. Discard any that remain shut. With a slotted spoon remove the mussels from the stock. Arrange them, on their half shells, on a large flat dish. Strain the cooking liquid into a jug and set aside to cool.

Make the mayonnaise. Blend the egg yolk, mustard, salt, cayenne and vinegar in a bowl. Using a balloon whisk, beat in the oil very gradually, drop by drop. When about half the oil has been added and the mixture looks thick and shiny, add the rest of the oil in a slow thin stream.

Stir in the lemon juice and reserved cooking liquid. Spoon the mayonnaise over the mussels and sprinkle with chopped parsley. Serve chilled.

SERVES 5 TO 6

SHRIMP OR PRAWN SALAD

½ cucumber
5 ml/1 tsp salt
2 lettuce hearts or 1 iceberg lettuce, finely shredded
60 ml/4 tbsp Mayonnaise (page 32)
30 ml/2 tbsp plain yogurt
225 g/8 oz peeled cooked shrimps or prawns
2 hard-boiled eggs, halved or sliced lengthways
black pepper

Slice the unpeeled cucumber thinly. Put the slices in a colander, sprinkle over the salt and leave for 30 minutes to drain. Rinse the cucumber slices, drain well, then pat dry with absorbent kitchen paper. Use the slices to line a glass salad bowl.

Lay the lettuce in the lined bowl. Sprinkle lightly with salt. Mix the mayonnaise and yogurt in a bowl, then spoon the mixture over the lettuce. Pile the shrimps or prawns in the centre of the dish with the hard-boiled egg halves or slices in a circle around them. Grind black pepper over the egg slices just before serving the salad.

SERVES 4

MRS BEETON'S TIP Place the cucumber slices side by side, just touching but not overlapping. A layer of radish slices may be added.

CRAB AND MANDARIN SALAD

50 g/2 oz shelled whole walnuts or walnut
  halves
400 g/14 oz drained canned or thawed
  frozen crab meat
75 g/3 oz celery, sliced
100 g/4 oz drained canned mandarin
  segments
1 lettuce, separated into leaves

DRESSING
  50 g/2 oz blue cheese
  125 ml/4 fl oz soured cream
  2.5 ml/½ tsp grated lemon rind
  salt and pepper
  75 ml/5 tbsp sunflower oil
  20 ml/4 tsp lemon juice

Make the dressing. Crumble the cheese into a bowl. Gradually work in the soured cream until smooth. Add the remaining ingredients and whisk until completely blended. Pour into a jug, cover and chill.

Set half the walnuts aside to use as a garnish. Chop the remaining walnuts finely and place them in a large bowl. Add the crab meat, celery and mandarin orange segments. Toss lightly, breaking up any large pieces of crab meat with a fork.

Arrange the lettuce leaves on a flat salad platter. Pile the crab mixture in the centre. Trickle a little of the dressing over the crab mixture and garnish with the reserved walnuts. Serve the rest of the dressing separately.

SERVES 4

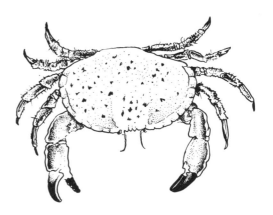

SEA BREAM MAYONNAISE

Sea bream is not one of the most common fish but it is caught around the coast. As well as the dark-skinned fish (black bream or sea bream), there is a red-skinned variety known as red sea bream.

  butter for greasing
  575 g/1¼ lb red sea bream fillets, skinned
  lemon juice
  salt and pepper
  125 ml/4 fl oz Mayonnaise (page 32)
  1 hard-boiled egg, chopped
  10 ml/2 tsp chopped parsley
  8 lettuce leaves
  tomato wedges to garnish

Grease a shallow ovenproof dish. Set the oven at 190°C/375°F/gas 5. Arrange the fish fillets in the dish, sprinkle with lemon juice, salt and pepper and cover loosely with greaseproof paper. Bake for 20 minutes. Flake the fish with a fork, remove any bones and leave to cool.

Mix the mayonnaise, hard-boiled egg and parsley lightly in a bowl. Stir in the cold flaked fish. Spread out the lettuce leaves on a flat salad platter, top with the fish mixture and garnish with the tomato wedges. Serve.

SERVES 4

SALAD NICOISE

Illustrated on page 158

salt and pepper
225 g/8 oz French beans, topped and
    tailed
2 hard-boiled eggs, cut in quarters
3 small tomatoes, cut in quarters
1 garlic clove, crushed
1(198 g/7 oz) can tuna, drained and flaked
50 g/2 oz black olives
1 large lettuce, separated into leaves
1 (50 g/2 oz) can anchovy fillets, drained,
    to garnish

DRESSING
    45 ml/3 tbsp olive oil or a mixture of olive
        and sunflower oil
    salt and pepper
    pinch of English mustard powder
    pinch of caster sugar
    15 ml/1 tbsp wine vinegar

Bring a small saucepan of salted water to
the boil. Add the beans and cook for 5-10
minutes or until just tender. Drain, refresh
under cold water and drain again.

Make the dressing by mixing all the
ingredients in a screw-topped jar. Close the
jar tightly and shake vigorously until well
blended.

Put the beans into a large bowl with the
eggs, tomatoes, garlic, tuna and most of the
olives. Pour over the dressing and toss
lightly. Add salt and pepper to taste.

Line a large salad bowl with the lettuce
leaves. Pile the tuna mixture into the
centre and garnish with the remaining
olives and the anchovy fillets. Serve at
once.

SERVES 4 TO 6

BEAN SALAD WITH TUNA

Illustrated on page 158

450 g/1 lb dry flageolet beans, soaked in
    water overnight
150 g/5 oz tomatoes, peeled, seeded and
    chopped
2 spring onions, finely chopped
1(198 g/7 oz) can tuna, drained and flaked

DRESSING
    90 ml/6 tbsp sunflower oil
    45 ml/3 tbsp white wine vinegar
    1 garlic clove, crushed
    15 ml/1 tbsp chopped parsley

Drain the beans and put them into a
saucepan with fresh cold water to cover.
Boil briskly for at least 10 minutes, then
lower the heat and simmer for about 1 hour
or until tender.

Meanwhile make the dressing by mixing
all the ingredients in a screw-topped jar.
Close the jar tightly and shake vigorously
until well blended.

Drain the beans and put them in a bowl.
Add the tomatoes, spring onions and tuna
and mix well. Pour the cold dressing over
the hot beans and the other ingredients and
serve at once on small warmed plates.

SERVES 4

SEAFOOD SALAD

The cod fillet must be fresh, firm and of excellent quality if the salad is to be first rate.

450 g/1 lb cod fillet, skinned
30 ml/2 tbsp lemon juice
2.5 ml/½ tsp sugar
salt and pepper
75 ml/5 tbsp olive oil or other salad oil
15 ml/1 tbsp chopped capers
30 ml/2 tbsp chopped spring onion
225 g/8 oz peeled cooked prawns, thawed
    if frozen
100 g/4 oz shelled freshly cooked mussels
4 ripe tomatoes, peeled and diced
30 ml/2 tbsp chopped parsley
1 courgette, diced
¼ iceberg lettuce, shredded

Steam the cod between two plates over a saucepan of boiling water for 10-15 minutes, until the flesh is firm and white but still moist.

While the fish is cooking, place the lemon juice in a bowl. Whisk in the sugar, with salt and pepper to taste. When the sugar and salt have dissolved, whisk in the oil. Stir in the capers and chopped spring onion.

Flake the cod into large pieces, discarding all skin and bones.

Place in a dish and pour the dressing over. Add the prawns, mussels, tomatoes and parsley, then mix lightly, taking care not to break up the cod flakes.

Toss the courgette and lettuce together and arrange on 4 plates. Top with the seafood mixture and serve at once, with hot fresh toast, Melba toast or crusty bread.

SERVES 4

HALIBUT, ORANGE AND WATERCRESS SALAD

600 ml/1 pint Court Bouillon (page 28)
4-6 halibut steaks
8 large lettuce leaves, shredded
125 ml/4 fl oz Mayonnaise (page 32)

GARNISH
orange slices
watercress sprigs

Bring the court bouillon to simmering point in a large saucepan. Add the halibut steaks and poach gently for 7-10 minutes until cooked. Using a slotted spoon transfer the fish to a plate and leave to cool. Remove the skin.

Arrange most of the shredded lettuce on a flat salad platter. Coat the fish in mayonnaise and arrange it on the lettuce. Garnish with orange slices, watercress and the remaining lettuce.

SERVES 4 TO 6

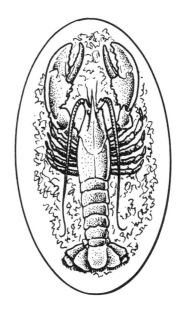

GLOSSARY

Aspic Clear savoury jelly.

Au Bleu This term is used for a method of cooking freshly caught freshwater fish such as trout. The fish must be freshly killed, then gutted, taking care not to rinse the natural coating off the skin. Scales are not removed. The fish is placed in a pan and a little boiling vinegar is sprinkled over it. The acid in the vinegar gives the fish skin a blue hue. Boiling court bouillon is poured over and this makes the fish curl, the second characteristic of fish cooked au bleu.

Au Gratin or Gratin A dish finished with a crumb topping which may include breadcrumbs, cheese or nuts and which is browned under the grill or in the oven.

Bain Marie A container such as a roasting tin which can be filled with water to create a 'water bath' in which a second container of food can be placed for gentle, even cooking.

Beurre Blanc Unsalted butter added gradually to reduced white wine and chopped shallots to produce a creamy sauce for boiled or poached white fish.

Beurre Manié A paste of butter and flour, whisked into boiling liquid as a thickening agent. Often added to casseroles of meat and poultry. Since the liquid has to be boiling when the beurre manié is whisked in, it may only be used to thicken the cooking liquid from fish and seafood once the fish has been transferred to a separate dish.

Beurre Noir Butter cooked to a deep nut brown – not black as the name suggests – then mixed with vinegar as a simple sauce. It is traditionally used with skate. Chopped parsley and capers may be added.

Bisque A soup traditionally made of shellfish in which the meat is puréed as a thickening. The crushed shells may be added to the soup.

Bivalves Shellfish with two hinged shells which completely enclose the creature when shut. Cockles, mussels and oysters are all bivalves.

Bouquet Garni A bunch of herbs, commonly a bay leaf, parsley sprig or stalk and thyme sprig, tied with string and added to a moist dish during cooking. Fresh herbs are best by far for bouquet garni. The compositions may vary according to the recipe; however dried bouquet garni in the form of small sachets are available.

Chowder A thick, wholesome soup, traditionally made from shellfish but now accepted as a hearty fish soup.

Clarified Butter Butter which has been heated and strained or allowed to stand in order to remove solids.

Cleaning Fish A fish that is cleaned has had its entrails removed. The term gutting may be used.

Court Bouillon Poaching liquid for fish, usually water, parsley and other seasonings with vinegar, lemon juice or white wine added. Unlike stock, court bouillon is discarded after cooking.

Croquettes Cork shapes of mixture, coated in egg and breadcrumbs, then deep fried. In the case of fish, a thick savoury white sauce forms the basis and flaked cooked fish is added with herbs such as chopped tarragon or parsley. The sauce is chilled until set, then the shaped portions are rolled in flour, coated, chilled again and deep fried. A double coating of egg and breadcrumbs is often applied to ensure that the filling does not burst out during cooking. When cut, the filling should be creamy.

Crustaceans Creatures with jointed limbs, segmented bodies and a carapace or exoskeleton. The category includes crawfish, lobsters, shrimps, prawns and crabs.

Cutlets Fish cutlets are cut across the central part of the body. They consist of two main portions of flesh attached to a central bone with two thin flaps which surround the body cavity.

En Papillote A method of cooking (usually baking) in paper. The paper (usually greased greaseproof) is firmly closed to trap all cooking juices and flavour. A method used mainly for individual portions, which are then opened at the table.

Fillets Portions of fish flesh cut off the bone and therefore taken from the length of the fish. The majority of fish fillets do not contain bones; fine bones may be present.

Flat Fish One of the main categories of fish. Flat fish are literally flat, for example plaice and sole, but they may be very large, as in the case of turbot and halibut. They swim along the sea bed, therefore the skin on their upper sides is often patterned or dark to act as natural camouflage.

Goujons Strips of thin fish fillets, coated in egg and breadcrumbs and deep fried. Plaice, sole and whiting may be used.

Gratin See *Au gratin*.

Gutting See *Cleaning Fish*.

Hard Roe The ovaries of the female fish.

Matelote Fish stewed or casseroled in wine, notably eels.

Meunière The term is used for fish cooked in butter. The cooking butter is seasoned and may be flavoured with lemon juice. It is poured over the fish for serving.

Molluscs Invertebrates (without a backbone), including shellfish such as mussels, scallops, clams, cockles, whelks and snails. Octopus, squid and cuttlefish are also classified as molluscs.

Oily Fish Another main category of fish, this includes mackerel, herring, sardines, anchovies and other species that have a high fat content.

Round Fish A category used for classifying fish with rounded bodies, such as mackerel and herring.

Scaling The term used for scraping the scales off a fish. Also known as descaling.

Scalloped A term used in cooking for food which is sauced and served within a ring of piped mashed potato, usually in a shell or shell-shaped dish (although not necessarily so), and browned under the grill or in the oven. The term is derived from the traditional method of serving coquilles Saint Jacques.

Soft Roes The testes of the male fish.

Steaks Fish steaks are cut across the body of the fish at the tail end. They have a central bone (the backbone) but they do not have an open section (the body cavity).

Trimming Removing the fins, tail and head, sometimes the gills, or other inedible parts from the outside of the fish or from fillets and other cuts.

Univalves Molluscs with one shell, for example whelks, winkles, snails and abalone (also a member of the snail family).

White Fish A category of fish, including species which have white flesh. For example, cod, haddock, coley, whiting, plaice, hake and so on.

INDEX

Abalone, 9
Aïoli, 32
Almonds, roasted, 69
Anchovy, 9, 49
Angels on horseback, 163
Angevin salmon trout, 83
Apricot-stuffed trout, 140–1
Aspic jelly, 28
Avocado
    butter, 109
    Ritz, 177
    sauce, 72

Bacalao dourado, 96–97
Baking, 122–3
Bass, Sea, 15
Batters, 94–95, 112, 121
Bean and sherry sauce, 69
    salad with tuna, 186
Béchamel sauce, 41
Black butter, 43, 81
Bouillabaisse, 46–47
Breadcrumbs, 30, 45, 93
Bream
    sabo-no-teriyaki, 106
    Sea, 15
Brill, 9
    and potato Mornay, 127
Brisling, 149
Butter sauce, 43
Butters, 43–44, 81, 109

Camargue mussels, 184
Cannelloni, crab-stuffed, 170–1
Cape cod pie, 143
Carp, 9
    stuffed, 86–87
    with mushrooms, 86
Casseroles, 59, 124
    see also Stews
Catfish, 9
Caviar, 9
Channel chowder, 47
Cheese dressing, blue, 185
Chicken stock, Chinese, 49
Chive sauce, 83
Chowders, 47, 52, 54
Clam, 10
    chowder, 54
Coatings, 94–95
Cockle, 10
Cod, 10
    and rice soufflé, 167
    au gratin, 124
    baked Murray, 125

casserole, 59
curried, 64
cutlets with shrimp stuffing, 96
golden grilled, 95
pie, 143
portugaise, 65
roe, scalloped, 161
salt: bacalao dourado, 96–97
seafood salad, 187
Southwold cod soup, 48–49
with cream sauce, 64
see also Smoked cod
Coley, 10
    provençale, 125
Coquilles St Jacques Mornay, 90–91
Corn and crab bisque, 51
'n cod, 124
Court bouillon, 28
Crab, 10, 149
    and corn bisque, 51
    and mandarin salad, 185
    au gratin, 163
    soufflé, 151
    soup, Mediterranean, 51
    stuffed cannelloni, 170–1
Crawfish, 10
Cream sauce, 64, 182
Cullen skink, 55
Curried cod, 64
Curry, prawn, 87

Dab, 11
Devilled butter, 44
    herring roes, 161
Dressing a fish, 172–3
Dressings, 185–6
Dunwich plaice, 135

Eels, 11
    casserole, 59
    conger, 10
    fried, 110
    matelote of, 58
    soup, 50
    stewed, 58
Eggs: garnish, 45
    stuffing, 31

Fish (general)
    and rice soufflé, 167
    ball soup, 49
    cakes, 104
    custard, 152
    fingers, 150
    forcemeat, 31

gefilte, 67
hot pot, 56
Irish bake, 128
Jamaican fried, 98
pie, Saltburn, 147
pudding, 65
scramble, 152
seafood lasagne, 171
slices, spicy, 97
soup, Norwegian, 55
    Spanish, 48
stock, basic, 27
    white wine, 27
terrine, 180
Fisherman's hot pot, 56
Flounder, 11
Forcemeat see Stuffings
French fish stew, 56
    fried haddock, 99
Fritto misto, 103
Frying, 93–94

Garlic butter, 44
Garnishes, 45, 173
Gefilte fish, 67
Gooseberry sauce, 106
Goujons of plaice, 100
Gravad lax, 177
Grayling, 11
    baked, 129
Grey mullet, 11
    baked, 129, 138
Grilling, 92–93
Gurnard, 11

Haddock, 12
    and fennel flambé, 98
    and rice soufflé, 167
    casserole, 59
    cullen skink, 55
    fillets, baked, 127
    florentine, 66
    French fish stew, 56
    French fried, 99
    ham and, 81
    omelette Arnold Bennet, 151
    Saltburn fish pie, 147
    with cider, 126
    with soured cream, 126
    see also Smoked haddock
Hake, 12
    and fennel flambé, 98
    sweet and sour, 68
Halibut, 12
    orange and watercress salad, 187

Ham and haddie, 81
Herb
  and lemon stuffing, 29
  butter, 44
Herring, 12, 149
  and tomato salad, 183
  baked, 130–1
    with olives and tomatoes, 141
  chopped, 181
  fillets, potted, 176
  marinated fried, 107
  Matjes, in cream sauce, 182
  roes, devilled, 161
    pâté, 174
    sauce, 174
  rolls, 181
  sabo-no-teriyaki, 106
  soused, 182
  stargazey pie, 148
  stuffed, 131
    with shrimps, 1131
  tails-in-air, 132
  with mustard sauce, 98
Hollandaise sauce, 42
Huss, 12

Irish bake, 128

Jambalaya, 167
Jamaican fried fish, 97
John Dory, 12
  au gratin, 128
  in white sauce, 70
Jugged kippers, 81

Kebabs, monkfish and bacon, 105
Kedgeree, 166
Kipper
  and tomato bake, 132
  grilled, 99
  jugged, 81
  mousse, 179
Koulibiac, 145

Lasagne, seafood, 171
Laver bread, 12
Lemon and herb stuffing, 29
  twists, 45
Ling casserole, 59
Lobster, 13
  bisque, 52–53
  potted, 175
  Spanish, 89
  thermidor, 89

Mackerel, 13, 149
  baked, with olives and
    tomatoes, 141
  marinated, 109
  niçoise, 71
  parcels, baked, 133
  sabo-no-teriyaki, 106

salad, 183
  with gooseberry sauce, 106
  with soured cream sauce, 133
Maître d'hôtel butter, 44
Marinades
  for herring, 107
  for mackerel, 109
  for perch, 110
  for salmon, 109
  for sole, 101
  sweet and sour, 68
Marinating, 92
Matelote of eels, 58
Matjes herring in cream sauce, 182
Mayonnaise, 32, 185
Mediterranean crab soup, 51
Megrim, 13
Microwave cooking, 63
Monkfish, 13
  and bacon kebabs, 105
Mornay sauce, 66, 67, 90–91, 127
Moules marinière, 57
Mousses, 178–9
Mrs Beeton's dressed
    whitebait, 104
Mullet see Grey/red mullet
Murray cod, baked, 125
Mushrooms
  red mullet with, 130
  sauce, 86, 102–3, 134–5
  stuffing, 30
Mussels, 13
  Camargue, 184
  in white sauce, 57
  moules marinière, 57
  paella, 168
  risotto, 170
  saucy angels, 163
  smoked, 150
  sole dieppoise, 136
  soup, 54
Mustard sauce, 98, 111

Niçoise salad, 186
Norwegian fish soup, 55

Octopus, 13
Olives
  and rice stuffing, 29
  and tomato sauce, 71
  coley provençale, 125
Omelette Arnold Bennett, 151
Onion sauce, 72
Oysters, 13
  angels on horseback, 163
  fritters, 121
  Rockefeller, 143
  smoked, 150
  stuffing, 30

Paella Valenciana, 168
Paprika cream, 88

Parsley
  garnish, fried, 45
  sauce, 161
Pasta, 165
  recipes, 169–71
Pastry: fleurons, 45
  short crust, 144, 147
Pâtés and pastes, 174–6
Perch, 13
  fried, 110
Pike, 14
  braised, 85
  quenelles, 85
Pilchards, 14, 150
  stargazey pie, 148
Plaice, 14
  custard, 152
  Dunwich, 135
  fish terrine, 180
  goujons, 100
  Mornay, 67
  portugaise, 134
  stuffed with prawns, 134–5
Poaching, 62–63
Pollack, 14
Potato and brill Mornay, 127
Prawns, 14
  and horseradish cocktail, 177
  avocado Ritz, 177
  celeste, 87
  cocktail, 177
  curry, 87
  potted, 176
  quiche, 144
  salad, 184
  sauce, 84
  sole with, 137
  Spanish, 112
  stuffing, 134–5
  sweet and sour, 88

Queens of the sea, 90
Quiche, prawn, 144

Redfish, 14
Red mullet
  baked in foil, 130
  with herbs, 111
  with mushrooms, 130
  with tomatoes and olives, 71
Rice, 29, 164–5
  recipes, 29, 145, 166–8, 170
Risotto, mussel, 170
Roe, 14, 149
Rouille, 32

Sabo-no-teriyaki, 106
Salads, 183–7
Salmon, 14, 150
  aurore, 142
  baked, 142
  boning, 172–3

creamed, in pastry, 146–7
gravad lax, 177
hot poached, 82
koulibiac, 145
mousse, 178
potted, 175
sabo-no-teriyaki, 106
salad, moulded, 180
steaks, grilled, 111
    with avocado butter, 109
Tweed kettle, 83
see also Smoked salmon
Salmon trout
angevin, 83
with avocado sauce, 72
Saltburn fish pie, 147
Sardines, 15, 150
baked fresh, 138–9
cassolettes, 162
Sauces
avocado, 72
béchamel, 41
black butter, 43
bonne femme, 136–7
butter, 43
chive, 83
cream, 64
dieppoise, 136
for spaghetti, 169
gooseberry, 106
herring roe, 174
hollandaise, 42
mornay, 66, 67, 90–91, 127
mushroom, 59, 86, 102–3, 134–5
mustard, 98, 111
onion, 72
parsley, 161
prawn, 84
shallot, 83
sherry and bean, 69
soured cream, 127, 133
sweet and sour, 68, 88
tartare, 32, 100
tomato, 43
    and olive, 71
tuna, 162
Veronique, 70
white, 41, 57
white wine, 70
Saucy angels, 163
Scallops, 15
coquilles St Jacques
    Mornay, 90–91
on skewers, 121
queens of the sea, 90
soup, cream of, 50
Scampi, 15
fritto misto, 103
in paprika cream, 88
jambalaya, 167
spaghetti alla marinara, 169
tails, fried, 112
Sea bream mayonnaise, 185

Seafood (mixed)
lasagne, 171
paella, 168
salad, 187
Shallot sauce, 83
Shark, 15
Sherry and bean sauce, 69
Shrimps, 15, 150
and cider bisque, 53
and rice stir, 166
potted, 176
salad, 184
sole dieppoise, 136
stuffing, 96, 131
Sild, 150
Sippets, 129
Skate, 16
fried, 107
in black butter, 81
Skipper, 149
Smelts
baked, 138
fried, 105
Smoked cod
and corn casserole, 124
custard, 152
roes: taramasalata, 175
Smoked haddock
chowder, 52
grilled, 99
kedgeree, 166
scalloped, 72
scramble, 152
Smoked mackerel pâté, 174
Smoked salmon: fish terrine, 180
Snails, 16
Snapper, 17
Sole
Anthony, 102–3
bonne femme, fillets of, 136–7
Colbert, 102
custard, 152
dieppoise, 136
Dover, 11
lemon, 12
meunière, 101
Orly, fillets of, 101
Veronique, 70
with prawns, 137
with sherry and bean sauce, 69
Soufflé
crab, 151
fish and rice, 167
Soups, 46–55
Soured cream sauce, 127, 133
Southwold cod soup, 48–49
Spaghetti alla marinara, 169
Spanish fish soup, 48
lobster, 89
prawns, 112
Spicy Fish Slices, 97
Sprat, 16, 149
paste, 176

Squid, 16
stuffed, 91
Stargazey pie, 148
Steaming, 60–62
Stews, 56–59
Stir frying, 94
Stocks, 27–28, 49
Stuffings
apricot, 140–1
egg, 31
fish forcemeat, 31
for carp, 86–87
for grey mullet, 138
for herring, 131
for plaice, 134–5
for squid, 91
gefilte, 67
lemon and herb, 29
mushroom, 30
oyster, 30
prawn, 134–5
rice and olive, 29
shrimp, 96, 131
tomato, 29
Sweet and sour
hake, 68
prawns, 88
Swordfish, 16

Taramasalata, 175
Tartare sauce, 32, 100
Tomatoes
sauce, fresh, 43
stuffing, 29
Trout, 16
apricot-stuffed, 140–1
baked, with olives and
    tomatoes, 141
hollandaise, 84
meunière, 108
poached, with prawn sauce, 84
with almonds, 108
see also Salmon trout
Tuna, 16, 150
bean salad with, 186
salad niçoise, 186
sauce, 162
Turbot, 16
baked, 139
dugléré, 140
marengo, 139
Tweed kettle, 83

Whelks, 16
White sauce, 41, 57
White wine fish stock, 27
sauce, 70
Whitebait, 17
Mrs Beeton's dressed, 104
Whiting, 17
baked, 128
    with olives and tomatoes, 141
fried, 100
Winkles, 16